GOING FOR THE
GREEN

ROBERT THOMPSON

GOING FOR THE GREEN

**ON THE LINKS
WITH CANADA'S BUSINESS
AND POLITICAL ELITE**

KEY PORTER BOOKS

*To Jennifer, the Princess
and the Pickle.*

Library and Archives Canada Cataloguing in Publication

Thompson, Robert, 1971–
  Going for the green : on the links with Canada's business and political elite / Robert Thompson.

ISBN 978-1-55263-993-1

  1. Businessmen—Canada—Anecdotes. 2. Politicians—Canada—Anecdotes. 3. Businessmen—Canada—Biography. 4. Politicians—Canada—Biography. 5. Golf courses. I. Title.

HC112.5.A2T56 2008   338.092′271   C2007-905427-7

**ONTARIO ARTS COUNCIL
CONSEIL DES ARTS DE L'ONTARIO**

The publisher gratefully acknowledges the support of the Canada Council for the Arts and the Ontario Arts Council for its publishing program. We acknowledge the support of the Government of Ontario through the Ontario Media Development Corporation's Ontario Book Initiative.

We acknowledge the financial support of the Government of Canada through the Book Publishing Industry Development Program (BPIDP) for our publishing activities.

Every reasonable effort has been made to trace ownership of copyrighted materials.

Key Porter Books Limited
Six Adelaide Street East, Tenth Floor
Toronto, Ontario
Canada M5C 1H6

www.keyporter.com

Text design: Martin Gould
Electronic formatting: Jean Lightfoot Peters

Printed and bound in Canada.

08 09 10 11 12 5 4 3 2 1

Acknowledgements

GOLFERS AT THE ELITE LEVELS of the game are supported by a wide array of people. There are swing doctors to fix your shanks and hozzles, your hooks and slices; psychologists to fix your head; physiologists to fix your body; and a wide array of managers, trainers, agents, and family. Regardless of their role, they each have a purpose. No one makes it even to a solitary middling finish on the pro tour without a lot of moving pieces.

And so it is with books, and specifically with this one. The crew who helped me create *Going for the Green* rivals the entourage that gets Diet Cokes and smokes for John Daly at a PGA Tour stop. In fact, the only difference between me and JD is that I've only been married once, and never to a stripper. Oh, and I don't have an RV worth $1 million emblazoned with "Hooters."

I'd like to offer my sincerest thanks to all of those who appear in the pages of this book and who took time out of their schedules to play a round of golf with me. Typically a game of golf is an opportunity to get away from your job, but these folks agreed not only to play golf with a reporter, but also to answer all the questions I could fire at them in four hours. I hope it wasn't too painful, but I'm not giving back any of the money I won along the way. Baby needs a new pair of shoes, don't you know.

I'd also like to thank all the fine crew at Key Porter Books who helped bring this book to life, including publisher Jordan Fenn.

After the demise of my "Going for the Green" column at the *National Post*, I was not sure it would ever be resuscitated, and I was thrilled that Jordan considered the concept compelling enough to finance my jaunt around Canada's great golf courses in search of interesting characters.

Of course, I'd be remiss if I didn't thank my editor, Carol Harrison. When we started I'm not sure Carol knew the difference between a bladed 7-iron and a fat wedge, but by the end she could distinguish a rusty cleek from a utility club, and could separate a penal one-shot hole designed by Doug Carrick from a par-5 with steep-sided bunkers created by Stanley Thompson.

A giant cheque (in size, not amount) should be sent immediately to Lloyd Davis, who dug through my copy for a second time. Hopefully golf balls were more interesting than donuts.

And a big hug for my agent, Hillary McMahon, who believed in this concept enough to pitch around and find me a deal. It took some faith, I'll tell you.

I'd also like to thank anyone who helped me along the way, arranging accommodations, cars, planes, or whatever got me (or in many instances my playing companions) to the course. That includes Andy Poon, my B.C. travel agent and hotelier; IMG's super-duper media guy, Dave Haggith; Sandy Hickman at Newfoundland Tourism; Andrea Nolan at Premier Danny Williams' office for putting up with all of my emails; Ken Villazor at Biovail; Jan Gear at ClubLink; Mike Taylor at Fairmont; Don Wanagas who gives political media flacks a good name; Sharifa Jordan, RJ's new executive assistant; Ruth Mcrea; Dean MacDonald; Bob Weeks for his time, and Porter Airlines.

A lot of individuals in the golf industry also helped by organizing games at their courses and occasionally joining the hacks for a trip around the track. Those worth applauding include Jamie Trenholme at Eagles Nest; Jason Plosz at the Elks Club; Elliott Isenor at Fox Harb'r; Joseph Murphy, GM at Scarboro G & CC; Ryan Beauchamp, the super at Glen Abbey; and Fred Veniot at Fox Creek.

And thanks to Dennis Firth at Angus Glen for letting me lay sod on his range while trying to find some semblance of a golf game so I didn't embarrass myself throughout the summer of 2007. Ted Manning at Titleist and Mark Dottori at Callaway supplied me and my victims with new balls to scatter all over the country. Paul Davies at TaylorMade helped procure my weapons.

A special thanks to my good friend Ian Andrew for his insight, criticism, and praise—who am I kidding, mostly for just the accolades—and to Steve Waxman, whose encouragement for this project came just as it was most needed. In exchange, Stevie, I'll flub a couple of shots coming down the stretch and let you take our next match. Or maybe not.

And my biggest shout out goes to my wife, Jennifer, who was always patient and supportive, even while pregnant and later with a newborn, as her husband flew around the country chasing a little white ball and playing golf with people who make more in an hour than I do all year. I'm convinced by the end of it our three-year-old, Sydney, was certain I paid the mortgage by playing golf. If only she knew how badly off we'd be if that was in fact the case.

In May 2002, I wrote my first "Going for the Green" column for the *National Post*. The concept was splashed all over the paper for days before it finally appeared. I'd taken a chance with my first attempt, asking retired Nesbitt Burns investment banker Brian Steck out for a round. He agreed and we played at Beacon Hall Golf Club, the kind of course that is hidden behind gates. Steck was interesting and led the conversation. I hastily jotted notes and tried to keep up while not hooking too many into the trees.

The following week I desperately tried to describe the experience of playing with Steck, including details of the course and the highs and lows of our round, all in under two thousand words. It was a struggle and I was decidedly nervous when I submitted my copy to my editor, Sarah Murdoch.

The next morning I came in to the *Post* and ran into Murdoch.

"Congratulations," she said flatly, in her own understated way.

I was worried she was being facetious, but it turned out she didn't hate it.

"I really enjoyed it," she continued. "You've not only got a column here, there's also a book in this."

It took six years, but I finally proved Sarah right.

Contents

Foreword

IN THE LATE SUMMER OF 2002, while playing golf with a business associate, I was asked whether I'd been following the series the *National Post* was running on the golfing abilities—or lack thereof—of some of Canada's corporate leaders. Although I was an avid newspaper reader, I truthfully had to answer that I was unaware of the stories. I was more of a *Globe and Mail* man than a *Post* reader, but I made mental note to check it out, then promptly forgot.

The next week it happened again when a friend mentioned he'd read an enlightening golf profile of a noted businessman. Had I seen it? I still had not.

A day later, a salesperson from my office sat down in front of my desk and again mentioned the column on the golfing business leaders, suggesting we should be looking to do something similar in *SCOREGolf* magazine, the publication of which I was editor. This time, the commentator was armed with a copy of the latest edition of Conrad Black's baby, slapping the folded journal onto my desk.

Finally, I read the story and was immediately intrigued. The tale was informative, the words lyrical and smooth. But for me the real question was just who was Robert Thompson? I had been writing and talking about golf for almost two decades in Canada and hadn't heard of this individual. I searched out a few more entries on the Internet and my interest was piqued. How, I asked myself, could this writer convince these power brokers to tee it up with him?

For most captains of industry, image is vitally important. Their appearances and speeches and even their dress are often managed by a cadre of executive assistants and PR flaks. They don't go anywhere without a plan rivalling the Normandy invasion. Yet, on the golf course they would be essentially naked, left on their own for the better part of four hours. With a journalist, no less.

Getting them to agree to this venture says a great deal about two things. The first is the respect they have for Thompson and his responsible, fair journalistic style (not to mention his ability to convince them to pick up his tab). Over the years, he has become known as someone who asks tough, often wince-inducing questions that may not make him any friends, but are absolutely necessary to understanding the story. More than once, he has startled a businessman or golfer with his pointed request for information, a request, it should be noted, that many reporters are too timid to make.

The second is that these power brokers simply love golf. It is the sport of business and having a low handicap and a membership at the right club can be as effective as a Harvard MBA in gaining traction on Bay Street. It's no secret that while business deals may not be consummated on the golf course, the relationships serve as the bonds from which these deals are forged.

Not many turned down Thompson's requests for a round at the course of their choice. He found that for many top corporate citizens, golf is somewhat of a soft spot when it comes to access. You won't get Eugene Melnyk or Ron Joyce or Ralph Klein to agree to sit down for four hours with any reporter, anywhere, but just mention the chance to chase a little white ball along a well-manicured pasture somewhere in Canada and they suddenly become like racehorses trapped in barns.

At least they did for Thompson, who managed to entice them not only to play golf but also to open up on a level that is almost startling.

What is truly remarkable is that in many cases, he managed to convince them to do it all over again. After the series ran out of gas in the newspaper, the idea of a book materialized and Robert went back on the fairways to get a Mulligan on many of his rounds with the big names in corporate and political Canada. Many of the profiles in this book are new but others are done from the vantage point of time passed. No matter into which category they fall, they're all astonishing for their clarity and for what they expose.

It might be difficult to classify *Going for the Green* as a sports book or, for that matter, a business book. It's more of a hybrid with a touch of biography. The profiles are varied and fascinating. Some deal with the business of golf, such as those of Golf Town CEO Stephen Bebis or prolific Canadian course designer Thomas McBroom. Others are of well-recognized individuals such as Ron Joyce, the Tim Hortons co-founder who owns his own luxurious golf resort, or Newfoundland and Labrador premier Danny Williams. And still others are of people not that familiar to the average Canadian, such as RBC's Jean-Paul Ouellet, but are equally interesting.

Each story reveals the man (and in one case, the woman) behind the name and the job title. And each allows a little glimpse into what is, in most cases, an obsession with golf. There are stories of playing with famous golfers such as Tiger Woods and Jim Furyk, or of tipping it up with prime ministers. There are revelations about the golfing abilities of some and the almost horrific lack of talent from others. Throw in a dash of ego, swagger, and personal history from each person and you have the ingredients for a riveting book.

These days, I no longer have to wonder about just who this golf/business writer for the *National Post* is as Thompson has become a friend as well as a contributor to *SCOREGolf*'s many media outlets (and I'm now a more regular reader of the *Post!*). He has established himself as one of the pre-eminent golf writers in the country and can not only command the attention of business leaders but also the golf industry: players, administrators, and executives.

For the record, Thompson has his own little obsession with the game and is a single-digit handicapper. But with a notebook or keyboard, he's clearly a scratch, which makes reading this book like a walk in the park, a park with sand traps and eighteen holes that is.

Bob Weeks,
Editor *SCOREGolf* magazine
January 2008

Prologue
On the Practice Tee

"Eighteen holes of match or medal play will teach you more about your foe than will eighteen years of dealing with him across a desk."
—Grantland Rice, American sportswriter

"HOW IN THE WORLD did you convince your editor to let you do this?"

I'd heard the question frequently, often asked with overtones of everything from surprise to confusion, jealousy, or occasionally even disgust.

This time it came from John Tory, then the head honcho at cable giant Rogers Communications, who on this gorgeous Indian summer day in early September was standing on the second tee of Rosedale Golf Club in Toronto. Blue blood runs through Tory's veins; with him was his father, John A. Tory Sr., one of the most successful business minds in Canada over the past three decades, who had taken Ken Thomson's billions and added a zero to the total. Tory's son, pre-teen George, rounded out our group.

John's question was a legitimate one. After all, I'd spent most of the summer of 2002 playing golf all over Canada with some of the country's richest and most successful individuals. I'd tipped it up at Ottawa's Hunt Club with Ron Zambonini, a hysterically funny Scotsman who at the time was running Canadian software giant Cognos. I'd flown in a private jet to Nova Scotia, where I was introduced as a guest of honour at a charity event held by donut baron Ron Joyce at Fox Harb'r, his seaside golf resort.

Over that first summer, I played the best golf courses that Canada had to offer—places like The National Golf Club, where the only truths you could be sure of were that you'd make double bogey by the end of your round and your wallet would be a little lighter, and Toronto Golf Club, where people sipped drinks behind a Victorian clubhouse that hadn't changed in nearly a century.

And yes, more than once I thought to myself, "Someone is paying me to do this?"

But it was while dining with pharmaceuticals billionaire Eugene Melnyk that I knew the crazy concept I'd dreamed up in the fall of 2002 might actually have some legs.

"I think this is great," said Melnyk, forking into his blackened mahi mahi while sitting on the balcony of his palatial home overlooking the ocean in Barbados. "You should take this to the U.S. or turn it into a book."

I should have told Melynk that, while *he* might be able to have his executive assistant pick up the phone, offer to send down his Challenger jet to pick up a top U.S. CEO, and fly them in for a game of golf, it wasn't that easy for me. Finding executives and politicians willing to play golf with a writer, and then have the results published in a newspaper, was not exactly as simple as sending an email. After all, most of these captains of industry might have belonged to some of the best clubs in the country, but only a few played golf more than a dozen times a year, and even then mainly in scrambles at charity fundraisers. It is a strange dichotomy—and more than once one of my playing partners would turn to me and say, "You know, I've only played here once this year, so this is a bloody expensive round."

I'd do the math and realize that the annual fees were usually the equivalent of a month's salary to me.

What I didn't tell Tory, the former Brian Mulroney aide and CFL commissioner who now plays the role of politician, when he asked me about my predilection for playing golf with the private-jet set, was that the idea stemmed largely from him.

In early 2001, things weren't so bright for Tory. As second-in-command at Rogers Communications, running the company's cable division, Tory was at the centre of a firestorm. The company's founder, Ted Rogers, a man known for bold business decisions—and, unfortunately, wrinkled baby-blue suits—had invested heartily in a California company called @Home, one of those seemingly well-funded startups designed to revolutionize the world. In this case, the goal of @Home was to bring high-speed Internet into homes across the United States and Canada through Rogers' cable connections. The problem was that @Home rarely lived up to its name. More often than not, home Internet connections powered by the company didn't work. Since people were paying fifty bucks a month for frustration, they turned on @Home and Rogers the way a pack of wild dogs rips apart a wounded animal. They jammed telephone support lines and the email boxes of Rogers executives. They screamed, they cajoled, and finally, they called the press.

For Tory, the easy solution would have been to simply unplug @Home and have Rogers build its own high-speed network. But Ted Rogers thought @Home was a great investment and had sunk millions into the company. "Keep using it," Tory was told. Apparently, Rogers hoped that if his company turned a blind eye to the problem, the technology supplied by @Home would somehow get better. It didn't.

As a cub reporter on the staff of the *National Post*'s business section, I was told to find out what was going on with Rogers' Internet meltdown. Over several months in 2001 I wrote a regular account of the woes of those who felt screwed by Rogers and its Internet service. Every morning, I'd open my email box and find it flooded by those who were disgusted, frustrated, and just plain pissed off with their inability to find solutions to their Internet problems.

With the situation becoming heated, industry analysts started to notice my stories. Rogers had bet big on the Internet—the company's future seemed to rest on it—and with @Home failing, customers were jumping ship faster than John Daly finds the local strip bar after arriving in a new town. The bosses at Rogers were noticing, too, and they weren't happy with me. The company's media flack regularly told me my stories were unfair and accused me of having a vendetta against the company. The truth be told, I was sick of the story after a few months, but my editor, Ken Whyte, loved it and sent me notes encouraging me to stay on it.

Eventually, Rogers realized that my stories weren't going to stop, so it decided to bring the enemy into the fold. Extending an olive branch, the company asked me to join several key executives—including Tory—at a box in the Air Canada Centre to watch the Toronto Maple Leafs take on the New York Islanders.

I said no. Why would I want to spend an evening with the same people who called me a liar on a regular basis during the day? To most people, a free ticket to a Leafs game—in an opulent box where drinks and dinner are gratis—is akin to winning a lottery; but for me, it entailed the unappetizing prospect of being sandwiched between overwhelming and overbearing public relations lackeys, sipping glasses of warm wine and making small talk with mid-level executives that I'd likely never see or speak with again. To some, the chance to take in a hockey game from a box is the height of luxury; to me, it sounded painful.

But after some prodding I eventually accepted the invitation—and only when I was told Tory would be making an appearance. We'd only spoken by phone during my interviews, and I thought it would be good for both of us to put a face to the name.

"Robert, it is good to meet you."

I was on the receiving end of the first of what would become many John Tory handshakes over the years. Tory isn't exactly an imposing figure. He's tall, but he's also a bit stiff—even these days, when he's trying to glad-hand his way around Ontario as a politician. He's rarely seen without a tie. In fact, if I were a betting man, I'd wager Tory wore a tie coming out of the womb. It's as if his security blanket consists of a blue blazer and red tie.

I'd expected to speak with Tory, and figured I'd get an earful about @Home. He surprised me. After the requisite small talk, he asked what I'd be up to that weekend. It was the first Thursday in April, and as far as I'm concerned there's only one thing any red-blooded male does on the first weekend of the fourth month of the year: watch the Masters.

"Yeah, I'm going to do that too," Tory said. "There's a charter that flies down to Augusta on Saturday. I've gone the past few years. We'll watch the tournament, have dinner, and fly home."

That wasn't what I meant when I said I'd be watching the Masters. My viewing, on a humbler scale, involved a twenty-eight-inch screen and a couple of beers.

But, regardless of whether we were speaking the same dialect, at least we were speaking the same language. Desperate to avoid talking about anything involving cables, we'd stumbled upon a subject in which we were both interested.

"Where do you play, Robert?"

I was a struggling public player, the type that tried to find courses that were inexpensive but still had greens that were, well, green. Tory, on the other hand, had never had to fight the hordes for a Sunday tee time. He'd grown up in a family with a membership at Rosedale, the hallowed course off Yonge Street that was home to many of Toronto's kings of industry—as long as those kings were of the type that prayed in a church as opposed to a synagogue. The Tory family had been part of Rosedale for nearly a hundred years. Tory's father was a member, as was his father's father and his father's father's father. You get the picture. The biggest issue that faced Tory was whether to continue to pay annual dues at Rosedale after he left law school and joined the family firm. His decision to join the family club was hardly a surprise. The club was, after all, in his blood.

"Well, Robert, I'd love to have you out for a game at Rosedale if you have the time."

In business circles, the casual invitation to play a round of golf usually has the same degree of sincerity as the shout of "we should have lunch" following a chance encounter with a former colleague in a crowded room. Playing golf with Tory seemed about as likely for me as teeing it up in a PGA Tour event.

When the hockey game ended and I managed to extract myself from the hangers-on hoping that some lukewarm pizza and a couple of equally warm beers would change my reporting tendencies, I went home and forgot about Tory's offer.

That changed a couple of weeks later when I received a note from him. "Here are the dates I'm available over the next few months for our game at Rosedale," he wrote. "Let me know what works for you."

I approached one of my overworked editors at the *Post* about taking an afternoon away from the office to go play a private golf course with one of the scions of Canadian business. Editors typically hate these kinds of requests, as they are chained to their desks, always convinced that reporters are out on the town, having a good time at their expense. It surprised me, then, when the editor in this instance not only agreed, but actively endorsed the idea.

We settled on a date, and a couple of days before the round, Tory called me. Did I know how to get to Rosedale, he asked, and would it be okay if he asked his father to come along?

"You'll probably find my dad interesting," Tory said. "He's the man who bought the *Globe and Mail* for Ken Thomson." Interesting, indeed.

With that in mind I left the office on a sunny afternoon and made the fifteen-minute drive from the *Post*'s office in Don Mills to Rosedale Golf Club in Hogg's Hollow.

Rosedale remains *the* course for those Torontonians with business and social ambitions, a golf club that leaves even the richest of the rich the ignominy of having to rest on a waiting list for more than a decade before being given the privilege of playing more than a handful of games annually. Created by Donald Ross, a Scot who left for the Carolinas and became a golf architect renowned for his innovative designs and the volume of courses he created over his career, Rosedale has been tweaked more than an aging socialite. It isn't the best golf course in Toronto, or even the best golf club—and there's a big difference between the two—but for those who are concerned about their position in proper society, it is the *only* club where one should be a member.

You know you've made it in Toronto social circles when you're allowed entrance to the club. Even after waiting years, some of the most successful businessmen and women in the city are denied access. Take, for example, the story of Canadian Big Mac king George Cohon, who found himself at the centre of controversy when he became the first Jew admitted to the club—in 1997. He might have brought the cheeseburger to Moscow, but that didn't mean he was going to get a wedge on Rosedale, at least not at first.

Though the club was very careful about who could become a member, they were apparently less concerned about letting ink-stained wretches hack up their fairways. I parked my Tempo next to a silver Mercedes, flipped open my trunk, and sat on the bumper while I put on my golf shoes. I probably received horrified stares from those around me who couldn't imagine changing their shoes while leaning on their car, but I was largely oblivious as I rushed to the pro shop, where I ran into a waiting John Tory. Even in casual golf attire, he looked the part of the professional businessman. His father showed up moments later and we took a few steps out of the old pro shop and onto the first tee at Rosedale.

The round was a blur of golf and conversation. I recall hitting my tee shot under a tree on the left side of the fairway, and reaching the par-5 eighth in two with a 7-iron.

What I recognized at the time was the insight I was getting into two of the top business minds in Canada at the time. Away from their offices, lawyers, suits, ties, and executive assistants, the Torys joked and poked fun at one another. For a family that seemed so conservative and so, well, uptight, it was enlightening to see they didn't talk about stock options, corporate marketing campaigns, and debt financing, at least not while playing golf.

Instead, Tory chastised his father for saying he was retired.

"Robert, ask Dad how often he goes into the office," Tory said, using me as his personal mediator.

"Well, how about it, Mr. Tory?"

"Only four or five days," he said, smirking. "But I don't go in on weekends anymore."

If that's retirement, I thought, kill me now.

As we wandered over Rosedale's pristine fairways, I learned that both men played out every shot, rarely—if ever—used a foot wedge to dislodge a ball from a tricky spot, and were encouraging and engaging playing partners. We talked about Tiger Woods, who was about to defend his Canadian Open title at Royal Montreal, and Conrad Black, who had recently sold his Canadian newspaper empire, including the *National Post.*

Most of all, I saw something closer to the real Tory family than any other reporter had in the past. I was given a passing glimpse of the relationship between a son and his father—one man still playing out his ambitions in public, the other so reticent that he rarely, if ever, offered press interviews. I found that the son who ran the cable company was unfailingly polite, even when his golf game went sideways—something it did on more than one occasion over eighteen holes. He was not easily flustered, something I'm sure has served him well, especially in recent years as his political career has gone in a similar direction.

His father, who played more frequently, often with former TD Bank CEO Dick Thomson at a Florida hideaway called Seminole Golf Club, was a better player, although, being in his early seventies, he rarely hit the ball very far. He was still careful about his remarks around a newspaper reporter, but by the end of our game the elder Tory had become less calculated and a bit more relaxed.

When it was all over, and we were walking up the fairway to the old green on the final hole with its crazed false front, my mind began wandering. Wouldn't it be a great concept to pitch a series about playing golf with Canada's power brokers? If they were all as intriguing as the Tory family, it could be enlightening, and besides, I'd get the chance to play a whole bunch of great golf courses along the way. How could I go wrong?

Over the next couple of months in the fall of 2001, I used my downtime between writing news stories to craft a proposal for a series of articles that would have me play golf with politicians and business leaders and write about it. It sounded so outlandish that I was sheepish about pitching it to Mark Stevenson, my editor at the time, who had put out a request to *Financial Post* reporters asking for new concepts for the paper. The problem is that most papers pay little attention to pitches from young reporters, and I was especially certain that my idea, which would see me spend the summer chasing a little white ball all over Canada, would be on the receiving end of a good chuckle and a yawn. Right, Thompson, they'd say, let's *pay* to have you play golf.

Undaunted, I pitched away, sending my concept to Stevenson.

Now, Mark, who currently runs *Maclean's*, doesn't appear to have the eccentric markings of a visionary, and if we're using golf as an indicator of personality, I can say I didn't learn a lot about him during our lone round one summer. I can say for a fact that he's not an avid player or single-digit handicapper. Quiet in demeanour, his wardrobe at the time seemed to consist of baggy jeans and golf shirts with sun-bleached collars flipped up in the style preferred by university freshmen in the 1980s. He was also new to the business section of the paper at the time, having been dropped into a co-editor position after a job cut a few months previous.

Surprisingly, he liked the idea, and offered to pay for me to travel throughout the country in the summer of 2002. The column would be called "Going for the Green," meant as a double entendre. Money *is* golf. Get it?

That whirlwind summer left me with little time to breathe between lining up victims for the columns, turning out a feature a week, and travelling all over Canada. It was also one of the most fascinating and enjoyable times I've had as a writer. I was hooked, and apparently readers were as well. They sent me tons of email, asking me about the little nuances I might have (inadvertently or not) left out of the articles.

For two more summers I travelled the country, taking on all sorts of Canadian businessmen and politicians in games where the bets were typically a few bucks, sipping draft beers on the patios of some of the best private clubs in the country, and generally hanging out in places reporters and the public rarely see.

It turns out that, even with drivers, personal assistants, and access to the greatest golf courses in the world, all the powerful really want is a reliable drive and the ability to get up and down from a bunker occasionally. They may have spent their days running some of the biggest companies in the country, but their ambitions on the course were usually not that grand. I found most Canadian power brokers were not unlike weekend hacks who take time out to play on a $25 municipal course.

Surprisingly few of them actually did business on the course. Issues relating to their companies would often come up, especially when golfing with other executives, but rarely would talk of a deal arise on a golf course. In fact, some got pissed off when business was brought up on the course. While it might come as a surprise to those who have never had the good fortune to set foot on Toronto Golf Club or the impeccable fairways of Mount Bruno, some clubs would prefer that business be dealt with elsewhere; in their minds, a club is a club, not a boardroom. Of course, that's not always the case, and in some more modern retreats—places like Frank Stronach's Magna Golf Club in Aurora, Ontario, an ostentatious golfing testament to his own ego—boardrooms equipped with sixty-inch flat-panel TV monitors are par for the course. But what I found was that, for most of the country's rich and famous, golf was more about developing relationships and learning about those with whom you worked and did business.

In 2005, the column ran out of life, the victim of an editorial change at the paper left "Going for the Green" poised for an early retirement. Call it the Seve Ballesteros of newspaper columns—it had spunk and occasionally could make birdie from some strange locations, but it wasn't built to last. The timing was probably not all that bad—after all, in thirty-six months I had turned out nearly eighty profiles of capitalist golfers and renegade politicians. It was enough.

The only problem was that, every so often, another email would drift into my in-box asking me about the column. I'd also bump into people in social settings who would tell me how much they'd enjoyed the series and ask whether it would ever reappear. At these times the idea of making it something bigger, something more fluid and thematic, would cross my mind. Then I'd give my head a shake, remembering just how long the series had taken to write and how much travel I'd put into it during those summers.

Still, the idea of revisiting it dogged me. It felt incomplete.

It took a couple of years, but eventually I found the time to spend another summer driving to Pearson International Airport, dumping my car in the lot, and frantically running to catch a flight to Moncton, or Victoria, or Calgary. The concept was simple: "Going for the Green" would return, but it couldn't just be the old columns regurgitated. Instead, I'd take fifteen of my favourite profiles and reinvent them with more detail, insight, and personality than a newspaper allows. That meant replaying all of the games—though the thought of returning to places like Shaughnessy Golf and Country Club in Vancouver, the Elks Club in Calgary, and Angus Glen in Toronto wasn't without its appeal.

The subjects I'd decided to hit up for a round were either the most intriguing or the most fun to write about. That meant going back to Eugene Melnyk, who had since departed Biovail, the pharmaceutical giant he created, and now owned the Ottawa Senators. It would allow me to drop in on Ron Joyce at his home at Fox Harb'r to play a few holes, two years after I helped him craft his autobiography. I also looked up Frank McKenna, fresh from the conclusion of a stint as Canada's ambassador to the U.S. and now spending his time as the vice-chair of TD Bank Financial Group.

I also felt the need to find some new playing partners—some of whom I had hoped to write about in the *Post* had the series continued, and some who had piqued my interest since then. That meant heading to The Rock to slice a couple with Newfoundland premier Danny Williams, and take a drive up Highway 404 for a torridly paced round with big-box entrepreneur Stephen Bebis, the CEO of Golf Town.

One of my last rounds during what became known around my home as "the summer of golf" was with McKenna, Francis McGuire (McKenna's former right-hand man and now CEO of Major Drilling Group), and Norm Keevil, the chair of the mining giant Teck Cominco. During our round, the former politician turned to me on the second hole of Fox Creek, a meandering public course outside of Moncton, and asked how my summer had gone.

Since my bags, including my golf clubs, had been sent into the limbo of lost luggage by Air Canada the day before, and my ever-expanding wife was at home seven months pregnant, I was in a bit of a self-pitying mood, both grumpy and tired.

"Oh, it has been a lot of work," I told him, eyeing my ball, which lay near some casual water on the right side of the fairway.

McKenna, sensing my situation wasn't as bad as I was letting on, paused for a minute, let me hit my wedge onto the second green, and then turned back to me.

"But I bet it was also a lot of fun," he said with a wide grin on his face, the look of someone who would rather spend more time on a fairway and less in a boardroom.

Indeed it was. Every hole of it.

CHAPTER 1

Jim Kinnear and Jim Balsillie
Capitalists and the Canadian Open

"Golf teaches success and failure. Neither lasts long."
—Glenn F. Kummer, American executive

JIM KINNEAR IS LATE. Not sort of late. Really late.

I'm not particularly surprised. Kinnear is the chief executive and founder of Pengrowth Energy Trust, one of the largest and most successful oil income trusts in Canada, and as such, he always seems to be heading in six different directions at once. He has seven different phone numbers (that I know of) and three assistants who handle his schedule. And even then they rarely seem to know where he's been, where he's at, or where he's going. He's frenetic, always on the move. One day he's in Houston, talking about the purchase of some junior oil company. The next, he's golfing in Scotland. In between, he might swing down to a PGA Tour stop to have dinner and a bottle of wine with Stephen Ames.

Which is why I shouldn't be surprised that Kinnear isn't on time to meet me on a glorious July morning at Angus Glen Golf Club, a remarkably popular public golf facility north of Toronto. Except this time I am caught a little off guard. Fifteen minutes from now, Kinnear is supposed to be standing on the first tee of the North Course at Angus Glen, warmed up and ready to play. And this isn't just any golf game. This one is with Garry West, the president of the Royal Canadian Golf Association, the organization that runs the

Canadian Open, and a guy named Jim Furyk, only the third-ranked player in the world and the tournament's defending champion.

Kinnear, you see, is late for his tee time in the Wednesday pro-am of Canada's biggest golf tournament. Furyk has already warmed up, West is on the range, and apparently whomever Kinnear has invited to round out the foursome is on the range doing calisthenics or at least stroking some on the putting green.

But the man himself is nowhere to be seen.

Now, I've heard of execs with memberships at private clubs where the annual dues total thousands of dollars per year, but who only play a game or two. "This game is costing me, let's see, about $3,456.22," one executive told me after doing the math in his head as he played his solitary round that season at his club. But Kinnear's costs for this particular round ran much deeper. He paid nearly a million dollars to have Pengrowth act as a sponsor of the Canadian Open, and one of the perks is a spot in the pro-am. Even assuming he makes the eight o'clock tee time—which is not a certainty with the clock ticking down to what is now just over ten minutes away—this has got to be one of the most expensive golf games in history.

As for me, I'm wondering if this is how all caddy gigs go. You see, even though I've played with Kinnear several times before, his crazed schedule prevented us from hooking up for a game this year. Instead, one of his assistants suggested that I should loop for the oil baron at the Canadian Open.

That sounded like a pretty good proposition. There's a strong lineage of writer/caddies who have chronicled carrying the bag for everyone from the notable (Rick Reilly's book, *Who's Your Caddy?*,detailing his time as the jam boy for the likes of Jack Nicklaus) to the less illustrious but equally entertaining (Michael Bamberger's *To the Linksland*, his account of working for practising Buddhist Peter Teravainen on the European Tour). Even Canadian golf-writing legend Lorne Rubenstein got his start caddying. It is a rite of passage.

So why not carry Kinnear's bag? Someone had to, and frankly it had to be easier to take notes while observing the game than playing it. At least it appeared that way in theory. The reality was different. When I should be buffing up Kinnear's clubs and suggesting whether to hit a draw driver or a fade 3-wood off the first tee, I am instead standing, sans golf bag or caddy bib, in the parking lot, waiting for my player.

I wander over to Tom MacMillan, the beleaguered media flack whose job it is to follow Kinnear during the tournament. Any idea where our oil exec is?

"I'm told he's on his way," he sighs, looking at his watch. His expression makes it clear that he's not certain Kinnear is going to make it.

But sure enough, within a minute Kinnear pulls up in a grey suv next to the registration table, jumps out, and immediately starts talking and shaking hands with those around him.

Fact one: Jim Kinnear is a social animal who stands out from a crowd just about anywhere he goes. He should be warming up, or at least be worried about making his tee time. Instead he's standing around, gabbing. The man loves to talk. I suspect that's why he's rarely on time.

Fact two: He's not worried about being conspicuous. On this day—as is common when he's playing golf—Kinnear is dressed in plus-fours, the common term for the anachronistic outfit of short knicker pants most commonly worn by golfers in the early decades of the twentieth century. Needless to say, amongst a sea of shorts and dress pants worn by those around him, even wearing a plain white golf shirt with the green Pengrowth logo emblazoned on the chest, Kinnear stood out like a bogey on Tiger Woods' card.

Fact three: He loves the colour green. Pengrowth's logo is green. Kinnear has tailored green trousers to match. And if wearing plus-fours doesn't bring enough attention his way, then the fact they are—you guessed it—sort of a hunter-green colour makes him easy to pick out of a crowd.

"Rob, how are you doing today?" he says to me with a big grin after he's done shaking hands, completely oblivious to the wave of chaos he is leaving in his midst.

"Umm, fine, Jim," I sputter. "We're on the tee in a couple of minutes."

It is only then that I look around and realize we have a problem.

"Umm, Jim, where are your clubs?"

"Oh yeah, clubs. I guess we'll need those."

This is off to a grand start.

Once we determine that Kinnear needs, at the very least, rental clubs, a glove, some golf balls (thankfully he had his own golf shoes), and has to be on the tee in two minutes, we began our walk up the hill to where our playing partners are waiting. Seconds later, as handlers from Angus Glen race up to the tee with a bag of rental TaylorMade clubs, a dozen Titleist Pro V1 balls and a left-handed glove, Kinnear is just settling in, which means he's chewing the ear off someone standing nearby. Despite the close call, he never seems flustered or anxious. Instead, he continues to operate as if everything were perfectly timed. The experience, in a nutshell, is a great analogy for his career, something that's been built on a self-confidence some might think is misplaced. But as far as I can tell, Kinnear never second-guesses himself. If he had, or if someone had convinced him of the folly of his ambition, he probably would not be standing on the first tee at the Canadian Open shaking the hand of one of the world's best golfers.

That said, Kinnear is only about five hundred kilometres from where he began his career—but in terms of how far he's come, well, it might as well be light years away. Having grown up in Montreal and worked as an energy analyst, Kinnear left in 1980 to join the energy boom in Calgary. According to the legend spread around Calgary's oil patch, he went west with nothing but a used Cadillac and $200.

"That isn't that far removed from the truth," Kinnear says.

It didn't work out well. Within two years, the Pierre Trudeau government announced the National Energy Policy and oil prices cratered. Kinnear could have admitted defeat, crawled back to Montreal, and found another mid-level position in some securities firm. But he never lacked in self-confidence, even when things were going badly, and instead of assuming the fetal position, he started Pengrowth, a company aimed at capitalizing on the aging oil properties that were no longer feasible for the biggest petroleum makers in the world.

The concept of the company was to find more effective—and profitable—ways of managing these assets. It wasn't as if these oil wells weren't turning out black gold; it was just that they didn't turn out enough of it to satisfy the massive needs of the multinationals that owned them. Kinnear eyed junior oil companies on the rise, which were often undercapitalized and unable to get their hands on the prize, or at least let it flow through their fingers as it was pumped out of the ground.

Kinnear launched Pengrowth in 1985 on a wing and a prayer, and managed to get the business to a public offering by early 1989. It took another five years before he could be certain Pengrowth would be a success. These days, the company has six hundred employees and is worth about $5 billion. He has also personally benefited handsomely from his huge gamble, having amassed a net worth that is surely in the hundreds of millions.

"I've done all right," Kinnear says matter-of-factly, as if "all right" equated to merely being able to make his car payments.

As Kinnear introduces himself to Furyk and West, I'm tapped on the shoulder. I spin around as quickly as one can do with a leather tour bag over one's shoulder, a dozen golf balls in one hand, and a notebook and pen in the other. In other words, I almost fall over. Golf balls could have gone everywhere. Hilarity would have ensued—at my expense. Thankfully, gravity doesn't take its toll.

"What the hell are you doing here?" the man asks.

Given the ridiculous anarchy of the previous few minutes, it takes me a minute to clue in to who is addressing me. Standing on the tee incognito, holding his driver and wearing a baseball cap pulled down fast over his white forehead, his eyes obscured by dark sunglasses, is none other than Jim Balsillie, the co-CEO of Research In Motion, the tech giant famous for the BlackBerry. As one of the sponsors of the Canadian Open—and one of the men searching for a title sponsor willing to put millions into the event—Kinnear hit up some key Canadian businessmen to join him at the tournament. Balsillie, an ultracompetitive billionaire who loves his sports, readily took him up on the invite.

At that instant, in the middle of the summer of 2007, there were few Canadians more notorious, more regularly in the headlines— and probably more loved—than Balsillie. An iconoclast who continued to doggedly promote his vision of the BlackBerry email pager when everyone around him said it would be bought by Bill Gates, lose to some other telecom giant, or fail outright, Balsillie had proved all of the naysayers wrong. Instead RIM's share price soared beyond $200, making him wealthy beyond his wildest expectations.

Though he's Harvard-educated, something he typically lets people know at the slightest prompting, Balsillie also comes across as understated, considering he's at the helm of one of the biggest companies in North America. He still lives in Waterloo, Ontario, and doesn't drive anything flashier than a BMW. Bald and in great shape from his extensive workout regimen, Balsillie isn't someone you'd pay attention to if he walked down the sidewalk beside you. Though he often speaks in public, it is pretty much only about BlackBerries and email. That changed in the fall of 2006, when Balsillie announced he was going to buy the Pittsburgh Penguins of the National Hockey League. That deal eventually fell apart, but Balsillie is nothing if not persistent. Instead of giving up his hockey dream, in the spring of 2007 he tried to buy the Nashville Predators and move the team to Hamilton.

The idea that Balsillie would increase the number of teams in Canada, taking one of them out of the hands of inept American owners who clearly had little sense of hockey or its history, appealed to the fabric of the country. That he offered $230 million for the team, vastly overstating its worth, then took deposits on season tickets for a team that he didn't yet own, and finally stood up to NHL commissioner Gary Bettman and the league's largely subservient ownership base, only endeared him further. It didn't really matter that he wasn't successful—Canadians have lauded him for simply trying. In many ways, Balsillie is as big a superstar as those on the ice.

I regain my composure, and, making sure the golf bag doesn't topple into the spectator behind me, extend my hand to Balsillie.

"You've been busy since I last saw you," I suggest, in what must be the understatement of the year. The last time I played golf with Balsillie, RIM shares were trading at $13 and there was no discussion of acquiring hockey teams. At that time, the company was worth hundreds of millions; now it is worth roughly the gross domestic product of a mid-sized European nation.

Balsillie smiles knowingly and turns back to grab something from his caddy. Suddenly, the crowd of a few dozen spectators quiets as I fidget to get the head cover off Kinnear's driver.

"Now on the tee, from Ponte Vedra Beach, Florida, the 2006 Canadian Open champion—Jim Furyk!" the announcer exclaims. Up steps Furyk, one of the greats of the game. He takes a quick practice swing and strides onto the tee at Angus Glen's dogleg-left par-5 opener.

There's no description that can accurately encapsulate Furyk's golf swing. Some would call it "loopy"; others simply see it as unorthodox. Certainly, all the commentators agree that it isn't a classic swing in any sense. He starts with his hands close to his body, takes the club away decidedly inside, and reroutes it on the way down, resulting in what golf announcer David Feherty once described as akin to "an octopus falling out of a tree." That might be a little harsh; in any event, it is a deadly effective swing. Furyk has earned more than US$35 million in his career, during which he has won thirteen tournaments, including the U.S. Open.

And today, the octopus must like what it sees—Furyk strokes his opening drive down the middle with a slight draw.

The Wednesday pro-am is an event unique to professional golf. There is no equivalent in any other sport. It is almost unimaginable that an amateur—a desk jockey at the best of times—would be invited to compete on the same playing field as a professional athlete. Accountants don't get to pitch to Barry Bonds; no software engineer would be allowed to step into the ring for a little tussle with Ultimate Fighter Chuck Liddell; and you're not going to try to return a Roger Federer serve. But the day before the first round of competition at practically every PGA Tour stop, from Pebble Beach, California, to Madison, Mississippi, golf's best tee it up alongside a group of businessmen willing to fork out thousands for the opportunity to chop the ball around with someone who can actually golf.

Now, these businessmen don't exactly play the same game. They play from tees that are, in total, more than half a mile closer than those used by the pros. And they use their handicaps—essentially a way to level the playing field for those that aren't very good at the game. Oh, and the worst score one can make on any hole is par. When all is said and done, it isn't uncommon to see a group of supposed Sunday hackers post a score of 56, meaning they carded a birdie on almost every hole. In a pro-am, not only can they play alongside a Tiger Woods, but they can compete—and, yes, even beat him. And every pro in that week's tournament field plays—whether they are Ernie Els or Skip Kendall.

These affairs sound like fun, and for those who have anted up the cash they often are. That's assuming that the pro they've selected in the draw prior to their round actually wants to be out and playing with a bunch of guys who slice worse than Jack the Ripper. The Tigers of the world tolerate the pro-ams, and some even use the five-plus hours they spend on the course to pick the brains of their CEO partners for stock tips. For other pros, of course, it is a painful process of watching those who are great at real estate, investment banking, or mergers and acquisitions hack it around a course set up for those who figured out golf's nuances before they left high school.

It is a good thing, then, that the players in our group occasionally make contact when they swing. In fact, all three are relatively accomplished golfers, which means that no one in our group, or in the crowd surrounding us, is likely to get injured by a projectile. That much is clear from the tee shots made on the first hole by West and Balsillie, though my man Kinnear is not as convincing—he hits a hard hook that jumps down just in the rough, short of the left fairway bunker. As soon as he hits his ball, Kinnear wanders up the fairway with his foursome. I, on the other hand, am left to switch his rental clubs to a more appropriate set and run up the fairway after the group.

Just then, Richard Zokol, the former Canadian PGA Tour winner who is standing next to the ropes, turns to me.

"You know the three factors that make a good caddy, Robert, right?"

Uh-huh. I think I know what's coming.

"Show up, keep up, and shut up."

Tell me again when this caddy gig gets to be fun?

It doesn't get much better for us when the oil baron takes two swings out of the thick wet rough to progress the ball into the fairway. But Kinnear is an optimist. When most would suggest that he pick up his ball and stick it in his pocket, he's still hacking away. When we finally make the green, we're left with twenty feet for par.

"Isn't this fun?" he asks, smiling, as I hand him his putter.

"Right," I mutter under my breath as I grab a wet towel to clean the grass stains off his golf ball.

Balsillie is an interesting casual golfer. True to form, he whips out his BlackBerry on the second hole (one of the models with the full keyboard) and begins frantically typing with his thumbs, all the while talking to Furyk.

"Like your BlackBerry?" Furyk comments drolly, though it isn't clear whether he's suitably impressed or being dismissive of Balsillie's lack of focus on the game.

"Yes. See, my wife is off to Europe today," the email king says. "Just got to send a quick 'see you soon—will miss you, honey.'" He types for a couple more seconds and turns to the golfer.

"Okay, that's done. So, where did you go to school, Jim?"

"Arizona."

"Arizona State?" Balsillie asks, sticking the BlackBerry back in this pocket.

"No, I went to *college*," comes Furyk's sharp reply, referring to the fierce rivalry between his alma mater, the University of Arizona, and its state-run counterpart. How much time he spent in class, as opposed to the range, is likely up for debate.

It is always fascinating to observe how successful businessmen interact with professional athletes. In my experience, regardless of the status they've achieved in the corporate world, executives are always in awe of successful athletes—even bald, slightly gawky ones like Furyk. Here's Balsillie, a man who can buy a team of athletes, hanging on Furyk's every word. Kinnear isn't much different, but truthfully, he doesn't have time to interact with Furyk on the first couple of holes, as he tries to find his swing.

It is also intriguing to see the disconnect sports fans have when they get up close and personal with stars. Sure, these athletes are superstars, and they regularly accomplish remarkable things, but they are still human.

On the fourth hole, a long par-3 that plays 207 yards over a small creek, the flag cut into the back corner of the green just past a small swale, Furyk stands on the tee and ponders his shot.

Balsillie wanders over to me while Furyk goes through his pre-shot dance.

"What do you think—7-iron?" he queries.

Not if Furyk doesn't want to go swimming. I hold out four fingers, indicating a long iron.

"No way," Balsillie says dismissively as Furyk cracks off a soaring shot that hits a peak over the green and tumbles to the ground like a butterfly with bunions on its feet.

"Hey, Jim, what did you hit there?" I ask as we walk to the forward tee.

"Soft 3-iron," he says.

Balsillie starts shaking his head, animatedly mouthing the words, "No way," as if he doesn't trust that Furyk is telling the truth. Four days later, Furyk will win the Canadian Open, thanks in part to a hole-in-one on this very hole, made with a 5-iron. I know that to be true because I looked it up in the official scoring record.

Balsillie, even in his mid-forties, has more in common with pro athletes than most executives. He's a fitness freak who regularly trains for triathlons. He also has a majority interest in a business that owns several golf courses near Waterloo, where RIM is based. His golf game is based largely around his physical prowess. That is to say, he's not a great golfer, but what he lacks in ability he more than makes up for through strength and strong co-ordination. His isn't a pretty game, but it is effective.

And he rarely plays, especially given the demands on his time, he explains to Furyk as they walk up the fifth fairway. Only three rounds so far this summer—Sage Valley, a mini-Augusta in the U.S. south; Bond Head, with Canadian pro golfer Ian Leggatt; and Öviinbyrd, an exclusive enclave in cottage country north of Toronto.

Like Kinnear, Balsillie regularly gets invited to play in pro-ams. He has even taken up the occasional offer. I often wonder if top-level executives ever get worried about playing in front of the crowds that come out for PGA Tour pro-ams. After all, they aren't being paid for their prowess on the golf course. Balsillie doesn't get nervous, he explains, but playing in front of its crowds can be hazardous.

"When I played in the Canadian Open pro-am in Hamilton, we were with Fairway Freddie," he explains, referring to the affable PGA

Tour pro Fred Funk, best known not for his length off the tee, but for his ability to find the short grass. "We were coming up the eighteenth—you know, the one with the creek in the fairway. There must have been a few hundred people on the hill around the green. I had a 4-iron in my hands at about 190 yards in. And I guess the swing didn't come off because I sprayed it to the right. You should have seen those people scramble!"

Scrambling to find their cellphones to call their lawyers, I'm sure.

Though he's not nearly as athletic as Balsillie and more than a decade older, Kinnear possesses a much smoother golf swing that occasionally results in long, straight drives. A golfer since his teen years in Montreal, Kinnear plays as regularly as his extensive travel schedule permits. West, the official representative in the group—and, interestingly, the lead auditor for RIM's books—stays quiet for most of the round, observing more than interacting.

So, what do two golfers and executives speak about when they walk up a fairway with one of the top golf pros in the world?

Jets, as it happens. Balsillie is praising the Falcon 50 that RIM uses for executive travel. "It's just a great plane," he says, walking to his ball.

"I think I need to get one of those," Kinnear says, as if he's talking about acquiring a new car.

So, is Jim Furyk a BlackBerry guy? As we head up to the eighth tee, I finally break Zokol's quiet-caddy admonition and ask Furyk the question: Does he like to type with his thumbs?

Instead of looking at me as if I'm from Mars, he takes the question in stride.

"I never use one. Really, I'm not even much of an email guy," he continues. "I guess I could be better at it, but that's what my agent does. My wife, on the other hand, she's attached to hers. At the British Open we'd be at dinner and I'm like, 'Turn it off, would you?' And she'd always say, 'Oh, just one more.'"

On the tenth tee, a nasty, uphill par-4, I get a real sense of what it means to be a caddy. After Furyk pipes another down the middle— he doesn't miss a fairway all day—our group scatters balls all over the property. West's shot flies right; Balsillie hits it straight, but short; and Kinnear hammers a hook into the fescue on the left. He trudges up the fairway, eating an apple. When we find the ball in knee-deep grass, I hand him a wedge, hoping he can hack it back to the fairway. He, in turn, hands me his half-eaten apple. Does he want me to hold on to it and return it after his shot? Deciding I have no idea what the protocol is for gnawed apples, I casually dump it into the grass behind me. Four shots in the grass later, I suggest to my loop that we pick up the ball and move to the green, where our group is watching with widening eyes.

"Good idea. Good idea," Kinnear says, pulling his hat down and pacing up to the green.

While Kinnear struggles, Balsillie's game picks up. On the eleventh hole, a long par-5 with water to the left along the length of the hole, the BlackBerry pusher pumps one up the middle and hammers a mid-iron to the front of the green.

As we walk down the hill towards the fairway, Furyk and Balsillie end up in an animated conversation about what has made RIM successful. Balsillie gives the golfer a quick synopsis, one he's clearly used before.

"Well, Jim, it comes down to this," Balsillie explains. "Brains plus a great product equals success."

So *that's* the secret. He makes it sound so simple that I wonder why I didn't think of it.

Within Canadian business circles it is clear that one of the keys to RIM's success has been the relationship between Balsillie and his co-CEO, Mike Lazaradis. In many ways, Lazaradis is Balsillie's antithesis. Balsillie is the jock, while Lazaradis is the egghead, more at home discussing theoretical physics than golf or hockey. But aside from covering the skills spectrum between them, both execs are notoriously competitive. Competition has fuelled a lot of what Balsillie has done with RIM—from legal battles to challenging some of the biggest companies in the world. In Balsillie, this competitive edge is readily apparent, even in a friendly pro-am. On the thirteenth hole at Angus Glen's North Course, a mid-length par-4 with a fairway that swings from right to left as water looms between the tee and green, Kinnear steps up to the tee after Furyk hits yet another fairway. He takes a mighty rip at the ball, and yanks it badly on a direct line over the water to the green. With the hole playing slightly downwind, the ball clears the water—just barely—and comes to rest twenty yards in front of the green. It is a magnificent—if magnificently unintentional—shot.

Meanwhile, Balsillie has been juggling clubs between his driver and a hybrid wood. But once he sees Kinnear's shot clear the water, his competitive nature gets the best of him. Though it's a shot with little chance of success, Balsillie is not about to be one-upped by his host. He takes his driver and, doing his best John Daly impersonation, rips one on the same line Kinnear took. The ball flies across the water, landing about where Kinnear's ball finished and bounding farther towards the green.

"There you go," he says coolly, placing his driver back into the bag.

I guess that's the attitude, spirit, and competitive edge one needs in order to take on the giants and win.

As we reach the final holes, I get a tangible sense of Balsillie's newfound notoriety. Golf crowds always swell near clubhouses and the beer tents. Most sports spectators don't want to exert more effort than it takes to raise their hands to their mouths. And that's exactly the case at Angus Glen, where people are swarming around the final holes of the course. Though Balsillie is playing with one of the world's most famous golfers, the spectators seem more intrigued by the bald executive than by Furyk.

"Hey, Jim, can I get an autograph?" one spectator says as Balsillie and Furyk walk together. Furyk turns and pulls out his Sharpie.

"No, not you. Him," the spectator says, pointing at Balsillie, who gladly comes over and autographs a BlackBerry using a silver marker.

"You're a celebrity," I point out to him.

"Ah, this just started since the hockey thing broke," he says. "It'll go away soon enough."

Maybe not. As our round nears its end, another spectator pulls me aside and asks if Balsillie will pose for a photograph.

"He's more famous than Jim Furyk!" the fan exclaims.

And, on this day, she's right.

As the round comes to a close, Kinnear appears relaxed and settled in. Not that he ever seems to be under too much stress. The man just doesn't seem to sweat anything. As we leave the sixteenth hole and walk past the grandstands behind the green, the oilman starts talking about his desire to save the Canadian Open. From 1994 until 2005, Bell Canada had been the "title" sponsor—meaning that the tournament was billed as the Bell Canadian Open. In 2006, Bell elected to assume a secondary role, taking an estimated $5 million per year in sponsorship money off the table. Kinnear, worried the venerable tournament might simply disappear, stepped in and offered some cash to help keep the event going. Part of that arrangement meant that Pengrowth became the sponsor of the Wednesday pro-am, something of which Kinnear was justifiably proud.

And though he was committed to the concept of trying to help the beleaguered tournament, Kinnear simply has too much going on to offer too much of his time. Even after two and a half decades, he can't find someone he trusts to run the operations of Pengrowth, a move that would free up time for more golf, travel, and rescuing golf tournaments from oblivion.

"Do you ever think of hiring a chief operating officer and slowing down?" I ask as we make the long walk to the seventeenth tee.

"I should do that, you're right," he says nonchalantly.

"Wouldn't it free up your time for things like this?"

"It would, wouldn't it? That's exactly what I should do. And maybe we should build a championship golf course in Calgary for the Canadian Open. Let's do it," he says, reaching into his bag for his 9-iron.

I wonder who the "we" is in his statement and question what role he thinks a writer and part-time caddy might have in building a multimillion-dollar championship golf course.

As we hit the final hole, a downhill par-4 that bends to the left and over a stream, Furyk cracks yet another ball down the middle of the fairway, this time with a 3-wood. Balsillie pokes one out shorter, and West finds the creek on the left. Kinnear pops a short one out to the right with his driver.

The round is nearing an end and Kinnear still hasn't uttered a word to Balsillie about why he was invited to play in the lead group in the pro-am. I suspect the decision was given plenty of consideration. Since the tournament lost its main sponsor, Kinnear has stepped up to help, and he wants Balsillie to join him. While he may not say as much to Balsillie during the round, the fans understand why Mr. BlackBerry is in the house.*

"Jim, help save the Canadian Open!" says one exuberant spectator standing off the fairway to the rolling two-shot sixteenth hole, hoping to high-five the exec.

Balsillie looks nonplussed, then turns to me as I lug Kinnear's bag down the hill.

"No way I could do that—I'm just the co-CEO now. I'm just a figurehead," says Balsillie, referring to the fact that he was forced to step down as RIM's chairman over a scandal involving stock options.

I laugh, but it is clear that Balsillie is only half-joking.

"I mean, Canadians seem to get sanctimonious about the concept of someone being CEO and chairman," he continues. "We had co-CEOs, so it was a natural hedge anyway. What did they think was going to happen?"

* In November, just months after the Canadian Open, Kinnear would assist the RCGA in landing Royal Bank as the main sponsor of the event.

We reach the fairway, and though he's nearly two hundred yards to the green, Kinnear decides to gamble and put it all on the line with one shot. Though he seems certain of his decision, his swing doesn't demonstrate a lot of confidence. His slightly pushed approach to the flag comes to rest at the bottom of a pond that protects the right side of the green.

Balsillie, on the other hand, yanks an iron, and his ball comes to rest in the bunker protecting the left side of the green. He plays a fine sand shot to four feet and points skyward—either a nod to the man above or to RIM's stock price. He still misses the putt, but it makes no difference when Furyk two-putts for par.

For my man, it is an unfortunate result that comes at the end of a fine round of golf. Overall, however, Kinnear plays a solid, if decidedly casual, game, in contrast to West and Balsillie, who are both clearly more serious. But we're not going to take any prizes—our team score comes in at ten under par.

Sure, a score of 61 sounds impressive enough. However, it left us ten shots behind the winner. Not that I think any of the ultra-rich execs playing is inflating their handicaps when they enter one of these tournaments. No, that's never happened. Right. Maybe the stars just aligned, and some 20-handicapper shot a score that puts "Mr. 59," Al Geisberger, to shame.

As our round ends, Furyk takes some time to talk to a television crew and Balsillie, hat pulled down and sunglasses firmly affixed to his face, walks briskly past a group of reporters wanting to speak with him about hockey. Though he spent five hours talking to anyone within earshot on the course, he's strangely reticent as he exits.

Kinnear, in typical fashion, doesn't seem to be in a race to go anywhere. He mills about, and then begins a slow, deliberate walk up the stairs that lead from the eighteenth green to the clubhouse. I follow, bag in tow, sweat running down my face.

As we walk to the clubhouse, Kinnear is ambushed by the same group of reporters Balsillie just blew off.

I hand Kinnear his money clip and keys and walk into the clubhouse, where an Angus Glen staffer is waiting to help me with the rental clubs. He begins checking all the pockets to make sure nothing has been overlooked.

"This must be yours," he says, handing me a Rolex watch.

"Indeed it is," I laugh, and walk down the stairs to return it to Kinnear.

A caddy's job, apparently, is never done.

CHAPTER 2

Rai Sahi

Breaking into the Club

"One of the most fascinating things about golf is how it reflects the cycle of life. No matter what you shoot, the next day you have to go back to the first tee and begin all over again and make yourself into something."

—PGA Tour pro Peter Jacobsen

THERE IS A LOT OF HEAD-SHAKING when I arrive at Glen Abbey Golf Club in Oakville, Ontario, as the light breaks over the horizon at 6:15 a.m. on a bright August morning. First, it is pretty damned early, even for those dewsweepers at the public tracks. But this isn't just any public course: this is a $250, max-out-your-credit-card-and-mortgage-your-kid's-future kind of course. And at these kinds of tracks, apparently, no one plays at such an uncivilized hour.

In fact, nobody is actually supposed to be playing until eight o'clock this morning, when a shotgun-style tournament takes to the fairways of the Abbey, arguably the most instantly recognizable public golf course in all of Canada. These days, the club is owned by corporate golf giant ClubLink, a company that controls a handful of top courses—most of them private facilities—in Ontario and Quebec. ClubLink likes corporate tournaments—after all, they pay regardless of the lousy weather, and no one asks for a rain check.

35

I walk towards the pro shop door, only to find it locked. One of the staff, busy prepping the golf carts and checking the tee sheet, turns and notices that I'm somewhere I'm not supposed to be.

"Sir, can I ask what your tee time is?" he inquires, with a perky tone that seems out of place at a time when most people are still in bed.

"Well, I think I'm supposed to be on the tee in fifteen minutes."

Um, right. He stares at me like I've just announced I'm Tiger Woods.

"No, you're not," comes the perfunctory reply. "No one is playing this early, unless they own the course."

"Well, as a matter of fact, that is exactly the case," I reply, pointing to the big fellow with the dark hair lumbering up towards the club. "That's Rai Sahi. And he just bought a majority stake in ClubLink. So, I may not own the course, but I am golfing with the person who does. Does that mean we can go and play?"

I think it was that last bit that made the employee sort of sputter for an instant, but he regains his composure enough to be ready to shake Sahi's hand as the real estate mogul wanders up towards the pro shop.

Five minutes, two coffees, and four practice swings later, we are standing on the first tee of Glen Abbey, a short opening par-5 that plays one shot less when the pros turn up, as they have twenty-three times since 1977, and as they will in 2008 and 2009.

Sahi, with whom I last played in 2003, steps up and with a slightly awkward, outside-in swing, smacks his ball 230 yards down the left side of the fairway into the rough. Owning ClubLink must be suiting Sahi well. His first swing is a vast improvement over anything he was capable of only a couple of years earlier, when it took him a couple of awkward-looking lunges to get one in play off the opening tee. It turns out that he's taken his eyes off his real estate empire—a myriad of holding companies with names like Morguard and Revenue Properties and related real estate income trusts. Instead, he has spent the past week batting the little white ball around the links.

"I just played with Paul," he says, his deep voice resonating over the empty fairway. "And I also had a golf tournament fundraiser for Dalton."

The first reference I take to be about Paul Martin, the former prime minister with whom Sahi did a large corporate deal at the start of his career by acquiring trucking company Kingsway Transport Group from one of the politician's many businesses. The two remained friends, and Sahi gives the appearance of being an avid supporter of the Liberal party, hence his backing of Dalton McGuinty, the premier of Ontario, who was then in the midst of a re-election campaign.

Is Sahi a Liberal, by chance?

"I support democracy," he says, chuckling a hearty, gravelly laugh. "Let's just leave it at that."

Since I manage to find the cup for a birdie on the hole, and Sahi struggles with a wayward approach that falls right near the trees bordering the green, I decide that letting the subject drop is fair. No need to grind salt into his wounds, because Rai Sahi isn't someone you want to aggravate.

Others—typically beleaguered, down-on-their-luck companies whose stock prices were sliding downhill faster than a putt from the back of the twelfth at Augusta—have tussled with the big man from India. And, almost always, they have lost. That's because Sahi has made a career of buying broken businesses, fixing them, and flipping them for millions in profit. Most times, Sahi has decided he can run their companies better than the current management. So, armed with hundreds of millions in cash and a proclivity for solving problems, he has completed takeover after takeover. Sometimes one isn't even complete before he starts another. He may be Canada's corporate real estate baron, but Rai Sahi is also Canada's hostile takeover king.

"I have never been afraid of doing a hostile takeover," he admits as our cart bobs up and down on the second fairway. "Too many of these guys take what I do personally. It is just business. The truth is, they didn't perform and I think I can do better."

And what makes Sahi's story so remarkable is that, typically, he's right.

No one would have figured this life lay in store for the burly former university wrestler when he arrived in Canada from India at the age of thirty-three on February 1, 1971.

"I even remember the exact time—noon—because my brother had to pick me up from the airport and had no idea what time I was arriving," he chuckles as we bomb down the fairway, heading up the cart path to the right so Sahi can play his ball from a greenside bunker. "I didn't even want to come. I was working at a bank and my brother convinced me to come work for a few years, make some money, and go home. But I'm still here."

The money part took a decade to come, but once the rising tide of the "greed is good" 1980s hit and Sahi became involved in his first corporate deals, he put the idea of heading back to the country of his birth permanently on hold. The corporate world was too much fun and presented too much opportunity, and the drudgery of returning to work in an Indian bank paled in comparison.

After slogging it out in the real estate department of the Bank of Montreal, Sahi, who is trained as a general accountant, leveraged all of his meagre assets and, along with several partners, invested in a manufacturing business. The group managed to double its revenues within a few years, presenting Sahi with the financial wherewithal to set his sights on bigger prizes.

Those rewards came quickly. Within a decade he had acquired and consolidated a transportation empire, turning it into the third-largest trucking operation in Canada with annual revenue topping $300 million. This success came in spite of the fact that he had no experience in the industry. In 1988 he sold his trucking company and soon turned his focus to another struggling business, auto parts distributor Acklands Ltd.

He eventually acquired a 24-per-cent stake in Acklands for $44 million. Within his first full year of controlling the company, he replaced Acklands' management and grew net earnings to $3 million from a loss of $9 million a year earlier, increasing operating income by 172 per cent in the process. Thus began Sahi's reputation as a corporate raider who had a knack for spotting broken companies, acquiring them, and fixing their problems in short order. He led dozens of takeovers while at Acklands, rarely shying away from a deal even if he encountered uncooperative management; indeed, he relished taking over companies that didn't want him. He ramped up the rhetoric with the best of them, assuring shareholders that he was better than existing management. More often than not, he was right.

Sahi claims to have done more hostile takeovers than anyone currently in Canadian business, though it is a hard stat to confirm. Acklands, however, was a deal he characterizes as "a soft hostile."

"Oh, I took that one out in parts," he explains, preparing to hit a tee shot on the sixth hole. "It wasn't what I'd call a true hostile takeover."

Regardless of the degree of hostility, Sahi's ambition and aggressive business tactics have generally led to financial windfalls. He eventually sold off parts of Acklands, a company that cost him $85 million to buy, for $400 million. He took the proceeds and returned to his roots in real estate, creating the Morguard group of companies through dozens of acquisitions and takeovers. Along the way, Sahi developed a reputation as tough and unrelenting, with a singular view of how a business should be run.

Those who encountered Sahi while he was building his empire often said he was gruff and aggressive. Some, like Prem Watsa of Fairfax Financial, told Rai he should tone it down. It was simply not Canadian to do hostile takeovers, and if he continued, Sahi would be rebuffed by the establishment.

"Like I really cared," he says, chuckling, as we sit in our cart preparing to hit our tee shots on the dramatic par-4 eleventh that plunges into the river valley. "Prem was wrong. I did what I needed to do."

His move into the real estate business, at least in recent years, seems to have taken some of the tougher edges off his personality. Maybe that's because real estate moves at a different pace, he says.

"Real estate is really business in slow motion," he says, as we search for his tee shot in the rough on the eleventh fairway. "It doesn't react quickly. Things don't change all that much in a few weeks.

"And it is a different business from Acklands and those others that I owned. There are assets that, if you sold, you'd never get back. Things like the St. Laurent Centre in Ottawa. If I sold that, we'd never have a chance to get it back."

Over time and through a series of mergers and takeovers, Sahi built up Morguard to the point where it manages more than $8 billion in real estate assets (half of which is managed for various pension funds), including apartments, industrial buildings, shopping centres, and hotels, with revenue of nearly $400 million.

Despite his success, Sahi is not all that interested in attention. In an industry full of big public personalities, he has flown relatively under the radar. His foray into the golf business has brought him more headlines than all of his hostile takeovers combined. That makes him very different from other real estate moguls, like Donald Trump, who have never met a camera they didn't like or a newspaper reporter with whom they wouldn't speak. Indeed, Sahi, whose name and photo rarely appear in the papers, doesn't trust that sort.

"Oh, I just don't believe most of what that guy [Trump] says. How could you?" he shouts, leaving our cart to play his shot.

But real estate isn't Sahi's only holding. He also runs Tri-White Corporation, essentially a publicly traded merchant bank that he has operated for the past ten years. It is through Tri-White that Sahi owns a piece of corporate golf giant ClubLink, which purchased Glen Abbey for $40 million in 1999. He clearly enjoys owning what is arguably the most expensive course in the country. Truthfully, Sahi must shake his head at his good fortune when he plays the Abbey.

The remarkable property boasts the first Jack Nicklaus course in the country, among the Golden Bear's first designs ever. Split between an upper bench of relatively flat land that encompasses the opening nine and a wide swath of valley that is home to the majesty of much of the final holes, Glen Abbey has stood the test of time and been tested by the best in the world. Though one might think he understood all of the course's mysteries, Nicklaus never won at the Abbey. But Greg Norman did. And so did Tiger Woods, in 2000, by lofting a shot that came down on the right side of the green and rolled into the fringe, beating Grant Waite along the way. And, of course, Vijay Singh broke the hearts of Canadians when he manhandled the eighteenth hole in a playoff to best Mike Weir, the finest homegrown talent the country has offered so far. Pretty much every modern golfer worth their saddle shoes has played the Abbey.

Sahi is a casual golfer at the best of times, with a loopy swing and a distaste for practising his short game, so his acquisition of a piece of ClubLink may seem incongruous given his real estate holdings. But like many of his business moves, this one had more to do with his opportunistic business acumen than with golf—more a question of happenstance and sensing the potential for a good payday than about his interest in the company's central product. On the Labour Day weekend in 2001, Dallas-based ClubCorp came knocking on his door—quite literally—seeking to sell its 25 per cent stake of ClubLink. At risk of breaching its debt covenants, ClubCorp had to unload some of its assets in a hurry. Thus, ClubLink founder and CEO Bruce Simmonds and James Hinckley, ClubCorp's chief operating officer, found themselves at Sahi's home for a late-night meeting to see if he'd be interested in acquiring the shares.

Although they had an appointment, no one answered the door. Unwilling to give up—and in a desperate situation—Simmonds and Hinckley walked around to the back of the house and found Sahi slumped asleep in front of his television. Their banging on the door awakened him, and he welcomed the pair in, ready to do business. Acting on a hunch that ClubCorp's stake would be a good investment, within forty-eight hours he had acquired one-quarter of ClubLink.

"ClubCorp said they needed to sell and close by Tuesday, and the transaction was around $30 million. Not many people could do it in two working days," he says as we ride along the fairway of the tricky par-5 thirteenth, a hole with a green protected by the fast-moving waters of Sixteen Mile Creek. "This was just pure opportunity. It has changed now, but at the time I wasn't sure what my investment would become."

The ClubLink concept was developed by Simmonds in 1989 after he acquired the struggling Cherry Downs Golf Club near Pickering, a suburb of Toronto. Three years later, while sitting on a beach in Florida, Simmonds dreamed up a concept of a network of private golf courses that members could play interchangeably. Within four years, he had raised $45 million and acquired a handful of new courses—as well as a lot of debt.

In truth, the ClubLink model appeared more attractive to members than investors. While the company invested in some of the best-known courses in Canada, including the dramatic and unexpected purchase of Glen Abbey Golf Club in Oakville, home of the Canadian Open, its share price slumped from a high of $15 to a low of $5.

Though Sahi didn't have immediate plans for his ClubLink investment, he studied the business and in 2002 launched an aggressive and unexpected takeover. He publicly battled with Simmonds and Bob Franklin, ClubLink's chairman at the time, claiming that senior management and the board had not capitalized on opportunities within the company. After a month, the battle reached a stalemate when a group of technology entrepreneurs from London, Ontario, led by Atkinson, acquired 15 per cent of the outstanding shares, pushing the stock price beyond Sahi's offer. When the dust settled in January 2003, three large groups of shareholders—including Bob Poile, the former vice-president of corporate development for the bankrupt Toronto retailer Dylex—agreed to place their ambitions on hold and not acquire any additional ClubLink shares for two years. Sahi became chairman, and Simmonds was ousted, replaced by Poile as CEO.

The triumvirate's deal remained in place for a couple of years, at least until Atkinson and Poile determined they would turn the tables on the hostile-takeover king and attempted a power play to take Sahi out. That was a mistake—when it comes to the businesses he runs, Sahi isn't about to be pushed around by anyone. He bought out Atkinson and Poile and installed himself as CEO. It doesn't matter that he's not an operations guy, he points out, because at its basis ClubLink isn't all that different from every other firm he's taken over in his thirty years in business.

"The basic principles are the same. In business it comes down to a P&L statement, to the bottom line. That's true in golf and that's true in real estate."

In many ways, owning Glen Abbey makes Sahi part of the Canadian establishment, even more than the office towers he controls in downtown Toronto or the shopping centres in Vancouver. It demonstrates that a man with a foreign accent, dark skin, and a gruff manner can take on Bay Street's blueblood culture and win.

For a man competing in a corporate business environment still largely dominated by white males with MBAs, Sahi says he has never experienced racial prejudice. My limited time with him suggests otherwise. Our first game was played soon after Sahi had lost the hostile takeover of ClubLink, but was holding the chairman's seat on the board. He invited me to interview him at Rocky Crest for the columns I was writing for the *National Post*. During our round, a photographer from the paper followed our game, taking photos. This fellow had the ability to quietly work his way into the background to get the shot, and soon found himself nearing the group in front.

The group's makeup was as one would expect for a course with a green fee of $175. That is, they wore the golfer's uniform of collared shirts, rode in a cart punctuated by beer cans even though it was only mid-morning, and hacked balls readily into the surrounding woods.

A few holes in, they were too involved in their game to notice that the photographer had crept to within earshot. However, one of the foursome *had* noticed Sahi's presence on the tee.

"Who the fuck let the Paki on the course?" he said, turning to his playing partners, who all laughed out loud.

Not long afterwards, while helping the group search for a ball, the photographer pointed out that the fellow playing behind them—the one who was actually from India, not Pakistan—was also the owner of the course.

At that point, you could have cut the tension with a sixty-degree wedge. Ashen-faced and suddenly as quiet as the final putt of a major championship, the group kept their distance for a couple of holes, finally complaining to a course marshal that the photographer was "bothering them."

Bothering their consciences, perhaps.

Sahi didn't hear the story at the time—it was told to me in the confines of a newsroom some time later. But as we sit in our cart on the eleventh hole, a monstrously good par-4 that features a tee shot that plunges nearly a hundred feet to the fairway below, I ask him about racism. He stares back at me unfazed. Prejudice, he says, is too often used by immigrants to Canada as an excuse for their lack of success. It is an excuse for not achieving.

"I think it presents something for people to blame for not getting what they want," he says.

That might be the case, but I find it hard to believe that a big man from India, one who was predisposed to tackling tough and often confrontational business situations in his career, was never on the receiving end of some racist remark.

Sahi considers that for a moment, and answers as he exits the cart and heads to his bag to grab a club.

"Well, maybe I felt a little bit of it when I first came over. But I don't think I get it much now."

Golf is clearly not a natural skill for Sahi. Given his thick build and aggressive nature, it should come as no surprise to find out that he was a wrestler. It was only after he came to Canada and became established in real estate in the 1990s that he decided to pursue the game. He joined Mississauga Golf and Country Club, not because he was particularly fond of its course, which had been hemmed together by a vast series of designers. No, he became a member because it was close to his home and allowed him the freedom to stop by on the way to work to pound balls on the range.

When we first teed it up a couple of years previous, Sahi had the touch of a man who builds massive office buildings. His swing, with its outside-in, throw the club from the top motion, rivalled that of former NBA star Charles Barkley. How bad is Barkley's swing? The basketball player was once paired with Tiger Woods, who told Sir Charles that a new Kmart was being built nearby.

"Where?" Barkley asked.

"Between my ball and yours," came Woods' reply as he promptly smoked one.

However, time—and apparently some hard work with the hundreds of pros he now employs at ClubLink—has been very kind to Sahi's golf game. While he once demonstrated a complete disdain for anything that resembled a short game, at the Abbey he plays a couple of delicate chips with precision and actually completes his putts. Four years earlier, he would have smacked the ball onto the green, picked it up, and moved on to the next hole. Then, the game was only about power. Sahi still likes to take a big rip at the ball, but he will also line up a putt and chuckle good-naturedly regardless of whether it finds the hole.

"Take a look at this," he says, full of confidence as he prepares to hit his approach into the par-5 sixteenth hole. "This is what ninety-three yards feels like."

Unfortunately, on this occasion, ninety-three yards must feel more like sixty, because his ball ends up short of the slope that leads to the green.

Though he never intended to run ClubLink, he appears to be having fun doing so.

With more than fifteen thousand members, almost double the number it had when Sahi bought in, the organization now boasts thirty-nine courses scattered over urban areas in Ontario and Quebec. Already there are rumblings among some members, many of whom have paid more than $60,000 to join the company's best clubs, that Sahi is more interested in the real estate value locked beneath the fairways of ClubLink's golf courses than he is in running golf, something the organization's new CEO denies.

The truth is that, while Sahi has had impeccable timing in the past with any corporate acquisition, only taking risks that he felt the markets would support, the ClubLink deal isn't as clear cut. In recent years, the golf industry in Ontario has been burdened with an oversupply of courses, all competing for the same dollars from the white-collar professionals that ClubLink courts. These courses were often built more as a testament to the ego of their owners than as actual businesses, meaning they can handle losses that would be unacceptable to a public company. That factor makes the economics of the golf business a challenge, something Sahi has discovered first-hand.

But he also loves the business. Maybe that's because it gives him an entrée into a world he could not easily be a part of, regardless of his financial success. After all, golf clubs are the only places that occasionally turn someone away based on their religion or skin colour, despite the fact they are ready to write a six-figure cheque to gain admission. Associates of Sahi's have told me the real estate mogul loves owning Glen Abbey. Controlling the club, where so much of golf history has been made in the last thirty years, effectively opens the door and makes him part of the Canadian establishment. He'd never admit to that, of course, but he does say he's enjoyed owning golf courses more than much of his real estate.

It may be hard to show off a shopping centre, but it is easy to impress with a golf course. And Sahi loves to show off his courses.

His daughter's wedding was held at a ClubLink course. There were hundreds of guests, he tells me, as we head over to the bunker of the right side of the fairway of the eighteenth hole, the one where Tiger Woods blasted a 6-iron onto the fringe of the green, en route to his victory at the Canadian Open.

"Were you here when he hit that shot?" he asks me.

I tell him I was standing not far from Woods at the time.

"I wasn't even here—I didn't have part of the company yet," he sighs. "But it looked amazing."

It doesn't matter whether he was in the crowd of fifty thousand that day because, by controlling Glen Abbey, Sahi owns a part of Canadian sports history. And even for Sahi, a man who has acquired companies only to fire the entire management, a man who would appear to be simply an unsentimental corporate raider, that has meaning.

CHAPTER 3

Frank McKenna
The Lure of the Game

"I have lived my life by certain standards, both off the golf course and
a lot more on it. I have been committed to certain beliefs...since I
was six years old. Those beliefs have not changed."

—Mark McCumber, PGA Tour pro

WHILE A GAME OF GOLF should always be played within four hours, I
enjoy being casual with the time that bookends the start and close of
a round. I'm one of those obsessive types who must hit a few dozen
balls before the body loosens up and starts communicating with my
brain. Without a couple of fast shots on the range—maybe a thin
3-iron and a wayward drive or three—I'll lack the confidence to exe-
cute on the course, at least for a few holes. And if my confidence is
lacking, my swing will get loose, shots will disappear into the ether
and I'm sure a lawsuit will commence when my ball resurfaces on
the patio of a nearby home.

This is all running through my head as I bomb along the Trans-
Canada Highway towards Moncton, New Brunswick, in desperate
pursuit of my 8 a.m. tee time. With twenty minutes to spare, I'm off
the freeway and onto the quiet city streets that lead into town,
emerging in suburban Dieppe. As I head south, the road becomes
residential and finally, as the clock ticks down, I pass the final row of
homes under construction and turn into the gravel parking lot that
is already full of cars at Fox Creek Golf Club.

Hastily yanking my clubs out of their travel bag and pulling on my shoes without lacing them up, I sprint towards the clubhouse. Apparently, in order to close for a tournament later in the day, the club is in the midst of a so-called shotgun start, which means that as many as thirty-six foursomes will start simultaneously, one on each hole. That explains the throngs of people standing around the clubhouse entrance. In the midst of this seeming chaos, holding court with a number of golfers, is Frank McKenna, one of the most successful political figures ever to emerge from Atlantic Canada, the former Canadian ambassador to the U.S., and the current vicechairman of the Toronto-Dominion Bank. He's also my playing partner for the morning.

I first played golf with McKenna in 2004. At the time, he was the chairman of CanWest, the media company that owns the Global television network and a couple dozen newspapers, including the *National Post*, where I worked. That made him the boss of my boss's boss, or something like that. Needless to say, everyone at the paper paid a surprising amount of attention to my round of golf. Since McKenna doesn't play at a club in Moncton, where he spends most of his summers, we golfed at the Rees Jones–designed Royal Oaks Golf Club, part of a housing development outside of the city. The club was built on uninspiring land that was matched by the resulting course, but I'll say this about Royal Oaks—it is the best course of its kind. Nevertheless, it served our purpose at the time, which was to whack the ball around and chat about his career.

This summer, McKenna has chosen Fox Creek, not far from Moncton's airport. Like Royal Oaks, Fox Creek, created by Montreal's Graham Cooke (the same designer behind Ron Joyce's Fox Harb'r), is also part of a housing community. But the golf course in this case is more attractive and challenging, winding its way through rolling land and between large pines. It is not an elite course—any track that plays among newly constructed houses and forces golfers to traverse a roadway will never be charming—but its large, rolling greens and general lack of water hazards makes it playable by practically anyone.

To my surprise, McKenna has rounded out our foursome with two heavy hitters, though more for their corporate clout than their golfing abilities. I immediately recognize one of the pair: Norm Keevil. He's been the driving force behind mining giant Teck Cominco for decades, and someone with whom I've had the good fortune to play twice (including once for this book, but more on that later). His quiet demeanour and love of the game always make him a delightful playing partner. He doesn't always fill the air with conversation, choosing instead to make pointed and careful remarks where he thinks they are warranted. I don't know the final player in our group. McKenna introduces me to Francis McGuire, who was New Brunswick's deputy minister of economic development and tourism when McKenna was premier and is currently CEO of Major Drilling, one of the world's largest companies involved in mine drilling. His connection to Keevil's mining empire is obvious, and his familiarity and camaraderie with McKenna are clear from his friendly and good-natured verbal jabs as we stand on the opening tee. McKenna clearly enjoys having his old friend along, affectionately calling McGuire a "public policy wonk" at one point in our round.

"Some say Francis was the brains of the McKenna operation," McKenna points out.

"Oh, you should have been so lucky," McGuire answers.

The banter continues over all eighteen holes.

A match is suggested as we stand on the first tee, a downhill par-5 with a landing area flanked by a large oval bunker that juts into the fairway and a slightly raised green with another cavernous sandy trap protecting the left front. Since McGuire and Keevil both sport matching 17 handicaps, and McKenna is a 15, they suggest that I play alongside the former premier. That's fine, I agree, adding it is much easier to take notes while playing if you're not shouting to your subject from across the fairway.

The question of the wager comes up quickly. Knowing my three playing partners earn vastly more than this ink-stained wretch, I jump in to recommend an appropriate amount. How about a $5 Nassau for the three executives? My personal terms would be somewhat different. If McKenna and I prevail, I suggest that appropriate compensation would consist of two seats on McGuire's board of governors and fifty thousand multiple voting shares from Keevil.

Silence.

It doesn't take me long to realize I've set the terms with Keevil at $1.8 million, and God knows how much a board member at Major Drilling gets paid, but it has to be more than the $15 I'd take home for winning our Nassau.

Despite my shit-eating grin, no one seems to know exactly how to respond to my offer; they don't seem willing to take it up, but nor does anyone voice an objection. I figure I must be proposing a fair deal; otherwise, someone would have protested—right?

For our group, there's general agreement that the blue tees at 6,448 yards are appropriate to the varying abilities. McKenna tees off, stroking the ball down the middle of the fairway with his driver. Keevil's ball goes careening into the woods to the left; McGuire takes a big cut with a 3-wood, depositing it in the rough, while my tee ball finds the protection of the right fairway bunker. After McKenna's approach sinks into the front bunker, and McGuire and Keevil struggle with the bentgrass chipping area to the left of the green, I come away with the only par. In a high-low match whereby everyone has to finish regardless of how well they are playing, McKenna and I quickly draw first blood, taking two points on the No. 3 handicap opener.

McKenna is an engaging partner. He likes to talk, and his deft touch and turn of phrase surely helped him during his ten-year stretch as premier of New Brunswick. He speaks relatively plainly, making him appear approachable and giving him that casual populist appeal that obscures the fact that, like most politicians, he's a lawyer. Since I last played with him, he has undertaken a tour as Canada's ambassador to the U.S., re-establishing his profile while raising awareness of the connection between the two nations.

Apparently, being an ambassador was also costly.

"I took a real hit in the pocketbook," he says after we tee off on the delicate, but short, second. In order to take the job, McKenna had to step away from his law firm and drop all of the numerous directorships he held.

He quickly garnered a reputation for, well, speaking frankly.

"I was really proud of representing Canada in that way. I wanted to be able to speak truthfully to those in power and to be able to speak up for Canada, especially when it was clear the U.S. was in error."

He took the job in February 2005, and immediately stirred the pot. He tried to educate the U.S. on its misperceptions of Canada, and called the U.S. government "largely dysfunctional." McKenna received more media attention during his time in the position than at any time since he resigned as premier in 1997.

"Let's face it: the government at the time under Paul Martin was a minority, so the U.S. became a whipping boy for a lot of people. But we also had some heady issues—softwood lumber, border issues, mad cow—that we had to deal with. In many ways, it was just like being a politician."

It all ended abruptly—too quickly, in fact, for McKenna and his wife, Julie, who were both enjoying their time in Washington, he explains, hitting a wedge from the fairway onto the second green.

After Martin's government faltered, it was clear McKenna's time in Washington would be limited, that he'd be recalled by new Conservative PM Stephen Harper. It wasn't about the results of his tenure—it was party politics, pure and simple.

Whether McKenna let it be known in Bay Street circles that he was looking for a new gig, or whether company executives just assumed he would be moving on, the offers came in quickly. "I must have had twenty board seats offered to me," he says.

We reach the third tee, which McKenna, who has played Fox Creek frequently since it opened in 2005, says is the hardest on the course. Even from the blue tees, it plays 421 yards, with a narrow fairway protected by water on the left and dense forest on the right. Not distracted by the conversation, McKenna hits first, finding the fairway with his driver. McGuire follows and also finds the fairway. Keevil isn't so lucky: his tee shot hits a tree left of the fairway, but careens out, coming to rest on the short grass, an awfully long way from the green.

Back in our cart, McKenna picks up where we left off. The best job offer came for an unusual role with Toronto-Dominion Bank. The bank's CEO, Ed Clark, wanted someone to help expand the institution's image, to help drive new business, and to shake all the right hands. Clark just wanted to run the bank's operations. He needed an outgoing person for the role he had in mind, and McKenna immediately came to the forefront.

"Ed was the most persuasive," McKenna explains as we walk from the cart to the centre of the fairway, where his ball rests 180 yards from the green. "He really wanted me to be the ambassador for the bank and free him up for the operations side of the business, the area he really excels at. It is a terrific opportunity. I like the bank and I like the space."

Perhaps most surprisingly, Clark wanted McKenna to continue to be a part-time politician, to push his agenda on issues like health care where he saw fit. Since banks are typically the most conservative of institutions when it comes to almost all matters, making Stephen Harper's Conservative party look almost socialist in comparison, even McKenna admits he was caught off guard by Clark's offer.

"Ed's view is that they've sought out my brand, and my brand is my interest in public policy and my profile across the country," he says. "He's of the opinion that a healthy public policy discussion is a good thing for Canada."

Public policy is one thing, but soon after landing the job McKenna had to wade into the issue of bank-machine fees, which was raised by Conservative finance minister Jim Flaherty—hardly one of those life-or-death issues that McKenna was hoping to address.

"A ridiculous discussion," he says, being unusually dismissive.

"A waste of your time, then?" I ask.

"Tell me about it. What a piece of shit to debate."

We reach the fourth hole, a long par-3 that plays over a pond, with bunkering between the water and the green. The hole is McKenna's Waterloo, and he tells our group he's been practising his long irons in an attempt not to massacre it. He lofts a bullet at the green, coming to rest ten feet pin-high, and is elated at the result, smacking hands with those in the group. Keevil's result comes up short in the bunker, while McGuire lands in the rough to the right of the green.

Keevil thins his second shot out of the bunker and over the green, while McGuire's chip comes to rest twenty feet from the hole. Though McKenna's putt comes up short, I also make par, leaving us with a commanding four-point lead.

Comfortable with our position, McKenna relaxes. Rather than wasting time on ATM fees, he wants to open a serious discussion about health care in Canada. He isn't an advocate for a huge over-haul of the current public system, but he wants the matter opened for debate.

"There needs to be more room for innovation from the private side," he explains, walking off the green. "And why should we feel bad about it? The most socialist countries in the world involve pri-vate interests in their medical systems. And I believe the public aren't bothered by it. It is the unions that are bothered by it."

Leave it to McKenna to make such a contentious issue seem so simple and practical. It is a level of candid discourse one doesn't typ-ically expect from someone with his influence. Those politicians are so careful as to make their comments meaningless. But today McKenna is a golfer, not a politician, and his off-the-cuff remarks and comments reflect that. Nearing sixty, McKenna stands five foot ten and doesn't sport the tall, thin build of most good golfers. He appears shorter than his frame would suggest, perhaps because of his thick and powerful build. As for his golf game, McKenna takes a balanced cut off the tee and the ball travels straight—sometimes straight into the trees, but straight nonetheless. He plays relatively frequently, and TD has made not-so-subtle suggestions that he join a private club in Toronto where he can host guests and the bank's high-profile customers.

"What does it cost to join one of those clubs?" he asks.

Anywhere from $50,000 to more than six figures, I tell him.

"That's crazy. I won't play that much," he says.

Of course he won't, but that's not the point. Those making seven-figure salaries with financial institutions are almost expected to have a pricey membership at a ritzy country club. It is part of the compensation package a bank vice-chair can expect, along with the executive assistant, the corporate speechwriter, a driver, and big, cushy leather chairs in a wood-panelled office.

As we walk up to the fifth hole, an aesthetically unappealing par-4 with power lines running the length of the fairway, McGuire asks McKenna how he has time to play golf, considering that federal Liberal leader Stephane Dion is in Moncton today.

McKenna is stone-faced, and instead of answering, he heads to the tee and hits a rescue club up the right side, where the ball comes to rest near the base of one of the power-line towers. It turns out McKenna isn't a big fan of Dion.

"If he'd take his hands out of his pockets more often and put them out to the crowd, he'd be better off," he tells McGuire. "Right now, he walks around like a penguin."

Given his skeptical take on the current Liberal leader, would he take a shot at the top job if it became available? Would McKenna consider returning to politics? I'd asked him the same question three years earlier. The response has not changed.

"The last time I said I was done, there was a lot of ink spilled on whether I was going to run or not," he says after extricating his ball from a fairway bunker. "I don't see a situation where I'd return."

One issue with any attempt at federal politics is that some in Quebec still blame him for pulling back on the Meech Lake

Accord, Conservative prime minister Brian Mulroney's plan to bring Quebec into the Constitution. As newly elected premier of New Brunswick in 1987, McKenna would eventually support the accord. But for a spell after he became premier, New Brunswick withheld its backing of the legislation. Even today, some Quebecers see it as a betrayal.

I mention this to McKenna, and it is the only time in our round when his unfailing self-confidence seems to weaken, if only for an instant.

"If I'd known they'd sabotage the accord, I'd have done things differently," he admits, standing off the green of the 165-yard par-3 eleventh, the only hole in our round where every player manages to salvage par.

Does he feel Quebec would be an impediment to his running in a federal election?

McKenna looks stricken for a moment, then turns to McGuire. "Francis, I think I was well liked in Quebec, don't you think?"

McGuire nods in agreement.

"I always felt well liked in Quebec," McKenna continues. "I think what I'd tell them is all I did was take the time to listen to the concerns of the rights of French-speaking citizens in New Brunswick and across the country. I signed on later and it was a shame it didn't succeed."

On the thirteenth hole, we hit the inevitable backlog one always encounters while playing a busy public course. As we walk off the twelfth hole, where McKenna struggles with a bunker, resulting in a double bogey, there's a group standing on the next tee, and another on the green of the short par-3.

As the group in front of us hit to the green and take off in their carts, McKenna kills time by raising one of the touchiest subjects in Canadian politics: what to wear and where to sit at the wedding the coming weekend of Liberal MP Scott Brison and his partner, Maxime St. Pierre. It is a political minefield, even though it is the social event of the season for Ottawa political types.

Former prime ministers Paul Martin and Joe Clark will attend, as will current Liberal leader Stephane Dion. All will descend on a small Nova Scotia town, a village that will likely be caught completely unaware of the turmoil that is about to rain down on it.

When he announced his engagement to St. Pierre two years earlier, Brison said he was looking forward to a time when the gay marriage of a politician "was not a story at all."

But it is a big story.

"Yes, Brison invited me to his wedding," McKenna says with a quizzical look on his face.

This seems to pique the interest of everyone in the group, though not in a homophobic way. It seems everyone has questions for which no one in our group has answers.

"Francis, do you know the protocol for a wedding like this?" McKenna asks. "I mean, Scott asked me to come, and though I was a bit surprised, Julie is really excited. But it isn't like any wedding we've ever been to."

McGuire chuckles, while Keevil has a look of chagrin.

"What do you want to know? What you should wear? What side of the church are you going to sit on, Frank?" McGuire questions quite seriously. "The groom's side, or the groom's side? I mean, how do you know which guy is the groom?"

"I don't know," McKenna answers flatly.

In the end, it doesn't matter. For a man who grew up in small-town Atlantic Canada, McKenna seems largely unflappable, even when presented with a circumstance that's out of the ordinary—like a gay wedding. When he heads to the wedding that weekend, he's stopped by newspaper reporters—and, of course, says all the right things about being at the affair to show support.

Our match is over on the sixteenth hole, where my par puts another point on the card, leaving Keevil and McGuire out in the cold without enough holes to recover. When it is all over, I shoot 75, while my playing partner McKenna records a 90. Keevil struggles on the day to post a 97, while McGuire plays steadily at 90.

Strangely, no offers of board seats or multiple voting shares are forthcoming. Apparently, McGuire and Keevil didn't take my request seriously. In fact, no money changes hands at all, though McGuire does email a couple of days later offering to send a cheque to cover his losses. I write him back to say thanks, but no thanks.

"Have I ever told you about the time I played with Chrétien just after I announced I was resigning?" McKenna asks as we prepare to tee off on the final hole, a 523-yard par-5 with a wide landing area off the tee and a unique green site cut into a hillside and protected by a small stream that separates it from the fairway.

I suspect McGuire has heard the anecdote, but Keevil shakes his head.

"We played at Ottawa Hunt. Soon after we start, he says, 'So, Frank, what do you want? A Senate seat?' I told him, no, all I wanted was $300 million for a highway program. Chrétien just nodded and laughed and we continued our game."

McKenna hits his ball from 175 yards onto the green of the par-5 eighteenth. It comes to rest on the fringe, twenty feet below the hole, leaving a strong uphill putt. After everyone else reaches the green, McKenna continues his story.

"Playing with Chrétien is always interesting. He never hits his ball straight, but he doesn't have to worry too much. He's got all those RCMP officers around. Sometimes he'll hit one in the woods and it'll come flying back out. Chrétien would always say, 'What's the use of having a national police force if they can't even find your ball?'

"Anyway, Chrétien and I have a bet going and I need a three-footer on the last hole to beat him."

McKenna attempts to do his best impersonation of Chrétien. "He says, 'You want that $300 million? Then you better be careful with this putt.' But I'm a competitive guy and I thought, 'Fuck you,' and I rammed it into the back of the hole."

What did Chrétien do?

"Oh, he stood there for a minute and then said, 'Ah, Frank, don't worry about it. I'll give you the money anyway.'"

The story tells a lot about McKenna. A man with integrity, a candid demeanour, and likable as well, he's also competitive and unrelenting to the end. At the end of it all, Frank McKenna is a battler, the type who never gives up. That fact leads me to believe, regardless of his comments, that he may not be ready to leave the minefield of politics behind him.

CHAPTER 4

Jean Pierre Ouellet
The Tiger and the PM

"Golf is the infallible test. The man who can go into a patch of
rough alone, with the knowledge that only God is watching him,
and play his ball where it lies, is the man who will serve you faith-
fully and well."

—P.G. Wodehouse

EVERY GOLFER HAS THE FRIEND who calls up Monday morning to
recall, often shot by horrific fat shot, every stroke he took during his
Sunday match. More often than not, such calls are simply unbear-
able, because the only one who can enjoy the blow-by-blow account
of a round with a mid-handicap golfer is the golfer himself. To those
afflicted with the need to offer up the details of their weekend
round, there's nothing more interesting. To those listening, there's
nothing more tedious.

And then there's Jean Pierre Ouellet. With a mix of verbal dex-
terity and wry humour that he uses to spice up his golf stories, the
banker is the consummate golf storyteller. One imagines him striding down the middle of a fairway, a golf bag over his shoulder and a
lit cigarette in his hand, at fairytale courses, places where he's a
member, like Pine Valley in New Jersey, Muirfield or St. Andrews in
Scotland, or Merion in Philadelphia.

What makes Ouellet a great storyteller is that he understands
that the fun is in the details and not the shots. It isn't about the 7-

iron that found the water; it's about the tales that arise from the personalities involved. He recalls little facets of long-gone games with subtle expressions and a clever turn of phrase, weaving them together with the precision of a watchmaker. His flat, somewhat laconic delivery—he rarely raises his voice—and his perfect English, honed by two years at Oxford and a lifetime of dealing with *anglais* businessmen, is punctuated with his distinct Quebecois accent. It all adds up to an engaging package.

And there's no story Ouellet tells that is more interesting, more intriguing, and more insightful than his take on his claim to fame— playing golf with BCE chairman Jean Monty, former prime minister Jean Chrétien, and the world's greatest (ever) golfer, Tiger Woods, during the pro-am portion of the 2001 Canadian Open. Even though he holds one of the most powerful positions in the banking industry—the Royal Bank's Quebec lieutenant to the province's biggest business names—Jean Pierre, better known as JP, has eschewed the limelight, rarely appearing in the media. Most outside of Canada's barons of business wouldn't even know who he is, but those who matter when it comes to high-powered corporate finance do. And that's what counts.

The setting for Ouellet's anecdote is perfect. Woods, a year removed from his fabled 6-iron shot that led to a victory at the Canadian Open, is at the height of his powers and popularity. At the time—and to this day—he is one of the most recognizable athletes on the planet. Add to that the presence of Chrétien, who was also enjoying immense popularity as the century turned, having thumped Stockwell Day and the Canadian Alliance to win a third majority government, making him one of the most successful prime ministers in history. And as chair of BCE, Monty was leading Bell Canada's transformation from the antiquated phone company into an Internet and media juggernaut.

Why was Ouellet in the group? He was the man with a boatload of corporate connections, a rainmaker who developed his network from years of working at the law firm of Stikeman Elliott before moving to the Canadian National Railway as its legal advisor soon after it was privatized. He was—and still is—the man who could pick up a phone and get a prompt return call from practically anyone.

In this case, he was in the group because he wanted a favour.

"When Tiger won in 2000 at Glen Abbey, with the glorious 6-iron, I was sitting at home," he explains, wearing the typical attire of the Canadian banker—a dark suit and tie—in the formal dining room at Mount Bruno Country Club, all the while munching on a sandwich and sipping a glass of white wine. "As soon as he won, I picked up the phone and called Monty, knowing that as the chairman of BCE, which sponsored the Canadian Open, he'd play with the champion the following year," he explains. "I left a message saying that I was sure I'd be the 299th person who would call, but that I'd love to play with him and Tiger the next year.

"We go back thirty years. That January, on my birthday, Jean called me up, like he does every year, and said, 'JP, I have a little present for you.' I asked what that might be. 'Well, I'd like you to play with me and Tiger in the pro-am at the Canadian Open.'"

Which is how Ouellet came to be the "mysterious" fourth in the group, as the *Montreal Gazette* characterized him in their recounting of the round. Hard to imagine how the vice-chair of one of Canada's largest banks could be described as enigmatic, especially since it is hard to find a hiding space under a boardroom table.

For Monty and Chrétien it would soon all come apart at the seams. Monty's dot-com strategy would falter, leading him to resign his position, and within a week of the pro-am, Chrétien would face the fury of 9/11 and increased turmoil from within his own party, as pretenders to his throne jostled for position.

But on a brilliant Wednesday morning, none of that was on the minds of the thousands who showed up at 7 a.m. to watch the prime minister and two business associates team with the world's best golfer.

"You can imagine the scene, Robert," he continues as we finish our lunch and walk through Bruno's lounge and into the ancient locker room to get changed for our round. "Here we are at the fifteenth hole at Royal Montreal. There are thousands of people around, and this is one of the toughest holes on the course. Tiger tees off with a 2-iron, hitting the stinger that he was known for, while both Monty and I find the fairway. Chrétien, on the other hand, hits it into the rough off the tee, and he doesn't really hit it very far. He finds it and hits it again, but once again it goes into the rough."

Now the PM is in trouble. With his shot sitting in long rough, and faced with a daunting iron shot over water to a well-bunkered green, Chrétien has it in his head that his ball is likely to find a watery grave. And the prime minister isn't the sort who wants to be embarrassed. However, with a difficult lie, and the crowd urging him forward, Chrétien ends up dithering in the way that would become synonymous with his successor, Paul Martin.

"Chrétien's ball was sitting in a little knoll," Ouellet says, holding his hands about six inches apart. "And from where he is, his feet are above the ball, and he has a stance where he's slightly downhill, over water, and he has to get it maybe ninety-five yards to the green. It wasn't a good situation.

"I was looking at the shot and asking myself that if I had it, how confident would I be of putting it on the green? And I'm a much better player than he is."

The options weren't great. Chrétien could blade it over the green. Catch it heavy and hit it in the water. Slice it off and end up in the water. Have the club turn and hook it into the water. None of the options were good, Ouellet says. The problem was compounded by the fact Chrétien had no one to turn to for advice.

"He just doesn't know what to [ask]. His caddy—a guy named Paul DeVillers, wasn't much more helpful," Ouellet explains.

I recognize DeVillers's name, but tell Ouellet that I can't place it.

"He ended up being secretary of state for amateur sport."

So, that's what happens to a caddy.

"Well, he was an MP at the time, but apparently he got his payback for carrying the prime minister's clubs."

Ouellet returns to his tale of Chrétien's difficulty.

"So they are debating what to do, and by this time Tiger has hit his shot and he and Steve [Williams, Woods' caddy] have walked all the way up to his ball. Monty and I are standing behind Chrétien, waiting for him to do something, and we can see Tiger in the distance getting fidgety. It is clear he just wants to get going, but Chrétien doesn't know what to do and the crowd is all over him, saying, 'Go for it! Go for it!'"

With the PM facing pressure he wouldn't experience again until his golf ball–juggling appearance at the Gomery inquiry, it was clear he needed support. Ouellet decided that that would be his role. "I just walked up to him and said, 'Prime Minister, announce there is casual water.'"

Under the circumstances, that would allow Chrétien to take a drop. And what did the prime minister do with this obvious bending of the rules?

"He nodded. 'Right, right,' he said. Then he just picked up the ball and dropped it in the fairway. But the crowd didn't like it and called him on it. He just pointed to me, like it was my fault," Ouellet says, shrugging.

After all of this there had to be a good outcome, right? Wrong.

"Chrétien then hits it a little thin and yanks it to the left, so it goes across the green and into rough."

By this time, the scene is devolving into something of a comedy. With Monty out of the hole after hitting his approach into the water, Woods decides not to wait any longer and chips onto the green.

"Once I get there, I go to my ball, which is just off the green, and get ready to play. Chrétien, however, has other ideas. He walks behind the green to locate his ball, and finds it in thick rough."

This is now his fourth shot?

"I guess so, if you don't include the drop for 'casual water' which wasn't there," Ouellet says flatly. "Anyway, he starts stomping down around the ball to try to improve his lie. Tiger is watching this, leaning in that familiar pose against his putter. And he's got this amused look on his face as he watches Chrétien stomp down the rough. So he reaches into his pocket and grabs a tee and throws it to Chrétien."

Tossing someone a tee in golf is among the most contemptuous gestures in the game. In a game where rules are largely self-enforced, throwing a peg at someone is akin to calling them a cheater. And it is something *le petit gars de Shawinigan* should have taken as an affront, a reason to get his back up. Instead, the slur flies right over his head.

"Chrétien doesn't get it," Ouellet continues. "He just continues to go about stomping until he's got a clear enough lie and then chips the ball to about ten feet.

"I chip up to just outside Tiger's ball—maybe about three feet. As I finish, Tiger comes up and says, 'Go putt out.' I tell him that it isn't my turn, that Chrétien has to putt first. 'He's hitting about twenty right now,' Woods replies. 'Is that with or without the illegal drop?' I ask him. Tiger just looked at me and said, 'We have a rule in a pro-am that once you reach net bogey you just pick up.' I told him that Chrétien was the prime minister—if he wanted to say something, he could. 'Well, JP, on the golf course we are all equals.' I said that's fine, but you go and tell him that. He was quite cool about it."

Did he go and tell him, then?

"Of course not," Ouellet says, a thin smile crossing his face. "Tiger just laughed."

It takes a while to get a grasp on JP Ouellet, but his story about Tiger and the prime minister gives away a lot about the man. He's a person for whom rules and etiquette mean a great deal, but who isn't blinded by history.

And perhaps more than anything, Ouellet is smart. On the golf course, and in conversation, he analyzes details. Nothing is lost on him. Thankfully, that doesn't make him uptight or too controlling. A bet is set on the first tee. In his own inimitable fashion, Ouellet pitches me a unique wager.

"How about this: we'll play for $100 per side, $100 overall."

I wince, thinking about my shrinking book advance should I lose, and the unlikely chance that I actually have $300 in my wallet in any case. I also wonder how I'd explain such a loss to my wife. Ouellet picks up on my discomfort quickly.

"But I'll apply a 99 per cent discount if you have cash."

I breathe a sigh of relief and we head out on the course, halving the first hole, while Ouellet's sharp putting and my lacklustre iron play puts me one down after two.

"I've never sought out publicity," he explains, the clouds looming ominously overhead as we head to the third hole, Mount Bruno's sharply bunkered par-3. "Even when I was practising law and did big cases, I never spoke to the press. There were other guys who, what's the expression, never saw a mike they didn't like."

One thing is for certain: Ouellet maintains the nastiest 8 handicap in golf, especially when playing at Mount Bruno, his home course since 1984. He may have more prestigious memberships—Pine Valley, for instance, is arguably the best course in the world, and the Honourable Company of Edinburgh Golfers, which plays at Muirfield, home to numerous British Opens, is one of the oldest clubs in the world. But his heart, it seems, is at Mount Bruno. In many ways Mount Bruno is an extension of his personality. It is a club that sits quietly out of the limelight. It is, on first inspection, not an obviously great course. But just like Ouellet, a man who is far from an open book the first time you meet him, the more time you spend at the course, the more apparent it is that Bruno is very smart indeed.

Not that he is a big fan of all of the club's quirks. Take, for instance, the club's insistence that members wear knee socks with shorts during Montreal's hot summers. When we head out to start our round, I almost choke on my Gatorade when I see Ouellet in his tan shorts, with his green socks pulled up nearly to his thighs. Though it may look ridiculous, knee socks worn with shorts have long been the custom at Montreal's most private clubs. But even Royal Montreal, the oldest golf club in Canada, has given up the rule. Mount Bruno members, however, like to stick to their traditions. It is a throwback to another time, and one that Ouellet doesn't appreciate.

"These damned knee socks are an anachronism, and you can quote me on that," he says, sneering downwards.

Remove socks from the equation and Ouellet's wardrobe demonstrates well the circles in which he travels. On his left hand he wears a golf glove emblazoned with the Augusta National logo, the home of the Masters, while the hat he wears to cover his balding head is from Merion, one of six clubs to which Ouellet belongs. He's a man who is accustomed to the best when it comes to golf.

He's not weighed down by his attire, and the dreadful socks have little impact on his game, which is sharp as a knife. His shot off the tee barely makes it over the lip of the forward bunker of the 153-yard hole, but it comes to a halt as if someone has yanked on a string, slowing and then striking the flagstick, eventually coming to rest three inches from the hole. He taps it in for a birdie, and even though I take a skin on the following hole, the match is never really close. Ouellet plays freely, shaping his draw off the tee to catch the left side of the fairway on most holes, craftily chipping and putting his way out of trouble on others, all the while swearing in French and chastising himself for his miscues.

Though he's not long off the tee, Ouellet plays golf like a surgeon, carefully targeting specific areas of the course where he knows he can successfully set up attacks at the pin. His golf game is smart, a reflection of the man himself, a not-altogether-surprising fact for a man that works as a tactician for a Big Four bank.

Given his nature, it isn't surprising to find that Ouellet was one of eleven Rhodes Scholars who went to Oxford in 1971, returning to Canada with a master's in law two years later.

"There's a myth about it—it is good if you've got it," he jokes as we make the turn and head to the short par-3 tenth hole.

Saying you are a Rhodes Scholar is one thing, but Ouellet found the social experience of being immersed in an English-speaking environment to be more beneficial for his career.

"Before I went to Oxford, my English was pretty good, but I was ill at ease in English social circumstances," he says. "But two years there did the trick. When I came back, it didn't matter where I was—Toronto, London, New York, wherever—it was second nature.

"That was really important if you want to be from Quebec and be successful in Canadian business. When I practised law, there were a lot of partners perfectly fluent in English. They could draft an English-language deal and they could plead in English. But if you put them in a social environment with anglophones, they would be ill at ease. It made them less successful."

Once he returned to Canada, an interest in capital markets led him to a position at Stikeman Elliott, one of the country's largest law firms. There he remained for more than twenty years, developing a reputation as a straight shooter, someone who was reliable and smart. It served Ouellet well as his career progressed.

"When I worked as a lawyer, and I say this in all modesty, I was a fair guy," he says, standing on the tee of the short par-4 eleventh, driver in hand. "People knew I wasn't going to fuck them and that I wasn't out for myself. And that's been great to me over time, because people can trust me. And now, when I pick up the phone to call someone, they call me back."

His work and seniority at Stikeman progressed, and in 1984 he became a partner. By this time, he had become embroiled in the decision to take CN Rail public. It would be the last thing he'd do at the firm. The spinoff of CN was so successful, and the principals involved were so impressed with Ouellet, that they offered him a job as the company's legal advisor. He jumped at the opportunity.

There he remained until 2000, when a headhunter representing RBC, which was desperate to make inroads into the Quebec market, came calling.

Sitting in our cart on the thirteenth tee, the high point at Mount Bruno, seems to be an appropriate place for Ouellet to relive his decision to jump ship from a job he truly enjoyed.

"You know, I could have stayed at CN for the rest of my career," he says. "It was a heart-wrenching decision to leave."

However, the job at RBC almost wasn't his in the first place. The bank, it seems, was reluctant to turn to someone in his fifties.

"They thought I was a little too old, being fifty-two at the time. I've spoken to Chuck [Winograd, the CEO of RBC Capital Markets] about it. He was hoping they'd get someone in their mid-forties who would be with them for a while. I guess they also thought they'd get someone more ambitious if they were younger."

Ouellet's deep corporate connections convinced them otherwise, and they offered him the job.

I'm sure leaving CN altered Ouellet's life at the time, but retelling the tale doesn't alter his focus on this day. On the toughest par-4 on the course, a downhill 436-yard monster with a green perched precariously on the crest of a small hill, Ouellet smashes his draw down the right side of the fairway, landing in the rough, while I snap a hook into the forest on the left. Bye-bye Pro V1. The banker then strokes a fairway wood onto the green to make a four, while I struggle to make double bogey.

As we head into the final holes at Bruno—including a wickedly tough long par-4 and par-3 combination—Ouellet explains the goal Winograd set out for his job at RBC. The bank, it seems, had developed a reputation for being the financier of big business. And for a spell, a lot of Quebec industry seemed to be off its radar. As the man with connections, it was Ouellet's role to change that.

"The idea was to re-establish the franchise in Quebec. It wasn't nearly as strong in Quebec as it was elsewhere," he says before blasting up the left side of the fairway to play his shot into the fascinatingly strange sixteenth green. "They wanted more business. Investment banking is very competitive, and you have to be proactive."

"What does that take?" I question.

"Thirty years ago, if a company needed to raise money for an acquisition, the CFO would just call the bank they had a relationship with," Ouellet says, making a determination of which club to hit on the dastardly 228-yard seventeenth. "Now everything is up for grabs. You can't sit in your office and wait for the CEO to call and say they are thinking of doing a deal. You have to go and talk to them—or better still, call and say, 'We are looking at your company and we think you should make this move.' Those moves change all the time, depending on the capital markets."

With Ouellet's presence, RBC has found solid footing in Quebec, working alongside companies like Alcan on its $38 billion sale to Rio Tinto, or advising BCE on its sale to the Ontario Teachers' Pension Plan. Of course that doesn't mean RBC advises alone. Ouellet's team of heavy hitters may put RBC among the most prominent investment banks in the world, but companies like Alcan and BCE want something more. They want the sort of reassurance that comes only from working with American corporate giants. Ouellet accepts that.

"If you sit on a board of a big company—a company with a market cap of $10 billion or more—and some unsolicited offer comes along, corporate law says you're not liable even if you made a mistake, as long as you relied on professional advice. So you go and get professionals. And if I'm sitting on the board of Alcan, I want a Canadian advisor because the Canadian capital markets are important in the equation, but I don't want to have to answer the question, 'Why didn't you hire Goldman Sachs? Why didn't you hire Morgan Stanley?' They are the biggest companies in the world, so you just hire them. We are always stuck as co-advisors."

As for where golf fits in to all of this, Ouellet has used his low handicap and connections to the best clubs in the world to foster inroads all over North America. And it doesn't hurt that he plays at Mount Bruno, home course to many of Quebec's top businessmen.

On this day he talks about how proud he is about convincing Quebec-based pharmacy chain Jean Coutu to jettison its ties to National Bank and take on RBC as its advisors.

"It is the kind of thing that three or four years ago would not have happened. That's not just because of me. But we are more aware, as a bank, of what is going on in Quebec business," he says.

And, as with most things involving Jean Pierre, golf plays a role. I mention that I'd heard Jean Coutu Sr., the family's patriarch, is a member at Mount Bruno. Ouellet's eyes light up, a clear indication that a client can be procured over eighteen holes.

"In fact, I played golf with Jean Coutu Sr. as my partner at Laval last week," he says, referring to the historic Willie Park Jr.–designed private course west of Montreal. "I came into the final hole one under par and made a fucking double bogey. And he was my partner, so I wanted to play as well as I could."

Like many businessmen, Ouellet is willing to use golf and his club affiliations to impress clients. But there is a certain protocol that must be followed.

"In truth, Robert, if any one of my clients wants to come and play Bruno, I'd be delighted. But I won't likely be talking any business, and they have to understand the etiquette of a place like this. Basically, it is about having a distinct respect for others."

And JP takes his game very seriously, a fact that has led some casual acquaintances to draw the conclusion that the man takes himself altogether too seriously.

He chuckles.

"They don't know me that well," he says, standing on the eighteenth tee, having won our match but still allowing me to cling to the desperate hope that I might win the back nine. That said, he's a stickler for the rules. A game with Ouellet isn't a casual affair. While most golfers take liberties that can't be found in the rules of the game, from improving lies in the rough to the liberal use of a foot wedge, Ouellet will have none of it. And he won't make any apologies for the way he views the game.

"Yes, I take the game seriously. When I'm on the course, I like to play by the rules and I like to play my best and I like those around me to try to play their best. It doesn't matter whether we are playing for a dollar or $100—I'm going to compete."

This certainly must lead to the occasional uncomfortable round, especially if Ouellet is playing with someone who lacks the same strident perspective on golf.

He continues: "I love the etiquette of the game. Bobby Jones once said that one of the pleasures of the game was its etiquette. And he is absolutely right—and not just on the course. Every club has its own characteristics and etiquette."

On this subject, Ouelett is as animated as I've ever seen him.

"There is a lot of difference between the atmosphere at Merion and Pine Valley, or Mount Bruno and Muirfield. There's a lot in common, but there are subtle differences. For example, there's something at Muirfield I really appreciate. When you go into the dining room there, you'll find big refectory tables. Long, long tables. And if you show up as my guest, and we play in the morning and then we get our jackets and ties on and go in for lunch, we just sit at the next available spot. You introduce yourself and get into a conversation. And I've met so many remarkable people from all walks of life at those tables.

"Once, I sat next to this guy and I asked him what he did. He told me he was a 'chicken strangler.' I thought that was a bit odd. Turned out he was the CEO of a poultry company. And the chicken strangler in question is part of the Muirfield Minstrels, a group that gets together to sing. And he speaks five or six different languages. Apparently, his home has one of the nicest gardens in all of Scotland, which he maintains himself. He's also a very competent golfer, and a good watercolour painter. A man should have a lot of interests."

We finish the final hole, beyond which Mount Bruno's club-house stands majestically in the background, with identical pars, although, as is often the occasion in golf, we take very different paths towards the same conclusion. Ouelett hits a nice, straight ball down the eighteenth fairway. I, on the other hand, catch a hook with my driver that would impress the women working St. Laurent Boulevard. I end up near the tenth green, but manage to punch a long iron to the front edge of the final area of short grass. Two putts later, it's all over. I'm thoroughly defeated, though our scores—78 for Ouellet and 81 for me—don't appear all that different.

"I gave you a pretty good thumping there," he says, shaking my hand on the final green. "You started out a bit sideways, but you got it going in the middle there. It was hard to get by my start."

That's JP. Largely unflappable, he's the kind of guy a company would want on its side when it enters into a financing worth hundreds of millions. He loves his golf, but his ambitions are bigger than the game. Though he is nearing a point where retirement should be in the picture, this man, with club memberships that would make Donald Trump envious, can't envision simply settling down to a regular morning game.

"It would be hard for me to stop and play golf. I can't play more than a couple of days in a row. I played in Scotland recently for five days in a row and it was hard to keep focused on the last couple of days. If you're a professional golfer, that's one thing. I'm not a pro. If I was, I wouldn't eat very well. And when I do retire, I'll do something else. Maybe write a novel."

Nothing seems to agitate him, nothing gets him flustered, except perhaps one of the few instances where his name ended up in print.

Which takes us back to his claim to fame: the round with Tiger. In a flippant remark, *Montreal Gazette* columnist Jack Todd called Ouellet an "RBC Securities veep." But it isn't the fact that Todd got his title wrong that leaves Ouellet seething with anger. No. According to Todd, Ouellet "did his best to educate Woods on Quebec culture by chain-smoking his way around the course, dropping butts on the carefully manicured greens."

Sitting in a white rocking chair outside of the lounge at Bruno, Oeullet relaxes, smokes, drink in hand, telling a story about his recent trip to Scotland. But he turns red when I ask him about the article, and I don't think it has anything to do with a lack of sunscreen.

"I'm pissed off with Jack Todd of the *Gazette* to this day. As you know, I'm a smoker, and I smoked a bit more that day, probably because I was nervous," he says as we walk down the path beside Bruno's pro shop that leads to my rental car. "Todd accused me, in his article, of leaving cigarette butts on the green, which is something I'd never, ever do. That's just crazy."

He pauses, stopping for a minute to collect himself. Only on the occasional bad shot during our round did Ouellet ever actually let his demeanour show through.

"I have not bought the *Gazette* since."

The incident, and Ouellet's response to it, says a lot about the man. At a time when many in business, and in life, have a certain moral pragmatism, Jean Pierre Ouellet thinks that in golf—and in business for that matter—some things are sacrosanct.

CHAPTER 5

Dee Parkinson-Marcoux
The Game's Solitude

"It is the most individual of all sports, and no amount of camaraderie
prior to the match can change the fact you're in it alone."
— Barbara Baldwin, author

THE RELATIONSHIP OF FEMALE executives to the game of golf is
strange and complicated. Over the past decade, more women have
entered the sport—and abandoned it—than ever before. In
Toronto's Bay Street community, which includes many of the biggest
businesses and banks in Canada, it is increasingly typical for top
women executives to hit the links as their male counterparts have
done for years.

For example, the former CEO of the Toronto Stock Exchange,
Barb Stymiest, plays dozens of times a year at her home club,
Toronto Golf Club, and at other country club haunts. Similarly,
investment entrepreneur Kiki Delaney likes the fairways at Magna,
Muskoka's Öviinbyrd, Collingwood's Mad River, and elsewhere. All
of this is public information—hidden in the online software used by
golf associations to track handicaps. The point is that women like
the game and are no longer intimidated to use it for business.

For decades, this was not the case. Even as women cracked the
glass ceiling that had limited them to certain areas of business, like
marketing, that were considered within their realms, they did not
take to the links. That has changed in the past few years, as women

more frequently learn the game and are no longer concerned about playing alongside business associates. Networking organizations for women executives increasingly offer a golf component, including golf schools designed to allow women to feel more comfortable about their games—and themselves—when they are on the course.

Considering all of this progress, Canada's top businesswomen are apparently reluctant to show off their skills. While male executives—even 22-handicap hacks who chop up the pristine fairways of their country club, a membership often acquired as part of their compensation package—aren't shy about displaying their inadequacies, the same is not true for many of the country's most powerful women. These women play at the top clubs and have games that rival those of many of the male executives at their companies. But they rarely show these skills off—or at least they wouldn't for me.

When I set out to plan this book and choose the subjects that would show up in its pages, I cast a wide net. Many of the executives were familiar with my writing, even if they weren't familiar with me, and eagerly agreed to join me for a game. Along the way, I approached ten female executives.

Only one, Stymiest, even bothered to turn me down. She had a media flack at the Royal Bank call back to say that playing with me "wasn't something she'd consider at this time."

"But I don't care how well she plays," I replied. "And, for the record, she plays pretty well. I mean, she just shot 89 at Toronto on Sunday."

Not surprisingly, all I heard in response was a dial tone.

In the end, one woman agreed to join me for a game. We'd played before, four years earlier. She didn't hit the ball very far—and still doesn't—but no one intimidates her.

I wish there were more women like Dee Parkinson-Marcoux in business today, those willing to offer frank discussions and talk about the implications of gender on business, all while chasing a little white ball around a course. But just as her solitary nature and keen insight separate her from many of her peers, Parkinson-Marcoux is unique in this regard.

To outsiders, the Oilmen's Golf Tournament has all the appearances of a secret society, the type of event where participants have to know a secret handshake or password to be allowed entry. Hidden away at such fabled Rocky Mountain golfing retreats as Jasper Park Lodge and Banff Springs, it has for more than fifty years been *the* social event for those in Alberta's petroleum sector. Each year at the end of August, more than three hundred senior oil industry executives, along with their spouses, turn up for a celebration and a competition on two of the country's best courses. Over five days they eat, drink, and play, taking over the courses during the day, having lavish dinners in the evening, and retreating to luxurious hotel rooms at night.

The affair is meticulously planned by an event chair who essentially dedicates a year to working through all the details, from a theme (past tournaments have been patterned around the Jazz Age, the Calgary Stampede, and even a less successful outer-space concept) to the extracurricular activities—ranging from hikes to bridge tournaments—for the wives who aren't participating.

"It is a hell of a lot of work for whoever has that position," says one industry insider who has been involved with the tournament for a decade. "Or at least it is for his executive assistant, who has to make the calls to set everything up."

The event itself mirrors what one would find at a weekly tournament on the PGA Tour. Electronic scoreboards broadcast the results, noting the winners and losers of each flight level of the tournament, which is broken down by the respective abilities of the players. A daily newspaper is produced for those who want to follow more closely. In the past, such golf pros as the legendary Byron Nelson were flown in to offer lessons and tips on the driving range, and golf schools and clinics are set up for those just getting a handle on the game.

But for more than four decades, there was one thing missing. Amongst the 224 golfers desperately trying to save face among their executive-level peers by beating their competitors, there were no women. Not one. Not a single female played in the matches, regardless of her handicap.

Part of that was because there were few women who had risen to the executive strata needed to be invited to the tournament. Typically, only C-level leaders—chief executives, chairmen, and presidents—were permitted entry, and women in those roles in the oil business were infrequent.

Then along came Dee Parkinson-Marcoux. An engineer by training, Parkinson-Marcoux started in the oil industry in 1976. By 1991, she had risen to a position no woman had ever previously attained: executive vice-president of Suncor's oil sands group. And a year after taking the job at Suncor, she was invited to the oil tournament, though not to play in it. "We went on the social invitation," she explains soon after we tee off on the first hole of the Sunshine Coast Golf & Country Club, Parkinson-Marcoux's home course for the past two years. She rubs her eye—an infection put our game in doubt for a while—and continues. "The first time you go, you can't even play. You have to volunteer twice before they'll even consider allowing you to play."

Parkinson-Marcoux is practical by nature. Practicality is likely encoded in her DNA, which should hardly come as a surprise, given her engineering background. And, practically speaking, since the tournament was where the oil industry's movers and shakers went, Parkinson-Marcoux decided she had to go as well. She didn't play golf, but given the policy, that was hardly a problem.

It sounds like a secret society, I say.

"That's because it sort of is," she adds. What she and her husband, Michel, found was something completely foreign to their experience. "Michel and I went off and when we got back to the hotel we traded secrets. Because I was the invitee and he was the guest—and they'd never had a male guest before—I was invited to the ladies' luncheon, which was for the wives of the invitees. Michel didn't get invited—because though he was the guest, he wasn't a lady. So we'd meet back in our room after it was all done and say, 'Who had the worst moment of gender bias today?'"

Parkinson-Marcoux chuckles, stops by her ball in the centre of the first fairway, and pulls out a 6-iron for the approach into the straightaway three-shot opener. She takes her standard wristy swing. The ball doesn't go particularly high, but it does head straight at the green, coming to rest on the fringe and giving her a shot at par.

She recognized the obvious chauvinism of the event, and though she isn't the type that takes slights well, Parkinson-Marcoux wasn't prepared to do anything about the tournament's single-gender makeup.

That is, until Candi came into the picture.

"She was a diehard type who had gone to the events every year for four decades—but looked like she was still twenty," says Parkinson-Marcoux, pulling her clubs to the second hole. "We were standing in a group, and Candi turns to me and says, 'Dee, if you were asked to golf, would you golf?' I didn't even think about it. 'Sure I would.'"

That wasn't the response Candi was expecting. Parkinson-Marcoux might be diminutive in stature, standing barely five feet tall and weighing about a hundred pounds, but she never backs down from a challenge. That's surely part of the reason for her rise in prominence in the energy business, a sector dominated by Calgary's oil cowboys.

"Candi went into a tirade," Parkinson-Marcoux recalls, teeing off on the tight 292-yard par-4 second. "She said she thought it would be a disgrace if they ever asked a woman to play. I understood why she was saying that. Candi, and those like her, all lived through their husbands. You know the trophy type of wife I'm speaking about."

I nod emphatically.

"But her comments made me angry. I don't think until then I'd ever even considered golfing. I turned to her and said, 'I heard everything you've said, Candi, but does your husband put this trip on his expense account? Because if he does, this trip isn't social. This is business. And if this is business, you can't limit it just to men.' Candi went off to complain to everyone about what I'd said. So then I became this *cause célèbre*."

It didn't take long for one of the male oil executives in attendance to hear of the altercation and ask Parkinson-Marcoux about it.

"One of the guys came up and said, 'Well, Dee, we would invite you, and you do qualify, but you don't golf,'" she says, a sly smile crossing her face. The gauntlet had been thrown down.

"I looked at him and said, 'Yes, I do.'"

Of course, that wasn't exactly true. In fact, she'd never played the game.

"Now I had them in a corner, and I was thrilled but also horrified at the same time. I told Michel that I better learn to play. I bought my first clubs in March and played in my first tournament in August."

As for Candi's shortsightedness—the catalyst that pushed her into the game of golf—Parkinson-Marcoux says she now appreciates the shove.

"She was just from her time," Parkinson-Marcoux says quietly as the mist falls while we play out the fourth hole. "I knew that time had passed. If she hadn't attacked me, I don't think things would have changed so quickly. If she hadn't made me angry, I wouldn't have bothered to learn to play. And I fell in love with it. She did me the biggest favour any woman could have done."

Parkinson-Marcoux has played at the Sunshine Coast Golf & Country Club since moving from Canmore, Alberta, to the coastal community of Roberts Creek in British Columbia in 2004. The idea was to head into semi-retirement, but continue to sit on a handful of boards and consult with various companies. It was in Canmore that she got into the habit of making early-morning calls to the Australian oil company for which she consults, then grabbing her clubs and heading out as a single to play Silvertip, a high-end mountain course created by a group of Calgary developers and oil millionaires.

Silvertip, which is perched on the side of a mountain, not far from the highway that leads into Banff National Park, was created by local resident and golf architect Les Furber. Built in a modern style, with boldly contoured fairways blown out of the rock, its holes often plunge a few hundred feet from tee to green. The huge shifts make riding the course on a cart akin to taking a ride at Disneyland.

The Sunshine Coast course couldn't be more different. "It is a workingman's course," says Parkinson-Marcoux. "It costs me so little to be a member here in comparison to Silvertip that it is a real bargain." The course is actually an amalgamation of two nines, built decades apart. The front nine, sculpted through thick underbrush and around massive pines, is narrow and difficult, with streams crisscrossing fairways, and greens with large swales. The back nine is the original part of the course, and in distinct contrast to the front nine, it is more open, with fairways punctuated by the occasional tree, and natural greens that fit the pattern of the land.

Partial to playing on her own, Parkinson-Marcoux hasn't exactly integrated into the Sunshine Coast's club of locals. I suspect she's regarded by those at the club as a bit of an odd duck, the short woman who keeps to herself and plays on her own. It is an unusual golfer that is willing to play the game for a personal challenge and doesn't revel in at least some of the game's social aspects. But that's exactly the case with Dee. Since her husband, Michel, prefers gardening to golf, Parkinson-Marcoux often plays in her spare time. And she's not about to wait around hoping for a group to invite her to join them. She's just as likely to hit a shot off the elevated first tee at Sunshine Coast and start walking up the narrow confines of the first hole. On those instances, her only company is her racing mind, and for Parkinson-Marcoux, that's more than enough.

These days, her game is tidy—she doesn't hit the ball very hard or very far, but it also rarely strays far off line. She plays effective and consistent bogey golf, and since she's rarely off the fairway, it makes conversation very easy. It is also a game well suited to her home course, with its fairways surrounded by thick swaths of trees. Even on a day when an eye infection is bothering her, she finds fairways and has par putts on the greens, making a couple along the way.

It is exactly this consistent play that maddened her opponents once she began competing in the Oilmen's tournament. Put into a group of other high-handicap golfers in 1995 at Banff Springs, Parkinson-Marcoux's steady play often yielded surprising results.

"The men I'd play with were also high-handicappers, so they'd blow out holes, but also had potential to put a good one together," she explains. "And I'd just drive them crazy by hitting it down the middle three times to the green."

Eventually, it had to happen—Parkinson-Marcoux would beat one of her male competitors in the match play, a section of the tournament where golfers competed head-to-head. Winners are determined not by how many strokes are taken, but by the number of individual holes they win. It didn't happen the first year, in which she was soundly thumped, but by 1996 she had clawed her way to a couple of wins. The first few men she dispatched took their defeats well, despite losing to a tiny woman. But that wasn't the case with everyone, especially in 1997. Her improving golf skills made Parkinson-Marcoux a force in her high-handicap flight. After winning the first three days, she was pitted against a senior oil executive—whom she doesn't name—with a high handicap and the type of inconsistent play that meant he would manage only a handful of well-played holes a round. More often than not, a hole would turn into a disaster of hoseled shots, shanks, and fat irons.

That Parkinson-Marcoux doesn't identify him is really of no concern. Lacking a name, the golfer in question becomes an archetype of the Alberta oil business, a largely male concern where egos are often matched to the size of one's oil discovery.

Her opponent became increasingly anxious as it appeared more likely that the woman whose ball regularly found the short grass would better him. Parkinson-Marcoux says it had little to do with whether he lost—he'd never been that successful in the tournament. It was more about the teasing he would receive at the hands of his colleagues when it became recognized he'd been the first victim of Parkinson-Marcoux's deft short game.

"He was getting pretty stressed. I could see it in the way he acted. He stopped talking towards the end," she says. "I learned a lot from the tournament about gracious winning and gracious losing. I was so conscious of winning and how it would affect him. He was a nice guy, normally. So for this to happen to him, he was going to lose face."

One up in the match with two holes remaining—a long par-4 and a par-3—Parkinson-Marcoux didn't like her chances. Both players had a horrible start to the par-4, but eventually the unflappable female oil exec hit what she describes as an "all-or-nothing shot." It found the green and she took the hole and the match.

You made a bogey to win?

"Oh, gosh no. I think I made an eight and he made a nine," she sighs.

But the game didn't end there. In her own inimitable fashion, Parkinson-Marcoux analyzed the situation and recognized the agitated state of her competitor. She told him he couldn't go into the clubhouse to face his fellow oil executives while angry and embarrassed at the loss. Instead, she took him for a drink and a conversation, returning him to his associates in a less demoralized state.

"In true sportsmanship, I didn't win with glee. He was worried about how he was perceived. I don't want to be negative about him. It was very tough for someone to lose to the first female, especially to someone who had only golfed for three years. You had to be very tender about the fact that it wasn't a match between a couple of guys, where you can stand up and say one outplayed the other. It was something altogether different. It wasn't a personal issue with me; he just realized how much he was going to be teased by his peers.

"But he really liked that I'd given him a run for the money. He knew he could beat me—he just didn't. I took it from him and he had the high ground in terms of being competitive. But he was sensitive about getting ripped by his peers. We finished the game properly."

Her rise was complete—she'd won her flight in the tournament. Call it the Canadian Open for the dig-and-drill set. Her win made Parkinson-Marcoux the Michelle Wie of the Calgary oil industry, I point out.

"I don't know about that," she says, wiping her troublesome eye. "I won to the despair of those poor men that I beat. It is very hard to win four days in a row, surrounded by all of those powerful men."

Okay, maybe not Wie then, but Parkinson-Marcoux is a pioneer. Maybe she's more like the Margaret Thatcher of the oil business, a woman with a focused vision of what she wanted to accomplish.

Either way, winning all four days was one of the most taxing tasks of Parkinson-Marcoux's corporate life.

"Winning every day is incredibly exhausting. I appreciate now when people say Tiger Woods can maintain his focus. It is very difficult to stay focused over a few days."

Is it comparable to doing a big corporate deal?

"I don't think I've ever done anything that so mentally exhausted me. Maybe it is comparable to doing a one-on-one negotiation. That's what match play is."

Having started her career in the 1970s, Parkinson-Marcoux spent much of the following twenty years working for a variety of energy and oil companies, ranging from Imperial Oil to Petro-Canada. She hit her peak in 1991, when she was named executive vice-president of Suncor's oil sands group. By 1996 she had been named president of cs Resources; its sale to PanCanadian Petroleum saw her move on to the position of president of Gulf's heavy oil division. That job lasted less than a year before a decision not to take the company public saw her jump to Ensyn Energy, which was developing oil-sands technology.

Her faith in the concept of heavy oil may have earned her the nickname "Queen of the Oil Sands," but it also gave her a keen insight into the differences between men and women working in the petroleum industry. Her career, she says, walking up the fifth fairway, is "more parallel" to those of her male peers in the industry.

"One of the things I've discovered is that if you read a lot of resumés and didn't know the person attached, you'd have a pretty good sense of the gender. If you read my resumé, you wouldn't guess. I don't mean that in a good or bad way. It is just that my experience in there would be much more similar to the men I work with."

She hits a wood towards the green and continues.

"I get a lot of calls from women asking for advice. A lot of them don't get the same satisfaction out of their careers in the way a man does. I'm generalizing, but a man gets a lot of satisfaction out of a thing he's built. Women get their satisfaction about making people feel good about stuff. That's not me."

That's one thing you learn from playing golf with Parkinson-Marcoux: she isn't going to pander to anyone and she never backs down from a challenge. That doesn't make her unfriendly, though I suspect some find her frank nature and quiet, but direct comments to be off-putting. She is willing to challenge preconceived notions and will raise a wide variety of topics, from corporate governance to the latest novel she's read, over the course of a single hole. It takes a sharp mind to keep up with her, and on this day I'm struggling enough to take notes and hit the ball (semi) straight.

Unlike those in what she refers to as the "pink side of the industry," a comment on women in traditional marketing positions, Parkinson-Marcoux is a builder. During her career in the oil business, her interest was in creating companies and moving them forward quickly. When that failed to come to fruition, she was unwilling to take what she refers to as "custodial" jobs.

"I'm the kind of person who dances because I've figured out how to build a new mine," she says. "I just don't think I get the same sort of satisfaction that comes to most women from their jobs. That doesn't make me less female. I have all sorts of female characteristics, though maybe not so much on the nurture side. Where I get my sense of well-being and satisfaction is similar to that of a man."

As our conversation rises to topics rarely discussed on a golf course, Parkinson-Marcoux makes a remark that her infected eye is not improving. She'll play one more hole—the 198-yard par-3 ninth—and then head home.

"But you stay and finish the round," she insists. "I want you to see the course. I'll go back to the house and you can come by after for dinner or some wine."

I slog around the final nine holes, as play slows in the groups in front and a light rain begins to fall. After finishing with a bogey on the final hole, an intriguing dogleg right par-4 with a tabletop green, I lug my clubs up the hill to the parking lot. I salvage an 86 on the day, while Parkinson-Marcoux cards a 46 on her half-round.

Fifteen minutes later, I'm sitting on a couch in Parkinson-Marcoux's open-concept home with its spectacular view of the open waterway that separates mainland British Columbia from Vancouver Island. Her husband, Michel, turns on some classical music and opens a bottle of red wine.

Jumping back in from where our conversation concluded, I ask about her "pink ghetto" concept that relegates women to certain roles traditionally held by females.

"The women who are the brightest and most analytical are on the financial end," she says, leaning forward from a seated position on the couch. "You just don't meet women who have run refineries."

That's the elephant in the room. The question is why not?

"Leadership that women exhibit is seen as soft, as opposed to what is required in those environments, which is hard," she explains. "I always say 'tough and fair.' That's all anyone wants: tough and fair. It is the guys that are tough and mean that fail. And it is the women who are soft and fair that fail. Tough and fair doesn't mean something ugly."

From Parkinson-Marcoux's perspective, education is the foundation for this divide.

"In school, we reward the academic side of things more than those that like to experiment," she says. "We don't reward the guys who like to blow up the lab because they are curious. Their learning methods are different. Women get such praise from doing well on exams that it becomes a style. Give me a female lawyer or a female financier and they'll be damned good. In engineering, women are always looking for the customer. Men are client-focused because they have to be, but they are always looking to build a project. Women are often more focused on the relationship, building a customer a bridge so they can build something else. That's okay. That's where they get their satisfaction."

She pauses.

"But for me, it is creating the goddamn bridge."

Interestingly, as she shows me around the house, Parkinson-Marcoux admits she feels isolated. The house and location are tremendous, she admits, but it is a lengthy ferry trip and drive away from Vancouver. She misses the bustle and action that came from being near Calgary. Though she hasn't directly been part of the oil industry in nearly a decade, Parkinson-Marcoux is still in demand on issues relating to corporate governance and sits on several boards, including those of SNC-Lavalin and, more recently, Sherritt International, the resource company based in Toronto.

Sherritt CEO Ian Delaney (also a golfer, who can be found playing at Aurora's Magna Golf Club) approached her about coming on board. It isn't an easy position to fill, given Sherritt's activities in Cuba. The Helms-Burton Act, a controversial U.S. law, bans certain senior executives and their families from entering Uncle Sam's land if they do business with Castro's nation. Sherritt has substantial holdings in Cuba, and by taking a seat on the company's board, Parkinson-Marcoux is virtually assured she won't be able to travel to the U.S., perhaps for the rest of her life.

But in her own inimitable fashion, Parkinson-Marcoux is pragmatic about the decision.

"Oh, yes, I'm on the blacklist," she says in a matter-of-fact tone, looking out the window towards the water. "Doesn't matter to me one bit. I haven't had any dealings in the U.S. in some time. These days, my destinations are more likely to be Australia or Chile. Places like that."

Sherritt wanted Parkinson-Marcoux for her practical experience, she says.

"Sherritt gets it. I'm on their board and they have finance experts galore. I know how to do transactions, but where they look to me is my feel. I have a feel for mines. I know what smells good and what doesn't smell good. I also have a feel for major capital projects. I understand a lot of areas that men are often good at because they have experience. I don't know whether they are intuitive about it or experienced about it. Either way, they've picked it up, while women tend to be more theoretical. My experience is a combination. I'm a theorist, but only after the fact. I always like to have the experience and then put a framework on the experience so it is useful to other people."

Is it the experience that leads to the demand for her skills? I ask.

"For sure. If I hadn't had the experience, I don't think I'd have insight. You need to live through it rather than just study it. Women are really bad sometimes at thinking knowledge is a substitute for experience."

So, taking more degrees is a substitute for not getting your hands dirty?

"Exactly. I've taken the schooling, but I've done something. And that's where I think there's a gap between a lot of male executives and their female counterparts. And that's neither a judgment nor a criticism. It is just business."

After our tour of her home, we return to her sitting room. In a long career, there have been few missteps. While reminiscing about her rise up the executive ranks, she admits she learned not to involve herself in areas that didn't interest her—though, truthfully, those areas and subjects that don't catch her fancy are limited and often quickly dismissed. This, apparently, is true in both her personal and professional life.

"I didn't do well on National Bank's board because I found it very hard to get excited about a quarter-cent margin," she says.

"Don't we all?" I joke.

"But that's what they do at a bank," she points out. "And I'd get very dissatisfied that they talk about risk and risk management, when they have such huge access to such huge pools of capital that they are almost in a position where they can't fail to make money. It is almost like a casino. But for me, that was entirely unsatisfactory. They don't build anything for me. When they talk about project financing they turn out to be the ones that kill off a lot of wonderful ideas. So, what do we get?"

She sips her drink. Canada, she worries, could be facing a breaking point as native resources are sold to foreign interests and innovation doesn't receive the support it needs.

"I'm on the board of Sustainable Development Technology Canada, with a miserable $500 million to give to new technologies. Where are the risk-takers anymore? We're awash in capital and no one will take a risk."

Parkinson-Marcoux may be a ground-breaker, but she admits that few women have followed through the door she opened. Sure, Linda Cook, an American, rose to prominence in 2003, when she took on the role of CEO at Shell Canada, Canada's fourth-largest oil company. But there haven't been many others, Parkinson-Marcoux acknowledges after taking the last mouthful of wine from her glass. And though some women have also followed her into the Oilmen's tournament, female participants have been infrequent. Many female executives simply dismiss the tournament, or participate without embracing the competitive spirit that is the event's foundation.

"I told these women not to say yes to the invitation unless they were prepared to compete," she says. "I don't necessarily like competing. I don't like some of the dynamics it creates. But unless you're willing to have that guy say, 'I beat her' or 'She beat me,' then you shouldn't be in the competition. If you are just dismissive and don't really try in the tournament, you defeat the purpose of what it was meant to be. A lot of women don't understand that, and men do. Women on the golf course tend to be more social, more collegial."

Parkinson-Marcoux's entrance into the game was based on competition, and even today, at nearly sixty, she's not about to make it into a social activity. That's why, she says, "I don't play Tuesdays with the ladies at Sunshine Coast.

"For me, I'm competitive against the golf course. It is me and my ability against the golf course on that day at that time. I'm trying to be thoughtful and not let a bad shot get me down. I get a thrill out of that, so I can golf on my own forever."

CHAPTER 6

David Miller

Placing His Bets

"Politics is the skilled use of blunt objects."

—Lester B. Pearson

CALL IT THE ANTITHESIS OF the ultra-exclusive private golf club.

Only a few hundred yards south of the constant commotion of rumbling, hissing, and honking cars that is Highway 401, and obscured from Yonge Street by a rising driveway that loses itself in a jumbled parking lot, Don Valley Golf Club is the quintessential municipal golf course. Owned by the City of Toronto (and, before it, the municipality of Metro Toronto) since 1956, the reality is that for many, Don Valley *is* golf in Toronto. In a good year, more than fifty thousand people pull up in their family four-doors to plunk down $50 and smack a white ball around a group of fairways perched precariously in the midst of a city of millions. They show up in droves, largely because the course's affordable rates make it among the most attractive golf experiences for miles around. Many golfers race to the pro shop when it opens at 6:30 a.m., hoping to grab one of the first tee times. These are dewsweepers, obsessives with one goal in mind: to race around Don Valley's fairways and hit the occasional green in regulation before the throng of several hundred cart-riding hackers smack, swear, and gash their way around the course for the remainder of the day.

These early risers ignore the course's obvious shortcomings— like the looming pomposity of the highway that circumnavigates the front nine and the ever-present graffiti that accompanies it. They aren't under any illusions that Don Valley is anything more than it is; they know the course is light years from those multimillion-dollar public courses with their $150 green fees and players who show up for corporate outings dressed in suits. It isn't a posh private track with lush fairways and attendants willing to cater to the golfer's every need. No one is there to shine their shoes or valet-park their car. They know the course won't offer them 7,200 yards of cumbersome water hazards and bunkers that suck balls in and never give them back. That's not the point. After all, the golfers who play Don Valley aren't Tiger Woods, and they will never hit a 300-yard drive, unless their snap hook finds the hard edge of a cart path. They park their rust buckets, pop open their trunks, and change their shoes in the parking lots before grabbing their bags of knock-off clubs, heaving them over their shoulders and trudging down the steps that lead to the pro shop.

They are passionate nonetheless, and while these golfers may not be shrouded in the more expensive pretences of the game, Don Valley offers them the opportunity to display their affection for golf. For many city golfers, it is an oasis. Those who understand the importance of public golf to the overall health of the game also understand the importance of places like Don Valley—and the thousands of other munis spread out across North America.

Don Valley is a lot of things. But it isn't a place where you typically find the high-profile and high-powered.

It is in this context that, on a stunning August morning, with the sun just peeking out over Toronto's high-rises and the city in the midst of a major budget crisis, I navigate my car up the rise and into the course's parking lot. Though Don Valley is well known for attracting the early bird, I'm still among the first to hit the property—not surprising since the shop won't open for nearly an hour.

One of the perks of writing about golf for a living has been the invitations I've received to all of Canada's most famed courses—private haunts like Capilano, on the mountain outside of Vancouver;

Calgary Golf and Country Club, where the oil business's establishment hang; and Aurora's Beacon Hall Golf Club, where $100,000 might get you in the door. But I'd never been to Don Valley. Sure, I knew where the course was—and I'd even once posed for photos for a magazine spread, hitting off the first tee. But I'd never grabbed my clubs and gone to play a round. That was about to change.

I walked towards the clubhouse and began rolling some balls on the green adjacent to the parking lot. Since land was at a premium in the city even when Don Valley was conceived five decades ago, there's no massive warm-up range at the club. There's an area with some mats that look as though they've been at the course since it opened, and some balls that might once have been hit by Bobby Jones himself.

Standing on the green, with its bare patches and vista of nearby condos, I stroke a few. That's when my playing partner makes his appearance, a full fifteen minutes ahead of our game.

It isn't hard to see Toronto mayor David Miller coming. For one thing, he's a big man, standing over six feet tall. He walks with a certain presence, one that makes him easy to spot from a distance, even though on this day, clad in the uniform of the everyday golfer—tan pants and a red golf shirt, but no hat—he could be mistaken for any of the crew showing up at the course.

He carries his clubs in a bag over his shoulder and ambles up to reintroduce himself. While I'd never golfed with Miller, I had interviewed him once a few years previous about his passion for the game. I'm not a huge fan of his politics, which typically lean to the left of the spectrum, but I came away from my initial encounter with Miller knowing that the man really loved both his job as mayor and his golf. He uses the game as a diversion from the attention he usually receives as the type of populist politician who is perpetually shaking hands. Tucked away at his home course—the understated Markland Woods, a small private club in Toronto's west end—Miller typically plays early and fast. His regular Saturday outings were not political in nature, nor even retreats with a couple of lawyer buddies.

You won't find him out with a couple of councillors or courting some federal MP stopping in town. Instead, he jumps in his car at the crack of dawn and goes down to bat the ball around with friends who are more likely to be teachers than business associates.

Given all of this, it came as no shock that he agreed to a game when I called his media handler. Miller has a genuine affection for the game—though he didn't start playing until he was thirty-six and was preparing to give up his first love: rugby. And though he plays at a private club, Miller has worked hard at positioning himself as a populist—the man who can correct the plight of Canada's largest city after years of neglect. So the suggestion from his handlers is that we tee it up at Don Valley, home to golf's average Joes. Some might see the clientele as the game's great unwashed, but to Miller the people who congregate at Don Valley are his constituents, the ones who voted him into office for two terms. And he's not about to forget that.

Golf was not something Miller had considered often when, as an immigration lawyer, he entered the world of politics in 1994. The game simply wasn't physical enough for a big man who enjoyed the rough and tumble of contact sports. His love for rugby didn't diminish after becoming a Metro councillor, but his ability to commit to the sport did. The long hours his new job demanded left little time for the training that is necessary to withstand the physical strain that one endures, even in a recreational rugby match.

"It was also difficult, once I was elected, to show up for council with black eyes or missing teeth," Miller explains. Seeking an activity to replace rugby, he turned to golf. In some ways, it is akin to a ballerina retiring to pursue ice hockey. It doesn't make sense, but Miller became increasingly enamoured of the game as he continued to rise in the political world. After serving two terms on Toronto city council starting in 1997, Miller threw his hat in the ring to replace outgoing mayor Mel Lastman. Few figured he had much of a chance in the November 2003 election: he'd floundered in attempts to crack the federal and provincial political ranks, both with the New Democrats.

Given Miller's unproven ability to win at big-time politics, most pundits felt former Toronto mayor Barbara Hall, who had strong ties to Ontario's provincial Liberal party, would take the centre-left vote, while John Tory, the former CFL commissioner turned businessman, would take the right-of-centre vote. But Hall's campaign struggled from the start, leaving Tory and Miller in a tight race. Miller prevailed by a slim margin, becoming Toronto's sixty-third mayor. The Harvard economics grad and avid golfer cleaned up in a second election in 2006, leaving him with few political rivals.

It is clear that Miller doesn't remember me from our interview a year ago, so I flag him down as he prepares to wander down the steps into the pro shop that overlooks the course. On our way, an employee of the club approaches us and asks if we want to play together as a foursome with two others.

"Well, I've got something I've got to do, so it'll just be the two of us," he explains. That means no playing partners today. It is a disappointment, because it means I'm not going to see how the mayor would react if paired with two choppers from Brampton who have used the city's roadways to pillage Toronto the Good's best municipal course.

Instead, we are whisked into the pro shop, where Miller pulls out his Visa card and plunks it down to pay his $52 green fee. I too hand off my credit card, and with two green fee slips to show the starter, we're off down the hill towards the first tee.

"We've got to play quickly," Miller repeats, half jogging down the hill.

"I have to do an interview with Andy Barrie at CBC radio," he continues. "He's been on holiday during this budget issue, so he wants to catch up."

I simply nod. Apparently Miller is so good at multitasking that he's going to do two interviews—one with me and one live on the CBC—all while playing golf. That means we have to be off and running, which explains why we're jogging down the hill to the starter's hut, handing off our receipts and wandering briskly down the cart path to the first tee. Miller has a tee in the ground as I'm still trying to catch my breath.

When I told a friend I was playing with Miller, he asked me to keep an eye out for whether his politics and golf game match. In other words, does the man with NDP ties hook it to the left? It doesn't take long for me to realize that political perspective and the golf swing don't always align. Perhaps Miller has made a sudden change in his political tack, because on the first tee he hits two massive slices into the awaiting trees on the *right* of the short par-4. "I didn't renew my NDP membership," he'll tell me a few holes later. In fact, on some holes Miller hits it right of Brian Mulroney. On others, he's left of Ed Broadbent. As a golfer, he covers the political spectrum within the first couple of holes.

It strikes me that the disarray shown in Miller's game could well be a reflection of the groundswell of reaction the mayor was receiving to his battle over Toronto's budget. To someone reading the papers, it would appear that the city was in crisis and could simply fall down around its citizens at any time. Some pegged the budgetary shortfall at about $400 million—or about the cost of using the 407 Express Toll Route to avoid the traffic at the top of the city.

Our game was to be played a month after a proposal by Miller to fix the city's financial woes was rejected by both his foes and friends in Toronto's government. Miller's proposal was to avoid cutting services—the heart of the city, he'd say—and to tax homeowners and those who drove gas-chugging, smog-spewing cars. He was soundly defeated in his first go-round, though after our game he managed to push through an altered tax plan.

Thinking Miller might focus on his game if he's able to talk about the situation, I ask the mayor if the money issue is on his mind. It clearly is—he rattles off enough facts and figures while walking up the narrow first fairway at Don Valley to set my head spinning. I still manage to hit the green in two, while Miller struggles to keep his ball in play. But his focus is now on dollar signs.

"Do you know that just one cent of the GST collected in Toronto would give this city $400 million? That's all it would take to fix our budget," he explains, reaching into his bag, pulling out his putter and walking to his ball, which rests twenty-five feet to the left of the pin on the narrow first green. "I'm just so frustrated that we as a city collect a lot of tax revenue and then almost all of it goes elsewhere."

"Exactly how much money are we talking about?" I ask.

"I don't know, Robert," he says, stroking his putt four feet to the right of the cup. "Every time I ask, the number I get is different."

Miller says he typically uses golf as a distraction, and though he is invited to every golf tournament for a charitable or business cause within the city, he turns them down. "Nothing worse than a six-hour round," he explains, frowning. "Well, maybe there is.

"I played in a Korean businessman's event a couple of weeks back," he starts, as we walk past the graffiti-covered pilings and underneath the 401 towards the long par-4 second. "And not only was it really, really slow, but there were also all kinds of people with cameras—some of them television cameras. The only thing worse than playing in those types of tournaments is being photographed at them."

We wander up to the third hole, and Miller makes a rather tentative swing with his driver, hitting it again to the right and into a nearby stream. He takes a drop and punches one back towards my tee shot in the centre of the fairway.

Today, apparently, golf isn't a big enough distraction for Miller. Powerfully built, he would appear to be the type that should hit the ball a long way. But he tends to swing reluctantly, flaring the club away from his body on the backswing. As we meet at the green, he admits there are things on his mind.

"This budget issue is about our city," he says, moving to his ball at the upper left side of the elevated green. "Toronto is one of the most important cities in North America, and this is about building it properly."

He pauses.

"I guess this is an issue most golfers don't have to worry about."

We walk to the fourth hole, a dogleg over a creek. I crack one down over the corner, but once again, following a slightly lunging swing, Miller's ball heads to the right. Just then his cellphone goes off. It is the CBC.

He's right that there are a lot of balls in the air to juggle, all while playing golf. Meanwhile, Miller, without giving any indication of where he is, wanders off to find his ball, engrossed in explaining to Barrie why the city is in such dire straits. No wonder he's distracted: most golfers are bothered by a passing beverage cart; Miller, on the other hand, has to explain to thousands of radio listeners why he can't fix the financial straits in which Toronto finds itself mired. When I think about it that way, it makes my 110-yard approach look pretty inconsequential.

By the time we hit the turn, what little game Miller started the day with is in danger of disappearing completely. He double-bogeys the par-5 eighth after hitting his tee shot wide right off the tee, but manages a bogey on the ninth, a short par-4.

Most would simply give up after the resounding thumping Miller has received, beaten by the fickle nature of the game and a golf swing that appears one day and disappears the next. But the most diehard golfers, those really intrigued by the game, tend also to think they can overcome the trials golf throws their way. Golfers tend to be pragmatic optimists, and that's pretty much Miller to a tee. He's also an idealist. He still believes that public service—like being mayor—is a calling for him. For Miller, golf is also a calling; but, like disappointing polling numbers, his game is now something he has to overcome.

Like most weekend hackers, Miller says his golf game is reflective of his general approach to sports. In rugby, if he wasn't playing well, he simply tackled harder. The idea that one could get ahead in rugby by simply playing more forcefully was something Miller translated to golf. The problem is that golf—even in the era of long bombers like John Daly—is as much about subtlety as power. Miller says it has taken him a long time, but he now understands that lesson.

"In every sport I've played, I thought I could fix my problems by simply playing harder," he says. "But in golf, that just doesn't work." Even while struggling to find any semblance of a game, Miller is fine golf company. He loves to talk, and is blessed with the ability to weave his way into almost any subject. Over the course of the first nine holes, we chat about everything from the designer who created Don Valley (Howard Watson) to the nature of celebrity (Miller has met Arnold Palmer, but was really floored when Doug Gilmour introduced his father at a celebrity event—"Doug Gilmour! He asked me for an autograph for his dad!" Miller exclaims) and the changing nature of municipal politics.

"I think my job is to fight for Toronto," he says, "and I don't think you can do that and be partisan."

He also sees himself as a man of the people, tapping me on the shoulder during one of our early holes to compare himself to Prime Minister Stephen Harper.

"More than 335,000 people voted for me," he says excitedly. "You know how many voted for him? Thirty-five thousand! That's it."

Disappointed, but not dejected, Miller makes an intriguing offer as we walk behind the wire fence that protects the tenth tee from the eighteenth green.

"Okay, I need to get focused," he says. "Let's put a wager on the final nine."

I'm surprised. After all, I had just played the front nine in one under par, while Miller didn't break 50, including some scoring adjustments for picking up his ball from the fifth fairway while doing his CBC interview. But I'm game, and we set a wager that gives Miller a stroke on every hole.

After seeing his game held together by duct tape and the occasionally lucky putt for the front nine, Miller steps up on the tenth tee and hits it a mile to the right, landing on a maintenance road that runs along the fairway. I pipe it down the middle and we walk up to find the mayor's ball punctuating the middle of a large puddle. He hacks it to the front of the green and bounces a chip up a swale, stopping on the fringe, twenty feet pin-high. My wedge shot comes to rest five feet below the hole. Miller gives the putt a quick look, studying it without overly examining the detail, and slides it down the roll of the green. It finds the bottom of the cup, and we halve the hole.

"Now, that's a lot better," Miller says as he walks to the eleventh hole, a 345-yard par-4. A hole that's straightforward, yet deceptively difficult, with out-of-bounds on the right, Miller manages to find the fairway and make another par. I suddenly find myself down in the match against a player who was self-immolating for the opening nine holes. Like Barbara Hall, the favorite heading into Miller's first mayoral campaign, who would have her hat handed to her by Miller's populist appeal, I've learned that the strapping mayor isn't one to be underestimated.

On the twelfth hole, the only par-5 on the back nine, he talks me into hitting a driver. He's persuasive: "Ah, come on, Robert. You've got to hit it once." Not surprisingly, for a successful politician, Miller gets what he wants. I pull my driver out of my bag and promptly snap-hook my tee shot into the woods on the left.

As Miller's game continues to improve (though we both bludgeon the twelfth), our conversation becomes more pointedly focused on the city's fundamental issues—transit, crime, and guns, the increasing flow of disenfranchised immigrants. It is all part of the mayor's portfolio. And even in a friendly golf game, the mayor is willing to talk about the issues important to him. He's not pushy about it—he just manages to get them into the conversation.

"It is like slow play in golf," Miller says, smiling, as we walk from the short fifteenth. "Some things should just be socially unacceptable. Guns should be unacceptable. As a society, we should just say these things aren't acceptable. I can't understand why we don't."

As he continues to talk, Miller continues to steadily improve, mounting a two-hole lead heading into the seventeenth. But he struggles to find the green, and I manage to steal one. On the final hole, I sense an opportunity to even our match and keep my money in my khakis. I hit my six-iron from the elevated tee to the right side of the fairway. It isn't a solid shot, but it won't hurt. It is what is colloquially referred to in golf circles as a "Camilla Parker-Bowles"—golf-speak for "it doesn't look good, but it gets the job done."

Meanwhile, Miller's difficulties from the previous hole continue. His looping swing is now letting him down, and he hits a hosel rocket off the tee, miraculously skirting trees on the left and flopping down a hundred yards away in the rough off the ninth hole. He hacks it back to the fairway, but his iron approach misses just wide of the green.

It is all about having his eye on the prize, apparently.

"I've got to stay focused," he says, wandering up to his ball, which sits a few yards off the right side of the green. He puts his bag down and continues. "That's the reason I'm not talking about tackling some other area of politics. I've got to be focused. You've seen that today."

He pauses for a moment to examine his shot, then clips the ball cleanly. It bounds onto the green and rolls to a rest five feet below the cup.

My chip nestles up next to the cup, inches below the hole. Miller walks up, picks up the ball, and hands it to me. With a stroke on the hole, he still has a five-footer for bogey to halve the hole and take the match. He looks at the putt from a couple of angles and then carefully—almost cautiously—strokes it into the centre of the cup.

"I hate to lose," he says triumphantly, walking back to grab his clubs.

"Mr. Mayor," I say, handing him my coin, "perhaps this can be put against the budget crisis."

Miller shoots me a look, then breaks into laughter.

"I'm going to get this framed so I can tell people about beating the golf writer," he says as we commence the walk up the hill towards Don Valley's clubhouse. Is he joking? I can't tell.

We both laugh knowing that in golf, as in politics, what people remember most is your final shot.

Postscript: A couple of months after our round, a Toronto golf radio show solicited comments from notable personalities on "birdies and bogeys," a bad euphemism for the highs and lows of their year. Miller called, saying his birdie was playing "a very well-known golf writer."

"I beat him one-up," he said proudly, before adding, "but it was also my bogey because how thick can you be to beat a guy you want to write a good article about you?"

CHAPTER 7

Eugene Melnyk

Changing Courses

"I learned that whatever I got out of life, I'd have to go out and get it for myself."

—Walter Hagen

"**EVERYTHING CHANGED** that day."

Sure it appears to be hyperbole, and yes, it is hard to believe exactly, given all that Eugene Melnyk has accomplished and experienced over the past two decades. How could any one thing alter the world of a billionaire?

But Melnyk says it convincingly. Typically careful in choosing his words—often prefacing them with, "Well, I've got to be careful here"—in this instance he appears compellingly sincere.

Melnyk's tone is usually confident and aggressive. Even his detractors can't discount that his personality is probably one of the factors that made him so successful. But as he stands on the driving range at Eagles Nest Golf Club in the Toronto suburb of Maple, hitting a warm-up bucket, his tone changes. It softens and gets quiet, as if he's about to confide some secret he doesn't want anyone to overhear, even though we're the only ones standing on the practice area on an unusually warm Saturday in September. He stops hitting balls—the first time he's picked up a golf club in months, he says—and steps towards me, leaning on his club. And he begins to tell the story about why he decided to exit the executive ranks of Biovail—

his baby, the company that he created and developed into the largest drug maker in Canada.

For Melnyk, the day in question was December 11, 2006. It is rare that people can pinpoint a date when their life was altered entirely, but Melnyk can. In fact, he can be even more precise: it was 9:30 on an unusually mild day when he prepared to signal the start of the day's trading at the New York Stock Exchange. For Melynk, then the chairman of Biovail, the drug company he'd founded in 1989, it was a monumental occasion. With Doug Squires standing to his left, the man Melnyk hand-picked to succeed him as the operational leader of Biovail, the billionaire rang the bell that launched yet another day of unbridled capitalism.

"My brother died the day I rang the bell," he explains, swaying back and forth as he prepares to head back to finding his swing. "I knew then that I'd change things. I wanted to do something else. I wasn't going to spend time doing what I didn't want to do. Things would be different."

He finishes his sentence, and goes back to being the Melnyk I have come to know over the past half-decade. He takes a big cut at an awaiting ball with his 7-iron, swiping more ground than ball. Sod flies forward, while the ball rolls twenty feet in front of us. Call it a lack of focus.

Even before his brother passed away, Melnyk says his head wasn't in Biovail. Admittedly, two years previous, when we played golf near his home on the east coast of Barbados, Melnyk also told me it was time to alter his life. Turmoil—both in a positive and negative sense—had been the rule in recent years.

That's not surprising. After all, how many people can say they were feted for saving a Canadian NHL franchise, and simultaneously roasted as a corporate fraud? While he was applauded for salvaging the Ottawa Senators from bankruptcy in 2003, he was being attacked in the business pages for alleged violations of U.S. and Canadian securities regulations. And it all came at a time when Melnyk was trying to reinvent Biovail and enter the U.S. market.

Securities regulators would dog him for the remainder of his days at Biovail.

All of which makes Melnyk a strange mix of contradictions. He flies to eastern Europe and gives millions to orphanages, but has been accused of playing dirty with those who don't agree with him. He loves Canada, but lives in Barbados. He doesn't seek the spotlight, but it finds him anyway, especially given his ownership of eight hundred racehorses and the Senators. He's a scoundrel to some, philanthropist to others.

Melnyk tees up another ball and takes a physical, lunging swing at it. This one slices off to the right, over the hill that separates the range from the course and disappears in the distance. He can be forgiven for the faulty swing. There's been little time for golf in the past year, he tells me, and commitments, as well as a bad back, have limited him to a few games over the past year. And truthfully, he likes the game, but he doesn't love it. Not in the same way he loves his other distractions: hockey and horses. And he doesn't have the typical physical makeup of a golfer. Not particularly tall, with a shock of wavy hair, and a slight paunch, Melnyk could be any corporate exec with a high handicap heading out for a weekly game. A golf pro he is not.

Despite this, with his responsibilities at Biovail wrapping up, litigation against him for a variety of securities-related issues on the verge of being finished, and with hockey season just about to begin, Melnyk seems happier and more relaxed than I've ever seen him.

Money, Melnyk says, should give one a certain freedom. He'd worked diligently to build his pharmaceutical empire. That success allowed him to move to the tax haven of Barbados, acquire a private jet, buy a stable of racehorses, and snap up a National Hockey League franchise. But his brother's death and his approaching fiftieth birthday led him to the conclusion that it might be time to step away from the corporate limelight.

"These days, I no longer have to do H&R [human resources] meetings and sit around a boardroom every couple of weeks with senior management and discuss hirings," he says, broadly smiling. "Now I fly in, go to a hockey game, fly to Florida and check in on the horses, maybe take in a race, and then fly back to Barbados.

"You've got to admit, that's a much better situation."

Yes, Eugene, it certainly is—if you've got the cake to fund it.

Fortunately for Melynk, money isn't an issue. His net worth is guesstimated at more than a billion, and he still owns about 28 million Biovail shares.

Decked out in a striped Burberry golf shirt, dark grey pants, and new golf shoes ("They were a Christmas present—but I haven't worn them yet"), Melnyk grabs his bag and hops into our golf cart. We head to the course, driving past the black Mercedes tucked into a nearby parking spot, where Melnyk's driver diligently waits for his boss to finish his game. With time for only nine holes before he has to head to a function in suburban Mississauga for his Ontario Hockey League team, the St. Michael's Majors, we tee off on the back nine at Eagles Nest, clear of the weekend golfers that commenced their rounds on the first hole.

Since Melnyk doesn't spend enough time in Canada to be bothered with joining a course, one had to be selected. Eagles Nest was my choice, and it was an easy one. It's close enough to allow us to play some holes yet get Melnyk off to his meet-and-greet in time. It is also, hands down, one of the best public golf courses in Canada, a rugged links on steroids. Of course, like most steroid users, there's something a bit artificial about it. After all, a links, with its dunes and sandy soil, must reside near the sea. Eagles Nest isn't near any body of water—unless you equate the manmade holding pond in front of the clubhouse to the North Sea.

Regardless, it is a remarkable course, crafted partially out of a disused aggregate pit and resting next to a former landfill. It doesn't sound attractive, but Canadian designer Doug Carrick used the landscape to fashion a golf course that's muscular and subtle at the same time. It is both fair to those able to skirt its defences and doubly cruel to those who can't. Its front nine wanders into a stunning forested valley before rematerializing back on the old gravel pit, where holes like the ninth offer views of Toronto's distant downtown core.

But it is the back nine that Melnyk and I will play—in my estimation the toughest, most intriguing, and most enjoyable part of the course. Winding through open areas exposed to the wind, the course rumbles around the outskirts of the property before ducking into the centre for a couple of holes. It emerges for a triumvirate of feisty holes—two par-5s and a par-4—that can reward golfers who are up to the challenge or, as is more likely, kick them in the teeth repeatedly until they acquiesce to its power, or pick up their ball— whichever comes first.

It is a good course to play with Melnyk, especially since our first encounter was also a nine-hole match. That game, in 2002, was played on the relatively blue-collar Barbados Golf and Country Club outside of Bridgetown. At that point, Melnyk was riding high: Biovail had a commanding stock price and looked as though it would break out, transforming itself from just a Canadian success story to an international power within the pharmaceutical industry. I joined Biovail's chief financial officer and a handful of other company employees on their corporate jet for a flight to the Caribbean. Even then, Melnyk was a flashpoint for controversy. For example, it turned out he had sold that very jet to Biovail after acquiring a larger model for his personal use. There turned out to be nothing to the story—Melnyk and Biovail had followed the appropriate procedures—but it was just another in a list of tales that suggested the billionaire didn't follow the same rules as everyone else.

He may have his own rulebook, but there's no doubting Melnyk is a genius of sorts. It is just that genius is not one of creation, but of refinement. Add to that the ability to gamble his career on a couple of occasions, and win big, and it is clear Melnyk is unique among Canadian entrepreneurs.

At the age of twenty-three, the son of a Toronto doctor founded his first company, Trimel Corporation. He had taken a single university course, then discarded the notion of higher education as wasted effort. Instead, he took a job at a firm that made advertising aids for the drug business. While at that job, it occurred to him that doctors just don't have enough time to read all the medical literature that arrives on their desks. So, through Trimel, he created crib notes for physicians. In 1989, he sold that company to the Thomson Corporation for $8 million. He was twenty-nine.

"I could have done anything," he told me during our first game of golf. "What was I going to do? Just play golf? I could have just gone to the beach and counted clouds or raced horses. But that would have bored me in twelve months."

Instead, he entered the ultracompetitive, and sometimes downright nasty, world of pharmaceuticals, a business where the biggest companies like Pfizer and Glaxo Wellcome employ hundreds of lawyers just to protect their patents. Still, Melynk sensed an opportunity and gambled the money he'd made on the Thomson sale in an investment in Biovail SA, a Swiss medical company. He also acquired a Canadian contract-research facility for conducting clinical drug trials. His concept for the company was to take a pill that people had to take four or five times a day and create a version that they would only have to take once. That's the basis of Biovail: applying time-release technology to other companies' drugs.

Success came relatively quickly. Initially, the firm worked with other drug companies, but by the mid-1990s it had decided to go it alone, marketing its own drugs in Canada and abroad. The company hit several home runs. Tiazac, which is used to treat angina, had an incredible run after being launched in the mid-'90s. Later, Biovail created the antidepressant Wellbutrin XL. It was another star for the company. Suddenly, it looked as if Biovail might compete with the giants of the industry.

As the company's fortunes swelled, so did the number of those who began to question its rise. It didn't take long for lawyers to come out swinging on behalf of Biovail, alleging that people in the industry were whispering in the shadows while shorting its stock. Melnyk has always had an element of cagey streetfighter about him, even if it doesn't materialize on the golf course, where he's typically congenial and relatively passive. But put him in a shootout with a Wall Street hedge fund or an analyst he thinks has slighted Biovail, and the gloves come off. The most notable mudslinging battle started in 2002 with Wall Street analyst Jerry Treppel. Treppel made some less-than-positive remarks about Biovail, causing the company's shares to crater. Later, Melnyk and Biovail accused the analyst of owning shares in a rival and orchestrating the assault on its stock. Inevitably, the whole affair ended up in the courts, where it remains as we get together for this game. When I ask Melnyk about it, he gets a mischievous look in his eyes.

"Treppel's dead in this one. He thought he could pressure us into a settlement, but that's just not going to happen," Melynk says. He really wants to explain the situation fully—you can see it in his face as we stand under the beating sun on the devilish par-3 thirteenth. Of course, as is often the case with his remarks, Melnyk then proceeds to show his cards, dumping out the whole sordid tale, before finishing with a quick, "But of course, that's before the courts."

Fair enough, I guess. But the Treppel situation is only one of a handful of variations on a theme that cropped up throughout Melnyk's tenure at the helm of Biovail. By the time he resigned, he had just settled a case brought against him by the Ontario Securities Commission over the disclosure of some trusts that held Biovail stock. Of course, it goes without saying that the trusts were in the Cayman Islands.

Melnyk hits his tee shot into the front bunker and starts to talk about the situation. Yes, there were trusts that held Biovail shares in the Cayman Islands, Melnyk says, but he didn't control them. And yes, the situation may have been a bit muddy, but he didn't do anything illegal. There was a line, he says, gesturing with the club in his hand, but he didn't cross it.

Regardless, he still paid a $1 million fine to finalize the situation.

I think to myself that I'm glad we didn't put a bet on this one and that I'm the one keeping score. Otherwise, I have a feeling a bogey or two might also fall into "muddy" waters. I tell this to Melnyk and he laughs.

So, if he didn't do anything wrong, why agree to settle the case?

"I wanted to avoid a six-week trial where I'd have to be in Canada and away from my kids for all of that time," he explains as we park the cart and walk to the green. "I guess you could look at it as $3,000 per day. That was the cost of being able to go home and see my kids."

Now *there's* a man who truly loves his children.

Of course, the whole osc affair, as well as Melnyk's ongoing issues with the U.S. Securities and Exchange Commission, raises more questions. And even if he is successful in this one—which he assures me he will be—it leaves people wondering whether he's simply another white-collar criminal fleecing the public. I ask him how he deals with that perception.

"I'm immune to it," he says, preparing to go into the bunker that guards the green. "I'm not really worried about what those people think of me. I know who my friends are."

Having a billion dollars, access to a private jet, 28 million shares in a drug company, and a hockey team might sound to most like the definition of fun, but it looks as though trying to manage it all has taken its toll on Melynk. Not quite fifty, he's aged significantly since we last golfed in Barbados in 2003. And his schedule, as he describes it, sounds frantic. As evidence, he was one of the first people I approached about joining me for a game, and though he immediately agreed, finding time on his schedule was nearly impossible. It took nearly a year for us to arrange this get-together. The osc case and his impending retirement from Biovail were certainly factors, but perhaps equally so are his increased interest in his hockey team and his racehorses.

"It was my uncle Leo who got me into horses. I was eight. Leo was—well, I guess you'd call him a gambler," Melnyk says, laughing.

"And he wanted a little buddy to take to the track—that was me. It was his way of convincing his wife that he should be allowed to go out there. He'd always be standing in front of her and say, 'Eugene, do you want to head to the track?'"

These days, he has a bank of horses—and by that I mean they are worth as much as a small bank. More than $50 million all told, he says. And horses are as tradable as stocks, it turns out.

"Oh yeah, they are as liquid as securities," Melnyk explains. "I could call up an auction house today and they'd have it ready to be sold in a couple of weeks. That's not in the plans."

It is clear that Melnyk juggles his various commitments with the finesse and skill of a circus performer. But nothing he owns or runs seems to supersede his interest—call it fascination—in his Ottawa Senators.

Always a hockey fan, he loves nothing more than to regale listeners with accounts of heading down to Maple Leaf Gardens to watch games as a child growing up in Toronto. As his fortune increased, so did his interest in re-establishing that connection with his passion by owning a team. There were few outlets for Melynk's aspirations—at least, that is, until the Ottawa Senators went bust.

The tale of the Ottawa Senators is one of failed dreams and endless possibility. In the late 1980s, the NHL felt the time was right to expand. Several cities made pitches, including Ottawa, through a partnership headed by Bruce Firestone. In a stunning turn of events, Ottawa was awarded the franchise. The only problem was that the ownership group didn't have the cash to finance it.

Firestone approached Ottawa businessman Rod Bryden for help. Bryden was a man with deep connections and was taken by the chance to orchestrate the financing of the project. Eventually he raised the cash himself and became a partner in the venture. But money was still in short supply. The Senators played their first game in 1992, but they were already in trouble, having been financed with what NHL commissioner Gary Bettman once described as "an expired Amex card."

The team played downtown at the Ottawa Civic Centre pending construction of their new home, the Palladium (later the Corel Centre), in suburban Kanata. By the time it opened in 1996, costs had ballooned to $216 million, almost all of which was financed by Bryden through a complex series of loans. Bryden then faced the perfect storm: a falling Canadian dollar and rising player salaries, which are paid in U.S. dollars. By 2002, his estimated debt for the team had risen to $350 million, and bankruptcy rumours were rife. A year later, Bryden's house of cards toppled. Even with the Senators riding high as one of the best teams in hockey, Bryden was forced into receivership and, unable to repair the team's ailing finances, had to step down as owner.

Melnyk, who had already expressed interest in the franchise, jumped at the chance to acquire the team. He was met with a luke-warm reception, especially since rumour had it that Melynk was planning to take the team to Hamilton.

"Gary took a meeting with me, but with a lot of trepidation," says Melnyk as we sit next to the seventeenth tee. One can bet that he wasn't calling the NHL commissioner by his first name at the time.

"I got off to a bad start with Gary. At our first meeting, he just looked at me and said, 'I don't want you to take the team anywhere.' Then he put his feet up on his desk. I think he felt I wanted to go to Hamilton, but that was never in the cards. In the end he was extremely helpful. He can be—when he wants to get something done."

When it was all finished, Melnyk snapped up the team and arena in a $130 million deal that saw him rescue the franchise, but agree to keep it in Kanata. In typical Melnyk fashion, to celebrate his tenure as owner, he hired the Eagles to play a private concert for season-ticket holders prior to the opening game of the 2003–04 season. He also rented two jumbo jets to fly friends to the game from Toronto and New York. Melynk, it is clear, never does anything by half-measures.

When discussing the current state of NHL hockey, Melnyk is both outspoken and cautious; comments often begin with the phrase, "Don't write this down, but…" However, since we're playing one of two consecutive par-5s that lead to Eagle Nest's tough closer, I have time to get some sense of Melnyk's thoughts. Why, I ask, aren't there more Canadian teams? Why are there teams in places like Nashville and Phoenix, but not in places like Hamilton? I conclude by asking why BlackBerry billionaire Jim Balsillie doesn't own a team in Canada.

Melnyk, who hosted Balsillie at a game after it became known that the Research in Motion co-CEO was interested in acquiring a team, says he's partial to having more teams in Canada, but "I have to be careful about what I say here." Spoken like a man who has spent a lot of time being judged in the court of public opinion.

Well, what about Balsillie? He has billions—why doesn't he have a team?

Melnyk says it is about perception. The same attitude among NHL franchise owners that initially made it difficult for Melnyk to get a chance to acquire the Senators also hurts Balsillie's chances.

"They don't like rebels, and they don't like someone who is going to rock the boat," he says as we walk to find Melnyk's tee shot on seventeen, which has discovered the rough that splits the double fairway.

"You mean like Mark Cuban?" I ask, referring to the notoriously outspoken owner of the National Basketball Association's aptly named Dallas Mavericks.

"Exactly."

I understand Melnyk's love for his hockey team, but I find it hard to imagine that it will wholly maintain his interest now that he has retired after twenty years of running a public company. I tell him as much as we tackle the final hole, a sweeping par-4 with blowout bunkering on the left and water running down the entirety of the right side of the fairway.

There's no plan to return to the corporate world. His business now consists solely of horses and hockey.

"It isn't whether Biovail interested me any longer," he says. "It is a question of priorities. I love the business. It is all I've done since I was in my twenties. And it comes so logically to me. It was always great fun for me to dream up new ideas for Biovail. But everything has to come to an end."

As does our game. When all is said and done, Melnyk plays pretty well for someone who hasn't touched a club in six months. He makes a couple of strong swings in the middle of our round ("In case you didn't notice, that's two fours in a row," he points out. "Better write that down."), and over nine holes shoots 48 to my even par.

As I drive our cart up to the clubhouse, Melnyk's driver stealthily pulls up the Mercedes. After the meet-and-greet for his junior hockey team, Melnyk will make a quick stop in Ottawa, then turn the jet south towards his palatial home which overlooks the Atlantic in Barbados. Some still see the islands as Melnyk's tax haven, but he says they are home to him now. Besides, no one in Barbados ever bothers him, and reporters aren't asking any questions when he sits in the dreary confines of Bert's Bar in Bridgetown and watches his beloved Sens on television.

"If I were in Toronto, reporters would always be watching me and people would be talking about where I've been," he says as our clubs are cleaned at the conclusion of our round. He doesn't sound paranoid about the situation, but he has clearly given the matter some consideration. "If I were in Ottawa, I'd have to go to things like the Snowflake Ball. Why would I want to do that? To see people I don't know? I've been in Barbados for sixteen years now. Maybe people are just bothered by the fact that I'm there, sitting on a beach, drinking rum with my friends."

Well, when it is put that way, it certainly has some appeal.

Yes, Barbados is home. But his heart seems to reside with his Senators. While he continued to run Biovail after acquiring the franchise, his focus, he admits, was often drawn to his hockey team. That reached a crescendo in the spring of 2007 as the Senators reached the Stanley Cup final against the ridiculously named Anaheim Ducks.

To hear Melynk talk about it, the only thing more painful and tiring than being an NHL player who loses the Stanley Cup is being the owner of an NHL team that loses the Cup. He makes it sound like a physically punishing trial, as if watching his hockey team play twenty playoff matches, only to fall in California to a team named after a Disney movie, was tougher than battling with the U.S. Securities and Exchange Commission.

Now, if the Sens had won, he says that all of Canada would have understood how a billionaire hockey lover likes to get down.

"If we'd taken the Cup, I'd have put on a party like nothing seen before," he says in Trump-esque fashion, shaking my hand and getting into the car. He closes the door and rolls down the window. "If we win it this year, Woodstock won't rival the party we're going to put on!" he shouts as the car drives off.

Hyperbole? Maybe. But like a lot of Melynk watchers over the years, I've learned not to underestimate his ambition.

CHAPTER 8

Raymond Royer
Sensitive Capitalism

"It's how you deal with failure that determines how you achieve success."

—David Feherty, golf commentator

"THE WAY OF THE *kaizen.*"

It sounds like a bad Japanese film, the type of action movie where samurai warriors thrust large metal swords skyward as they run through a sprawling field to clash with an opposing army in slow motion. It sounds a bit ridiculous, in fact.

Don't tell that to Raymond Royer. To him, it is very serious indeed. That said, it is hard to imagine a time when Royer, with his flowing white hair worn slightly shaggier than that of most executives, is not serious. Sure, every so often he offers a quick smile that comes across like a slight grin, but you won't have to spend much time with him to sense that this is a man who considers his every move.

"I'm not sure what you want to talk about," Royer says, greeting me in the parking lot behind Mount Bruno Country Club. Our last interview was in 2004—one of only a handful of media requests for one-on-one time to which Royer has ever acquiesced.

"Well, your least favourite subject—you," I reply, shrugging my shoulders and lugging my clubs out of the suv.

It is always a good idea to get a ride to Mount Bruno. Though I've been several times, the course is one of the true hidden gems of the world—and by "hidden," I mean literally hard to find, as opposed to overlooked. Royer, being aware of this, has sent his driver, a former Canadian military type, to pick me up in a Lexus SUV so I'll be on time.

Located a half-hour southeast of Montreal, in the suburb of Saint-Bruno, the course is situated at the end of an ordinary drive to the suburbs. The route takes you through a seemingly endless series of overpasses and four-lane highways, past the Saint-Basile-le-Grand train station before arriving at a group of faceless strip malls. It is hard to imagine that a golf course of any quality could be hidden up a bumpy road from a Jean Coutu pharmacy (whose namesake CEO, it should be noted, is also a member at the golf club), but that's exactly where Mount Bruno can be found, just a short ride up a tree-lined hill, around the corner from a group of modest homes.

It isn't surprising that Bruno appeals to Royer. Sure, he's held high-profile positions, first as a rising star at Bombardier, where he ran the company's mass-transit division, and now as the chief executive of Domtar. A few years ago, a noted former Canadian executive and investor told me that Royer may well be the smartest and best CEO in Canada. High praise indeed, considering Royer doesn't go out of his way to draw attention to himself.

But the attention has come—it always does when one runs a business as massive as Domtar, with thousands of employees. And the spotlight is sure to shine more brightly since Domtar's merger in early 2007 with rival Weyerhaeuser, effectively creating the largest paper company in the world.

All of which brings the conversation back to *kaizen*, a management theory that Royer is once again trying to implement—for the third time in his career.

He first learned about *kaizen* while watching television in 1977. The program detailed how the concept, conceived by Edward Deming, had revolutionized Japanese car companies, specifically Toyota, by motivating employees and management alike and creating a team concept that brought the company together to work as one. The idea was to eliminate activities that added to cost but didn't create value. These days, the concept of a "team" approach to management is cliché to most, but not to Royer, who has spent most of his career as an executive trying to convince people that it is in both the business's and their own best interest to excel at their specific skill set.

I'm skeptical. *Kaizen* sounds a little too much like a New Age business philosophy. And having motivational talking head Anthony Robbins lift part of the theory in order to flog his public appearances doesn't exactly add credibility. But Royer is a believer in the pure concept.

"Continuous improvement," which is essentially the rough translation of *kaizen*, can be applied to almost any situation, apparently. Maybe golf doesn't qualify, though—at least, it doesn't look that way off the first tee when Royer hooks his Hogan golf ball into a spot of difficulty just to the left of the fairway.

Of course, maybe it isn't fair to suggest Royer's difficulties have anything to do with a management theory. It might have been the passing thunderstorm that put him off his game at the start. It could also be the fact that, for most of the previous two years, he's been working on a massive $3.3 billion merger with Weyerhaeuser designed to save Domtar from a rising Canadian dollar that has decapitated the nation's manufacturing sector.

"I have fourteen thousand employees, and I'm trying to create an environment where they can feel they can grow and remain competitive," he explains, taking our cart on the short ride to the par-5 second. "The goal is always the same: to beat the shit out of our competitors."

Frankly, I'm taken aback by his honesty and language. Harsh comments rarely flow from Royer's mouth. Typically, he comes across as the genteel executive, carefully considering his words before anything is said. But even when he claims that Domtar is going to "beat the shit" out of its rivals, Royer's voice rarely rises above his typically understated quiet tone.

On the third hole, Royer turns the tables on me. Maybe he feels I'm ready for it, having finally hit a halfway decent tee shot and an approach with a 9-iron that comes to rest on the subtle but nasty third green a few feet inside Royer's own shot. Or maybe—though I think it's a lot less likely—he's just always wanted to play the role of journalist for an hour.

"If you want to understand *kaizen*, I'll need to ask you a few questions," Royer says.

Okay, I'm game.

"Well, let's start with this," he says, lining up his putt. "Of all the things in your life—and I'm talking about things and not people—what is the most important? But don't tell me the answer. Just think about it."

It wasn't the kind of question I was expecting. Most of the golf talk I have with friends involves which course is better than some other track, or whether Tiger Woods is truly the best golfer of all time, or the problem they are having getting enough height out of their approach shots. Simple stuff. The kind of discussion that is rarely considered once the round is over.

Royer isn't prone to that kind of conversation. He's not exactly a big talker—he comes across as a bit reticent. But he's friendly, good-natured, and quick with a compliment.

I'm still thinking about the answer when we hit the fifth hole, a monster 465-yard par-4 that falls slightly downhill, twisting to the left before finishing at a tricky green. It is one of the best, and hardest, holes I've ever played. It is also the kind of golf hole that demands the golfer's entire attention. The problem is that my attention is now squarely on the question being raised by my interrogator, so it doesn't come as a surprise when I snap a pull-hook that barely gets by the tree on the left side of the fairway, coming to rest 260 yards away in the fairway. Royer has apparently gone through this drill so often that it is no longer a distraction for him. He smacks his tee ball up the fairway, but the wind hits it, knocking it down forty yards behind my shot.

By the time we reconvene at the green—Raymond on his third shot, me resting just on the front of the green with my second—I've come up with an answer.

"Okay, what is it?" he asks.

"I guess the most important thing in my life is my job, my ability to write. It supports me and my family. Yeah, it would be my writing."

"Well, let's take money out of the equation. Let me ask you this: Is your writing easy, something you can do with your hands tied behind your back, or is it something that takes effort and work?"

Hmmm. More cryptic questions. Royer has suddenly turned into a golfing version of Yoda. But I'm willing to play along.

"Sometimes it takes work, and sometimes it comes easily. I guess it depends on the subject and what I'm doing," I reply, walking away from the fourth hole with my par, one shot better than Royer's bogey.

"Okay. Let's say you do a good job, but people don't recognize it. How does that make you feel?"

I feel like I'm sitting with my therapist, not my golfing partner. I tell him that I can recognize a good writing job, even if no one else does, and that makes me feel pleased.

"Sure," he says, pulling his Callaway driver from his bag and walking to the next tee. "But what if you do a really shitty article? What happens if people come up to you and tell you that the shitty article was really great, even though you know it wasn't your best effort? *Then* how do you feel?"

Apparently, we're elevating this discussion. Shitty articles? I've had a few (or maybe more than a few, depending on whom you ask). And it is always strange when someone compliments me on an article that I know wasn't one of my best. What is one to do? Thank them for the accolades, but tell them in fact they are wrong? Tell them the story was really the job of a hack typist who could be replaced in a job cut by a series of ill-trained monkeys? That makes the answer to Royer's question clear.

I tell Royer that I get more personal satisfaction from the good stories, even if they don't stir much attention.

"Can we say that at the end of the day, when you do something well, it makes you happy?" Royer questions.

Yes.

"Well, then, I think we can safely say your first goal is happiness and that happiness comes from accessing your talents," he says softly.

We finish the hole (Royer makes a nice up-and-down for bogey, while I three-putt, a waste of effort that *kaizen* frowns upon), and take the short cart ride to the sixth hole, a nasty, uphill, two-shot beast. Royer continues his line of questioning.

"Who is the most important person in your life?"

I don't have time to give the idea too much thought before Royer, leaning on his Callaway driver, interjects.

"And let me say this—if you say someone other than yourself, I'd suggest you are being dishonest."

It is perfect Royer, choosing his words carefully. What he means to say is that all people are inherently selfish, but will lie about it. But Royer is too nice to call someone a liar.

"Think about it," he says, lining up his tee shot. "You might give someone a kidney, and you'd be generous in doing so. But we've already concluded people do things to make themselves happy. So there would be a reason for giving up a kidney. Maybe, in being generous, you feel good about yourself."

At this point, I'm thinking the conversation has taken a strange, heady turn. I rather prefer to be the one tossing out the pointed questions, rather than having them turned on me.

By the time we hit the eighth, a 191-yard one-shot hole that plays slightly into the prevailing wind, my head is spinning, and it isn't from the thirty-degree heat. If you want to muck with a golfer's game, just start talking about serious philosophical issues that take his focus off the task at hand. After destroying the seventh hole, a relatively easy par-4 that flows down the land, I again bludgeon the par-3, while Royer hits a clever 3-wood into the front of the green and two-putts for par.

"Local knowledge," he insists, before adding, "It isn't always easy to play when you're being interviewed, is it?"

We dump the cart off at the side of the ninth tee box, a sleeper of a hole with a fairway that rises sharply in the landing area, and a green where an elephant appears to be buried on the right side, creating a nasty hillock that chews up and spits balls out like a tobacco-chewing good ol'boy.

Maybe the momentary lack of time away from my fairway MBA lecture gets into Royer's head. Or maybe he just plays his more typical game. Either way, his tee shot slices wide to the right, landing in a clump of trees. On the other hand, my anger and disgust over my play on the previous two holes manifests itself in a 3-wood rocket down the middle that finds the upper shelf, and one wedge and two putts later I'm feeling better, thank you very much. At least good enough to turn the tables back on my host.

It turns out that one should get a corporate version of Utopia if *kaizen* rules are followed. At least that's Royer's take, standing next to the clubhouse on the tee of the tenth hole.

"If you have the right people and place them into situations and the right environment based on their talents, then the leader of a company can do what he has to do to maximize its team. If you can create this environment, and manage with principles, then at the end of the day, what you'll have is a group that works together for common goals. And that's how you create a winner."

Interestingly, his business philosophy also makes Royer decidedly against labour unions, or at least those in Canada. In the U.S., unions are more understanding of their place in the overall business environment, Royer says. In Canada, the unions seem more interested in being in business for themselves.

"I think they fight for principles that have nothing to do with the employees they represent," he says. "Take, for instance, a construction firm. If you create a unionized environment where workers can only lay a certain number of bricks each day, well, you're creating an artificial atmosphere and targets that are not going to satisfy anyone."

All of this would lead one to believe Royer might have a difficult relationship with the employees under his command. But while running Bombardier's mass-transit division, Royer's *kaizen* philosophy put the company into the lead in North America. Employees bought into their boss's concepts wholeheartedly, he explains, as he stands in the lumpy fairway of the 537-yard, par-5 twelfth.

"I still get Christmas cards from shop floor workers from Bombardier," he explains. "And I think that's because *kaizen* unites employees and management. It creates one dominant factor: we are all employees of the company."

It was at Bombardier that Royer made his reputation as an executive prone to thinking a little differently from the typical boardroom crowd. His background, as an accountant and lawyer, wouldn't have led anyone to pick him as a business radical. A university friend of Laurent Beaudoin, the son-in-law of Bombardier founder Armand Bombardier who eventually ended up as the head of the company, Royer joined the firm in 1974, eventually working his way to the position of president and chief operating officer.

It was at Bombardier that his great management experiment began. Given the company's interests in transportation, it made perfect sense to look at the Japanese, who were then making inroads into the North American auto market. Royer contacted a Japanese car maker and asked to send along some employees to observe *kaizen* first-hand.

"They thought I was going to send four or five people over," he says, a smile creeping across his face. "I think they were surprised when we sent sixty.

"I told those who went over that I wanted them to give me a report of three things the Japanese did better than we did," he continues. "When they came back, they had dozens of suggestions. It was incredible. The results came so fast. We reduced rail-car construction time by 12 per cent."

But Royer wants to be crystal clear on one thing: the success of the Japanese was about methodology, not the quality of employees.

"We knew we could do better than the Japanese. It isn't in the workers; it is in the method. Our employees just loved it. There was a big change in the pride of our employees."

For a while, one of Royer's roles included running and developing Belfast-based Short Brothers, an aircraft and component manufacturer acquired with the aim of making Bombardier a global business. Taking over Short Brothers at the height of the Irish Troubles, Royer spent a great deal of his time in Belfast being driven to work clandestinely through a different surreptitious route each day for fear he could be a target of bombers.

One of the few things he could do safely in the city involved his favourite pastime—golf. Royal Belfast Golf Club was hyperaware of the city's terrorism problems, and visiting dignitaries could typically play the course without worry, though also under the constant watch of men carrying large guns.

Though he was credited with some of Bombardier's biggest successes, Royer left the company abruptly in 1996. He says the departure was amicable, but it was also apparent that he would never lead Bombardier. Some in the Quebec business community have gossiped that everything he's done since leaving the transportation maker has been devised to prove Beaudoin and Bombardier wrong.

He dismisses that notion out of hand.

"I'd done all I could do there," he says, his voice becoming almost a whisper. "There was nothing left to do."

Instead, only months after his surprise departure from Bombardier, he made yet another bold move, taking on the role of chief executive at Domtar, which, burdened with heavy debt, was struggling through a period of uncertainty amid rumours it was about to be taken out by a competitor.

Royer immediately learned everything he could about Domtar's pulp and paper business, and plunged the company into adopting *kaizen*. It worked, at least for a number of years. By 2003, Royer's success at Domtar was getting him some recognition, something he would never personally seek out. He was named CEO of the year by *Pulp and Paper Week*, and Domtar seemed to be quickly on the rise.

That's about the point when things started to go wrong. On the golf course, you can tell a lot more about a person by how they respond when things go badly than when they go well. The same is true in business. With Domtar's situation turning suddenly bleak, Royer reacted as one would expect—decisively and with a deep sense of the ramifications of his actions, which included thousands of job cuts.

It is one of business's great contradictions. How can a man so seemingly decent, so caring about those around him, be willing to cast out hundreds, even thousands, through layoffs? After all, Royer doesn't even use the word "employees," preferring the term "colleague" when speaking about those who work for Domtar. Regardless of the wording, under his leadership, Domtar slashed nearly two thousand jobs in 2005 alone, amid a rising loonie and skyrocketing labour costs. Even when faced with few other options, I suggest to Royer that cutting thousands of jobs must be tough.

Royer's answer demonstrates the degree of pragmatism in the man's thinking.

"What are my options?" he asks, getting out of the cart and pulling his putter before walking to the tenth green. He stops and turns to me. Maybe he's agitated at the question, but his tone never varies from the rest of our conversation.

"I'm doing what is best for Domtar's workers. If I don't act, if I don't take action to change our cost structure, I could risk the entire company. And what's better: job losses of a few thousand, or taking the entire company down?"

Still, you get the sense from Royer that he takes personal responsibility for Domtar's issues. He should have foreseen the rise in the Canadian dollar and hedged against it, he says.

How? I ask. By using a crystal ball that tells the future? He smiles meekly.

"I don't know, but I know I should have been ready for it. I'm always asking myself how much I should have seen coming. If I'd just known, I would have done so many things differently."

In 2005, with Domtar still struggling to keep costs in order, Royer began to consider bigger solutions. By August 2006, he stumbled on an intriguing one: merge with Weyerhaeuser to create a massive paper firm with $6.5 billion in sales and less exposure to the surging Canadian dollar. So, nearing seventy, at a time when many expected he'd retire, Royer is at it again, preparing to implement *kaizen*, this time throughout the entire merged company.

"Now we have the critical mass to fight against anyone," he says. "It is great, because I never wanted to retire anyway. I wanted to create value for shareholders and for the company with my mental and physical abilities."

Thankfully, there isn't a lot of blame assigned in *kaizen*, because that would simply take time; and, since wasting time is, well, wasteful, there's no emphasis placed on it. That element of the philosophy must be why Royer feels so comfortable on the golf course. He's serene when playing, rarely letting himself get upset, even when the game doesn't go his way.

"Ah, Raymond," he will occasionally exclaim after a poor performance. But nothing more than that. No cursing in French. Not even the casual toss of a club or a swipe at the ground.

Or maybe Royer's attitude comes from his comfort level at Mount Bruno, without doubt one of the quietest great private golf clubs in Canada. There is no way an outsider would stumble on the club—unless, that is, they were looking for the Jean Coutu pharmacy situated near the entrance and happened to make a couple of wrong turns. Certainly, there is nothing nearby that screams "expensive, ultra-private golf course here," unlike many clubs with their ostentatious houses casting a blight on the surroundings and garish signs alluding to the wealth of its members. All too often, private golf clubs are just extensions of the massive egos of those who belong, with flashy clubhouses overlooking average golf courses.

That's not the case with Mount Bruno. The club balks at the typical trappings of those private clubs that seem to be more a celebration of wealth than they are about golf.

Truthfully, the club's two hundred or so members would like to keep the outside world unaware of its existence, except for those rare instances when one of its aging members dies and a new one must be recruited. The clubhouse at Bruno doesn't even have air conditioning. That's because it was built as a temporary structure, but construction of a permanent clubhouse hadn't yet started when the Depression hit and the economic boom of the 1920s faltered. So, the stately Victorian building, with its distinctive red-and-white colouring, still stands. Everything in the members' building is a throwback to an era when Sir Robert Laird Borden was prime minister, from the understated bar and lounge—which are punctuated with a handful of chairs that appear to have seen better days—to the metal lockers in the change room. There's nothing fancy or overdone; in fact, it looks as though it has been eighty years since anyone changed a thing in the place. And that's probably the case. But there's comfort in familiarity, which is why Bruno remains unaltered.

Royer is impressed when associates ask to play at Bruno. He's also a member of Royal Montreal Golf Club, the oldest golf club in North America, and more often than not, friends and colleagues will first ask to play there. But he seems most attached to this venerable old track, with its magnificent flashed bunkering and devilish greens that can easily make one look foolish.

Royer has been a member long enough to be aware of the areas where mistakes can exponentially increase your score. That's always the advantage a member has over a guest—he knows the spots where double bogeys loom. He's not a long hitter, but he's a consistent player, and diligently works at his game under the tutelage of Hocan Olsson, Bruno's remarkable head pro. Unfailingly polite, Royer compliments my game throughout the round, even when a blocked drive flies into the maples. "Oh, you hit that one very well," he says. "Very well indeed. I wish I could do that."

Those comments often make me laugh, especially when they come as he strokes another 250-yard shot down the middle, as he does frequently on the final half-dozen holes. Neither of us finishes well, however, as my drive finds one of several bunkers that aggressively guard the landing area on the 384-yard eighteenth hole, while Raymond's approach comes up short and he fails to make par.

But one gets the impression that it doesn't really matter to Royer how well he plays. He just likes the personal challenge golf brings him. That, and the fact his family can all play.

"Ah, yes, I see golf very much as a family sport," he says, which is why it is not surprising when his son shows up at the club during our round. His successes at both Bombardier and Domtar have also afforded him the financial ability to be a member of several clubs—including Lake Nona in Florida. He's also chased his dream of playing all of the top ten courses in the world—Cypress Point Golf Club, with its unparalleled oceanside setting, gets the nod as his favourite.

Our game comes to an end with Royer shooting an 82 to my 80. As we finish, he tells me to take my time getting changed, as he has a conference call to take. As I'm preparing to duck back into the Lexus and head back to Dorval to catch my flight, Royer comes dashing out of the clubhouse with my golf shoes in hand.

"My call didn't last long," he begins. "Let's just say it was with an American official quite high up. The fellow was a Republican and started by saying that he wanted to know what he could do to keep one of the mills open that we're closing. He told me I should do the right thing," Royer says with a knowing smile, acknowledging our previous conversation. "I told him that, in the politician's world, there must be plenty of instances where he could take the easy road or make the right decision."

"Like making the tough decision to cut employees to save a company, versus risking the business and not firing anyone?" I ask.

"Exactly," Royer says. "And the guy was quiet for a moment and then said, 'Touché.' After that, the conversation went well and didn't last long."

That's Raymond Royer in a nutshell—the concerned capitalist, the thinking man's executive, and the philosopher CEO who confounds his opponents with logic.

CHAPTER 9

Danny Williams
Playing It His Way

"By the time you get dressed, drive out there, play eighteen holes, and come home, you've blown seven hours. There are better things you can do with your time."

—Richard Nixon

HOW DO YOU KNOW Danny Williams is at his summer retreat? Look for the blue-and-white Dodge Viper parked in the driveway.

It is hard to say how many Canadian premiers drive their own version of the traditional American muscle car. But this much is certain: it is hard to envision other Canadian politicians heading out on the highway and testing out their sports car after a hard day in the legislature.

Not so with Williams. He's a different type of politician, one who gives away his salary, who battles former Beatles on television, and who gets the occasional speeding ticket in his Viper. He walks to his own beat, regardless of the repercussions. He's feisty and spirited—some would say to a fault. At the very least, he's unique (especially among staid political types), something most in Newfoundland recognize.

"Whadd'ya at?" says the attendant at my downtown hotel in her thick Newfoundland lilt. Come again? I'm not sure what she means, so in my dazed state, having just flown in, I tell her I'm not from Newfoundland, as if that needed explaining.

She laughs, says, "Oh, I knew that, honey," and asks what I'm doing in town. I guess that was probably her first question, now rephrased for someone not from here. I mention I'm off to meet with the premier the next morning.

"Aaaah, Danny Millions!" she exclaims.

Yep, that's the one. The nickname cuts both ways, sometimes used in praise of Williams's success, but occasionally as a comment on what some perceive as his showy affluence. It is also a clear indication that Williams is unusually rich by the standards of Newfoundlanders, and certainly atypical of politicians, many of whom land cushy, well-paying jobs as advisors to law firms once their time in the limelight is over. Their money is made on the back end of their careers—not before they enter the political landscape. Not so with Williams, a successful criminal and personal injury lawyer who sold his cable-TV business to Rogers Communications for hundreds of millions before entering politics, and who still has two golf courses held in trust for him while he is premier. He's been a developer, an advocate, an entrepreneur, and now arguably the highest-profile politician ever to rise out of The Rock. He's been debated on CNN, scolded in the pages of the *New York Times*, and gained headlines across Canada.

He's also a golfer and a course owner, which is why my car is parked in the makeshift lot of The Willows Golf Course at Holyrood, a club owned by Williams located forty-five minutes south of St. John's. I get out of the car, check in at the pro shop, and am told to take my car out of the drive and make a quick right at Williams's nearby summer home, where I'll meet the premier before our game. No bodyguards are in sight, and there's no media flack nearby. I'm on my own. Protocol in Newfoundland is apparently a little different from other parts of the country.

I knock on the door and am greeted by Williams, who is sitting at his kitchen table, wearing tan pants and a black-and-white golf shirt. He's both a bit shorter and a bit burlier than I expected, with neatly parted grey hair. He offers a friendly handshake and welcomes me into the cottage as he gets his shoes on for a short walk along a pathway that leads back to the club. We exit promptly, walking back down the path, across the parking lot that apparently doubles as a basketball court, where we meet the pair that will round out our foursome: Trevor Morris, a golf pro who helps run the family's courses and is married to Williams's daughter Jill; and Williams's brother Ed.

On a beautiful summer day, the club is busy, full of golfers looking to test themselves under the hot July sun, so we head to the first tee. For a populist politician running with a nearly unprecedented approval rating at more than 70 per cent, Williams is left alone by the patrons of the course as we quickly jump in our cart for the short ride to the steps that lead up a steep slope to the first tee.

"They say I'm the luckiest guy—horseshoes up my arse," Williams proclaims through his thick south shore accent, a testament to the province's mix of Gaelic heritage. I think he's talking about golf—but he could be talking about his life. In his fifty-eight years, he's been a Rhodes Scholar, a successful television cable operator and personal injury lawyer who dabbled in criminal cases, a backroom political benefactor, and, finally, one of the most popular regional politicians in Canadian history. Horseshoes, indeed.

The first hole is a short par-3 that plays off a hill that rises above the course, which is, without doubt, one of the strangest (and hardest) one will ever encounter. It isn't long—in fact, at 5,694 yards, it is short by modern standards. But it is odd, in large part because it was never intended as a public golf course. Williams owned the land when his daughter Katie began showing a talent for the game. Initially, the course was intended to be Katie's personal practice area, with only a couple of holes. Over time, it grew and expanded, though not in the same way as a typical golf course. The Willows grew organically, with pieces being added over time to eventually make up the existing nine holes. Little (if any) land was moved, so that means the holes flow on the existing property, which is a mix of rising hills and rocky outcroppings.

That's why it starts with a slight, downhill par-3, and ends with another downhill par-4 that plays to an elevated green. In between there are some terrific holes, like the three-shot third, a nasty 610-yard par-5 with a green guarded by bunkers, or the seventh, a dogleg par-4 that runs uphill before ending at a green etched out of the side of a hill. That's the good part.

There are also holes that make you wonder what the designer was drinking—except, of course, a proper golf architect was never involved in the layout. For instance, there's a blind par-3 (the eighth) and a par-4 (the fifth) where players scale a hill and tee off over the fourth green in an attempt to navigate a large pond—perhaps finding the green in a single shot, or reloading until they do.

Not that this really matters to Williams. He was just pleased to have a golf course, one of only a handful on the east side of the island. Williams expanded his holdings to include three courses at one point, but that's down to two now, the other being The Woods, part of a residential development in St. John's. Golf, to Williams, was a fun distraction from his busy life, and to a large part, it still is. Before we tee off, he admits to being a very average player. And he's never made an ace on the opener (hence the horseshoes comment), though he tells me that Dean MacDonald, the executive who ran his cable empire, has carded a one on the hole.

"He'd been out for drinks the night before and was late for his round when he showed up," Williams explains. "He took one swing and made a hole in one. I think he took a 14 on the next hole."

Williams's tee shot finds the front greenside bunker, and we're off. The premier plays the role of congenial host, speaking loudly and telling stories, some about the course's development, others about his daughter's golf experiences. He's clearly relaxed—some necessary downtime before his fall election campaign kicks into full swing.

Frankly, there's no real need for Williams to campaign, as the opposition has little chance against the premier's Conservative juggernaut. The fighter in Williams is disappointed in that fact, he says.

But he accepts that his popularity has grown because he hasn't played the traditional political role that many expect.

"In politics, people always told me you can't say, 'Trust me,' because they won't trust you," he says, scowling. "At least that's what I was always told. But I said they *will* trust me. That's why I'm here. That's what I'm supposed to do. And if they don't think that I'm working in their best interests, then that would be it—I'd just move on."

It's this level of frank conversation that sets Williams apart from his silver-tongued peers. With Williams, you get the sense he's laying it all out for you, not cloaking his real thoughts in political verbiage. Williams continues talking after hitting his sand shot to the fringe.

"I'm different than a lot of the rest of them. I say what is on my mind. I have a reputation for being very frank and very blunt and very forthright—good or bad. I can't keep things in. I just have to get it off my chest. That's the way I've operated in politics, and the people in the province see it, and know it and like it. I'm not saying it in a pompous way. There's no self-praise here. I got into politics because I didn't like what was going on. I didn't like the giveaways. I didn't like the way we were being treated by Ottawa. I told everyone what I was going to do when I went in, and I've stuck to it."

Though Williams doesn't present an imposing figure, he does elicit intriguing reactions from those involved in our game. I'd guess Danny has been the centre of attention at every party he's ever been to. It comes naturally to him, even if he overshadows those around him. His brother remains relatively quiet throughout our game, only occasionally interjecting and letting Danny do the vast majority of the talking.

But Williams apparently strikes fear into the heart of his son-in-law. At least that's what I gather from Morris's insistence on using rather formalized honorifics when addressing or referring to Williams, even in a casual setting like a golf course.

"Well, as Mr. Williams says..." Morris says on the second tee. I do a double take. Then he says it again. Mr. Williams this, Mr.

Williams that. It goes on and on. Eventually, I just have to ask Morris about it.

"Trevor, why do you call him Mr. Williams? It seems, well, strange. I just call my father-in-law John."

Morris looks a bit dumbstruck.

"Well, that's what I've always called him," he sputters.

Williams doesn't say a word, and just stands to the side smiling, quiet for the first time in our round.

Maybe Williams likes the more formal approach. After all, to most Newfoundlanders, Williams is Danny, and that's exactly how he likes it. The lack of formality is also a sign of respect, making Williams appear just like any average Newfoundlander, though he's never been average at anything.

Respect, not personally, but for the province, is what Williams says he's been fighting for since becoming Newfoundland's ninth premier in 2003. He has been more visible—and more controversial—than perhaps any premier in its history. He has been labelled as Newfoundland's version of the radical Venezuelan leader Hugo Chavez, has taken down Canadian flags to protest what he sees as unfair treatment of the province by the federal government, and entered into two wars of words with Canadian prime ministers.

"Jeffrey Simpson, from the *Globe and Mail*, said Newfoundland is just a small province that should do what's best and align itself with bigger provinces. What he's really saying is that we in Newfoundland should know our place," Williams explains, as we head to the second tee. He speaks forcefully and passionately on the subject, but still takes the time to pause the conversation and explain the hole's odd tee shot, which plays blindly over a ridge before falling to a green near a swampy area. Can't fault him for lack of focus. I hit my shot into the trees on the right, and the conversation starts up again.

"We need some respect," he says. "We're known for having snow and high unemployment, and we're much, much more than that. We need respect from Ottawa and we demand it."

And you'll let the rest of the country know by lowering flags?

"I was pissed and I had to let Canada know how serious I was about it," he says.

Maybe it is the nature of the conversation, but by the time we hit the third hole, the longest on the course at 610 yards, Williams's focus on his golf game falters slightly. His quick backswing, slightly out-side-in downswing, and lack of shoulder turn practically guarantee a slice, which is exactly how he strokes his first ball, pushing it into an area where it will not be found by anything but snakes. He tees up another after everyone hits, sending a short ball down the left side, where it finds the fairway. In golf, as in life, Williams is of the impression that if you hit something hard enough and long enough, eventually you'll find the short grass. He'll card a double bogey on the hole, but never seems flustered by it, taking it all in stride.

His flair for drama also surfaces during our round. Anyone who has seen him speak, or witnessed his face-offs with political foes, knows the premier has a great sense of theatre. He understands the benefits of mass media and how they can be used to his advantage. He's not subtle, but subtle gestures are often lost on the masses.

It appears Williams learned this lesson from his legal practice. Midway through our round, he regales me with the tale of his dal-liance with criminal law. He started with a "street practice," eventually moving into the more lucrative area of personal-injury law. However, for a short time in the late 1990s, Williams took a handful of criminal cases. Maybe the cable company was making enough cash that he could try something new, or maybe he was hop-ing to raise his profile in the province in advance of his entrance into politics. Regardless, three of the cases were murder trials. He won all three, but he tells me the story of the 1999 trial of William Hardy, an American swordfish boat captain who took a crew of reprobates out on the high seas.

"There were four of them, all HIV-positive and druggies," Williams starts, sitting back in our cart. "He inherited the crew from hell."

The way Williams explains it, the boat experienced a fuel problem, which forced it to come into harbour in Newfoundland. After a night of drinking, the crew attacked the captain, only to find their leader had armed himself with a shotgun. He killed one of his attackers, a man named Gary Feener. That was the end of Hardy's immediate problems, but he found himself charged with first-degree murder.

Williams took on the case.

"It is why people go into law, but you don't normally get [cases like this]. This could have been a movie," he says. "The captain's problem was there were three eyewitnesses telling a different story."

So it was just like an episode of *Law & Order*?

"Exactly. At one point my law partner [Steve Marshall] and I went down to the hotel to see the guys that were making the allegations. The guy at the hotel said the fellows weren't talking to anyone because the RCMP had been in, people from the U.S. embassy had been in, and insurance people had been in. So I went out to the car and I had a jacket that I'd gotten from the cable company that said 'CNN' across the back. I went down to their room and knocked on the door and told them I wanted to have a chat with them. They welcomed me in."

For more than an hour one of the witnesses "spilled his guts," as Williams says, telling a very different story from the one told to the police and Crown attorney.

"The next time they saw me I was in the court room. If you've ever wanted to see a guy shitting in his pants, this was it. He just about died," Williams says. "There was nothing illegal about what I did. They'd just spilled their guts, so I knew what had gone on. I got him at the preliminary inquiry. He didn't even show up for the trial.

"I got one of the other guys on the stand, and he was a bit shaky. I said, 'Do you have any previous convictions?' 'Well, I've got a little assault charge,' he replied. 'Is that it?' I asked, walking to where my partner, Steve, was sitting with a folder. All it had in it was a cable bill, but this guy didn't know that. So I asked him if that was the only charge. 'Are you sure?' 'Yes,' the guy said. So I went over to Steve and got the folder. I was looking at the back side of a cable bill. 'Are you sure that's it?' 'Well, I've done a little dope. And, well, I have done some trafficking,' he said sheepishly. 'Trafficking what? Pot?' 'Yes, some pot?' 'Anything more serious?' 'Well, maybe a little heroin.' I figured that was it, but I asked once more. 'And…?' 'Well, we did beat up a police car with a two-by-four.'"

Williams bursts into laughter as he recalls his good fortune. After a year, Hardy was acquitted of the murder charge. One wonders what Williams might have accomplished if he'd stayed in criminal law, but he had a different calling.

His ability to command an audience also came into play when Williams decided to debate former Beatles bassist Paul McCartney and his then wife, Heather Mills, on *Larry King Live* over the issue of seal hunting.

Williams chuckles and a broad smile creeps across his face when I mention it. His triumph over McCartney and Mills demonstrated his moxie and coincided with his rise as one of the country's most vocal and visible political figures.

Was he a Beatles fan? I ask on the fifth hole, a strange par-4 with a tiny green perched next to a steep slope. Williams takes a 4-iron and smacks a shot out onto the fairway. After I hook two balls into a hillside of well-tended flowers, he answers.

"I was in England at their peak," he says, referring to his time spent in the U.K. after being awarded the Rhodes Scholarship. "So, sure I was a fan—who wasn't?

"But I had heard Heather was hot-tempered and could be goaded into saying stupid things. I knew she didn't know that much about the seal hunt, that she was just being used. And that's exactly what happened."

While McCartney and Mills became increasingly agitated, Williams coolly recounted the facts as he saw them. The *coup de grâce* was delivered when Williams corrected McCartney's claim that he and his wife were in Newfoundland. They weren't—by that time, they were in Charlottetown, Prince Edward Island. The confrontation drew international attention. Most of it was positive, Williams says, after chipping onto the diminutive fifth green.

"Emails and phone calls were 80 per cent in favour of what I've done," he says, putting his club back in his bag. "Of course the other 20 per cent wanted to piss on my grave.

"It was terrific," he says.

After playing the fifth hole, we climb the stairs that lead up the hill beside the green, destined for the sixth hole, heralded by the club as its "signature hole." Signature holes were a creation of golf designer Robert Trent Jones, and used largely as a means of selling or promoting a course, as well as the real estate that was often associated with it. More often than not, it is the hole a club will show on its website or in media press kits. In this instance, the sixth is a slight par-4 measuring 283 yards off the tee. A large—and clearly artificial—holding pond rests in the middle of the fairway, while the left side is protected by scrubby underbrush. Since the golf match—for all of us—has largely deteriorated into a gabfest, we give the green a go. I hook one into the left rough in a pathetic attempt to drive the green. Ed lays up, and Morris nails one, nearly making the putting surface. The premier, perhaps emboldened by Morris's effort, also takes a shot at the green, yanking the ball into the scrub left of the fairway. He quickly plops down another and hits it low and thin, with the ball running to the left, just short of the pond. You can't fault him for persistence, or for trying a shot that is clearly beyond his abilities.

Overstepping his bounds is something Williams has spent his life doing. When he was still in Dalhousie's law school and had yet to launch his career, Williams cleverly recognized an opportunity when he was approached to make a bid to form the first cable television company in Newfoundland. Most university-age students would have considered the idea to be a bit batty; Williams took it as a challenge.

"I had no idea what I needed to do," he confides. It turns out that Williams was sharp enough to understand that if you don't know what you're doing, you should get a hockey star to promote it. That's why Williams, who is more avid about hockey than he is about golf, turned to former NHL player and announcer Howie Meeker to help rally a group around the cable proposal. Williams admits that even he was surprised when Meeker, who was in St. John's to produce a hockey television show, agreed.

"I said, well, I'd need someone who could draw people right out of the gate, so I asked him," says Williams. "I asked him if he was interested in an opportunity, and he said yes. So we drew twenty-one people together, and damned if we didn't get it."

That meant Williams, at the age of twenty-three, was in charge of creating the province's first cable company, which got its licence on Christmas Eve 1974. Though he had no money, Williams managed to borrow $2,500 to start the business. It turned out to be the wisest investment of his career.

"And since I was the youngest guy, I just kept taking people out when they were ready to sell. I just kept stepping up, and as I went through, I eventually ended up getting all of it."

Though business was always just one of Williams's interests, he kept at both his law practice and the cable company until the lure of politics and the desire of Rogers Communications to enter the Atlantic Canada market coincided.

"We owned the St. John's cable market, but consolidated the main ones in the province," he says. "Then we tried to do all of eastern Canada. But the problem was these cable companies were homegrown family businesses and wouldn't let go. Eventually, we sold to Rogers when we could get the top price in the market. We did really well."

In Williams's view, $228 million is considered doing "really well."

His decision to sell the cable company was prompted by his desire to move out of the backrooms of politics, where he spent money to raise cash for Conservative candidates, and take the limelight himself.

"You can't be premier and run a cable company. You just can't run the province and send out thousands of bills each month," Williams explains.

Still, he loves the speed at which private enterprise moves, as opposed to the glacial pace of government.

"It is a real balancing, and juggling, act to get things done in government," he says. "And my problem is I'm used to go-go-going and getting things done and moving on to the next thing. But you just can't move as fast as you'd like to. Government is absolutely more difficult than dealing with a company. If you are Frank Stronach, what you say goes. If you are Ted Rogers, people in your company do what you tell them to. And you live or die by that decision. But in this business, you have to make sure all the stars are aligned before you can make the next step."

Playing a familiar golf course is always easier than playing one you've not experienced before. There are always hidden hazards, areas where you can't extricate your ball. Such is the case with The Willows, where, given its naturalistic feel, odd little areas crop up regularly. Knowing the nuances of the course is paramount, and given that I don't know them, and take some wayward iron shots, I get beaten up. Familiarity breeds comfort, I guess.

Politics, at least in Newfoundland, is similar. As premier, Williams's constituency consists of more than seven hundred communities spread over twenty thousand square kilometres. In typical populist fashion, he says he knew many of these areas from playing hockey or practising law. But there are only so many arenas and so many hockey games, so when he entered politics in 2001, he went out to meet the people that make up his province. And, like golf pros John Daly and Davis Love III, both of whom travel to tournaments in their luxury recreational vehicles, Williams bought a motor home and hit the highway.

"First thing I did when I got into politics was buy an RV and head out on the road. I had three wonderful summers doing that. I took some of the kids and the grandkids. I wanted a flavour of the province.

I had played hockey around the province and had done court cases around the province, but I hadn't gotten into 50 per cent of the communities. When you get in an RV and weave your way through the northern peninsula and Labrador, well, it was just fabulous for me. The pictures of Newfoundland always show us covered in snow. And the place is nothing but a rock. But it is a spectacular province."

His time spent learning geography benefited him when he hit the campaign trail, he explains as we hit our final hole of the round, a downhill par-4 that measures 410 yards and is bisected by a creek.

"One of the highest moments for me in the last three years was last year, when I was campaigning and I knocked on a door and this woman said, 'Do you know where you are?' I told her I knew I was in Bishops Falls. She said, 'You're at the house of one of your workers.' I told her that was a good thing, and I think things are going well. 'Well, if you'd have come by thirty-six months ago, I would have slammed the door in your face. We had to go on strike and lost a month's work. But I see where you're going and see what you're doing, and I believe in it and I thank you.' It was a huge change."

With our game concluded (I card a 43 on the slight track, while Williams barely breaks 50), Morris announces he has another match in the afternoon, while Ed quietly disappears after thanking me for the round. Williams isn't finished talking, though, and he invites me to his place for lunch. We walk back up the path, through a small garden and past a swimming pool. The home is far from fancy—and cottage is probably the correct description. With its rustic interior and blue carpet, the interior is not exactly what you'd expect in a house owned by a man worth hundreds of millions of dollars.

We sit down and he offers me a beer. We start talking, and fifteen minutes later a club employee shows up with a bag of takeout food. Nothing fancy—just ham and tomato subs.

Williams has been using the cottage as a retreat following a fishing trip. The goal is to refuel before the fall campaign gears up.

"Even a month ago, I told my staff I was getting tired and I was taking some downtime. You have to do that because it is the small things that end up pissing you off. It is the little things that beat you down after a while."

It may be the minor elements of daily political life that bother Williams, but the grand gestures have helped him gain a certain amount of notoriety. Soon after becoming premier, Williams gained attention for pushing Ottawa to let the province have its cut of the revenue from its increasingly lucrative natural resources, specifically oil. The province had been burned in the past, Williams says, chomping down on his sandwich. He points to the Churchill Falls hydroelectric project in 1969—under the guise of promoting national unity, the federal government talked Newfoundland into awarding power to Hydro-Québec at a low, fixed rate without an escalation clause.

"That would have given us an extra billion a year," he says, wiping his face with a napkin. "If we had that now, it would turn us into a 'have' province overnight."

Though he's not a particularly competitive golfer, Williams is tough to shake in almost any other matter, from politics to hockey. Getting a better deal for Newfoundland became his cause as soon as he became premier, and his emotional brand of politics led him into altercations, first with Prime Minister Paul Martin, and later with Prime Minster Stephen Harper.

Just before Christmas 2004, Williams was riding high, certain that he'd convinced Ottawa to give the province a break. He flew to Winnipeg to meet Finance Minister Ralph Goodale, but a deal didn't get done. The premier first felt defeated, then defiant. And then, in Williams's typical feisty fashion, he ordered all the Canadian flags taken down from provincial buildings as a sign of protest.

"I remember feeling emotional; I was welling up, thinking my province had made it. I felt it, and I think that's why I was so angry coming back. I felt jerked around and I told my staff I was taking the flags down. My staff told me I couldn't do it. But I told them I damned well was. My staff is protective—you know that—because I'm a guy that shoots from the hip and they want to temper that."

Some accused Williams of entering the flag flap because of his own bruised ego. He admits he likes Martin as a person, and eventually worked out a deal worth billions in royalties to the province for its natural resources. Then Martin's Liberals were defeated by Stephen Harper's Conservatives, and the whole affair started all over again.

"Harper not only broke his promise to us, but he went one step further," says Williams, anger showing in his face. "He broke the accord that had been agreed to by the previous government. So with him, it was a vendetta. He came into this—I'm told by people close—with the impression that Williams was perceived to have won over Martin. And his take was that he wasn't going to make an example of me."

Williams then tells me to turn off my tape recorder and recounts an early meeting with Harper. I promised not to offer the details, but I will say the word "fuck" is used more expressively and in more ways—apparently by both Williams and Harper—than anyone might expect.

"It was twenty minutes of 'Fuck you,'" Williams acknowledges.

The feud between Williams and Harper now has personal overtones. The men don't appear to be able to cast aside their personal animosity and find a resolution. That has led Williams to become determined to actively work against Harper.

"My goal is to get him out. I don't want to see him get a majority government, because that could be very dangerous. But in a minority government, well, obviously, Newfoundland is going to get the short end of the stick as long as he's there. So my only hope is to have him replaced and have someone in who will give us a fair shake.

"He's trying to promote a super-strong Harper. His federalism is decentralization. But he has a disdain for Atlantic Canada. He said there was a culture of defeat out here. There might be some truth to that, because if a people get pushed back enough they might start to feel that. But you don't state that going into a region."

These days, as his own popularity soars, Williams is focusing a great deal on Harper, playing a high-stakes game of chicken in the hope the prime minister will blink first.

"I'm a student of his work. I've read the books that have been written on him. I've read his speeches, and some of the things this guy has said in the last decade is nowhere close to where he is now," Williams says as a warning. "I've spoken to the Federation of Students. I've spoken at the Economic Club of Canada. I've spoken in Saskatchewan. I'm getting the message around. And when I speak of him, I talk about what he was, what he stood for, and what he is now. And he's changed his colours as he goes."

With our beers finished and the subs eaten, our lunch concludes.

"I'm eight years in politics already," he explains, getting up from the table to show me out. He extends his hand and shakes mine warmly as if he hopes my last impression of him will be positive.

"At the end of my second term, I'll be sixty-two," he says. "And you only have so many good years."

Indeed, that is the case. Williams also understands that time is ticking, and after two hours spent on the course and a couple more over lunch, it is time to get back to the task of moulding his vision for Newfoundland.

CHAPTER 10

Bruce Simmonds
Owner of the Game

"Golf is typical capitalist lunacy."

—George Bernard Shaw

GOLF IS OFTEN A GAME of memory. Golfers frequently relate special moments of their lives to things that happen on the course. Some of these are directly connected to incidents that happened on course— an ace on a celebrated par-3, or a hole where a son first beats his father. For golfers, courses are special places, and though it has often been overstated, they can almost take on spiritual overtones. It is sentimental and often silly, but it's why many golfers insist on having their ashes scattered over their favourite courses.

But the typical connection golfers hold to some stretch of hallowed ground doesn't quite measure up to the significance the first hole at King Valley holds for Bruce Simmonds.

It really has nothing to do with the hole, exactly. It isn't about the fairway bunkers that flank the right side, or the way the green rises at the back. It has nothing to do with some spectacular feat Simmonds has achieved on the hole. No, it is about something deeper and more significant. And the signs are there, if you look for them.

There's the tree planted near the first tee in recognition of Simmonds's involvement in creating ClubLink, the corporate golf giant that owns the parkland layout. Not far from the first green sits the company's corporate headquarters, an unremarkable white building that housed his office for more than a decade when he was CEO. He still has a space, but he admits it is used infrequently. And, of course, the club must hold Simmonds's focus—not just as a golfer—given its significance in helping to create ClubLink in the first place. King Valley is many things to many people. But to Simmonds, it is much more than simply a golf course. For years, it was a way of life.

In most respects, throughout his career, Simmonds would have simply noticed the course's warts. Like most golf course owners and operators, his worries were more practical and less esoteric. Were the fairways cut to an appropriate level? Were the bunkers raked? Who was the idiot who dropped a beer bottle in the rough? Rather than being simply a good walk spoiled, golf became a game where Simmonds had to carry a garbage bag.

It's different now, he admits, hitting a shot with a fairway wood that stops short of the opening to the first green. He doesn't have to worry whether every blade of grass is perfectly aligned, or whether a member is going to get angry because a rake has inadvertently been left resting precariously halfway to the left fairway bunker.

More importantly, it is different because these days Simmonds runs a series of customer service call centres, not a group of golf courses.

"I can really enjoy myself when I play now," he says. "I'm not picking up the garbage or the candy bar wrappers anymore."

Not that Simmonds ever really wanted to enjoy himself while playing golf at King Valley, located in King City, a small village outside of Aurora, Ontario. That may sound like a strange remark, but Simmonds truly wanted to continue running ClubLink and to continue to be worried about garbage on his fairways.

The only problem was that the owners of ClubLink, three separate groups of investors who wrestled for control of the company in 2002, decided they didn't want the company's founder around any longer. Therefore, they showed Simmonds the door—though it was a long goodbye, with the retirement party lasting through almost all of 2004.

I ask him if it was hard to leave a business that had played such a big role in his life for more than a decade, and to lose it to a group who had very little experience in the golf business. Standing on the fourth tee, the first hole that dips into the valley with a tee shot that swings around a looming pond, Simmonds answers promptly.

"It really wasn't that hard," he says, pulling a fairway wood from his bag and clocking one down the left centre of the fairway, only yards from the water, but in prime position to tackle the difficult and well-guarded green. I hit my tee shot—into the trees on the right—and throw my bag over my shoulder while Simmonds continues.

"It was decided in January and I was done in October, so I had nine months to say goodbye in what was a busy year. We opened Glencairn Golf Club that year, and it was a great success. We were hosting the 100th Canadian Open and had the Skins Game in Montreal. It gave me lots of opportunity to get out. I just had a lot of time to wind it down."

Except that that is not what really sets the year apart in Simmonds's mind. In the midst of all that was going on, and while the company he built from scratch was being pulled away from him just as it was finally becoming an unquestionable success, Simmonds had a life-altering experience.

Some people wouldn't want to address such a subject, figuring it has no effect on their public life and is therefore private business. But that's not Bruce Simmonds. A round of golf with him is one lengthy conversation, commencing on the first tee and ending with a drink at the club. Everything is fair game with him. And though you might not always get the answer you're hoping for, Simmonds is rarely coy.

It's not out of character, then, when he mentions his personal mishap in June 2004, only three months before his scheduled departure from ClubLink.

"Two days after I had our last annual meeting, I had a little heart attack," he says.

"There's no such thing as 'a little heart attack,'" I respond. "It's like saying you're 'a little pregnant,' or 'kinda dead.'"

Simmonds smiles at my attempt at wit. Not surprisingly, his heart condition manifested itself on the golf course, during a round with former Bell Canada CEO John Sheridan. Though he always prefers to walk while playing—something that likely kept his once-burly frame in check—Sheridan had considered the looming weather and decided on taking a cart.

"We got to the fourth hole, and I really wasn't feeling well, and it started raining hard, so we decided to go in and see if it would blow over. We had a coffee, and it was clear it wasn't going to end, so we scrubbed it.

"I came into the office and climbed the stairs to the second floor and said to Jan, my assistant, that something was off. I said we better call my brother-in-law, who is a cardiologist. We got him on the phone—which is unusual—and she described the symptoms. He just said, 'Don't take no for an answer. Call an ambulance and get him to the hospital.' So she came and said, 'He said I have to call an ambulance.' I said, 'There's no way we're doing that. Not a chance. I'm not going out of here in an ambulance.'"

It isn't that Simmonds has some phobia of ambulances. His decision was much more pragmatic.

"If I do that, no one will get any work done around here for the rest of the day," he says seriously. He told his assistant to drive him.

"She asked what she'd do if something happened. I said, 'Don't worry about it. I won't hold you responsible. Let's just leave quietly.' We pulled up to the hospital, and they were standing outside waiting for me because my brother-in-law had called. Sure enough, I was in the midst of having a heart attack."

We reach the green of the uphill, par-5 fifth, where Simmonds is left with a touchy downhill putt. He barely touches the ball, rotating it enough to get it started and letting gravity take over. It picks up speed and rolls slightly to the right before dropping into the cup for par.

The heart attack practically ended Simmonds's tenure at ClubLink. And if there's such a thing as a good time to have a serious medical issue, well, Simmonds's timing was impeccable.

"Running any company is intense," he sighs. "Though I deal with stress well, there's always underlying stress. And, given that, it wasn't bad timing, because there was a lot of extra stress at the time. I'd built the company and I had a couple of large institutional shareholders, but basically I ran it. Then it moved to three large shareholders, all of whom lived locally and were fairly involved, with different ideas."

"They knew enough to be dangerous," I say.

"Exactly," he replies. "If you play the game of golf, you think you know something about it. Others think they understand it. It is like education. Everyone went to school, so everyone thinks they know something about it."

Still, he admits he received a nice pat on the back as he was shown the door, rather than a kick in the ass. The management he put in place still runs ClubLink, and he still sits on the board of directors, occasionally finding time to play golf on the company's courses.

When I called to ask him to join me for a round, Simmonds was more than willing. We'd played together several times, especially when he was running ClubLink. The smart businessman often liked to head out for a round with key reporters and columnists, often picking their brains for industry gossip and opinion. And though he could have picked any of two dozen courses surrounding Toronto for our game, his selection of King Valley demonstrates the significance the course held in his career. The acquisition of the course played an integral role in Simmonds's development of ClubLink. Today, it remains the flagship of the company's empire that now totals more than thirty courses scattered near cities like Toronto, Ottawa, and Montreal.

King Valley is significant for another reason: it was the first course of any note for Doug Carrick, who has become one of Canada's best golf designers. Yet when Carrick was hired to design it in 1986, it was supposed to be the young architect's breakthrough into big-time Canadian golf. Later in his career, his best courses— places like Eagles Nest Golf Club, the three at Osprey Valley near Toronto, and Humber Valley in Newfoundland—would capture the imagination of Canadian golfers with their splendid mix of strategy and often-showy aesthetics. Carrick, a quiet man, let his courses do the talking—and they shouted at anyone who would listen.

But King Valley came before Carrick was established as a man who could turn a rustic, rough piece of land into a work of art, and well before he was a known and marketable quantity, able to command large design fees and heralded as one of the best in the business. King Valley was Carrick's coming-out party. Too bad that party received more than its fair share of rain.

He started the project, crafting a routing on a site with broad natural valleys and plateaus, wetlands, and some relatively flat regions. But when it was time to break ground on the $3.5 million course, the original owners flipped it to a second group of partners. Though the course was already designed, the new owners were worried that their rookie golf designer lacked the recognition to sell the project to perspective members. "Doug who?" they asked. Thus, in one of the first obvious marketing ploys used to sell a golf course in Canada, the owners hired Curtis Strange, fresh off his first U.S. Open win, to become the property's "designer." Though Strange would make a solitary design visit to the course, when construction was well underway, he was heralded in King Valley's marketing material as being responsible for its creation.

Regardless of Strange's level of involvement, Carrick's work demonstrated he was a new force on the Canadian golf scene. Despite having a relatively small budget and moving little land, he created a course where everything is out in front of the golfer, with fairways emboldened by flash sand bunkers that lend a distinctive appearance to the course, punctuated by a series of small ponds that toughen tee and approach shots.

Sometimes, however, a good golf course cannot salvage a flawed business plan. Trouble continued for the project, as membership sales were slow, and King Valley was flipped to Mark Fry, heir apparent to the Fry's Chocolate empire. Fry, who was snapping up golf courses at a brisk pace, often paying far more than they were worth, decided King Valley would be his flagship and commenced building a palatial clubhouse for four times as much as it cost to build the entire course. Unfortunately, members didn't seem to care about the flashy clubhouse, and simply didn't bother signing up.

We walk past the clubhouse, and I joke to Simmonds that golf clubhouses are the rich man's versions of a dick-measuring contest. He laughs as we wander up the hill to the tenth tee.

"Golf also becomes a very big ego play and has often been the investment of choice for people who have made a fair amount of money," he says. "If you have $200 million to spend on your ego play, it is a sports franchise. If you only have $20 million or $30 million, then it's a golf course. I guess private jets are part of the same realm."

It turns out that this was one phallic showdown that didn't work out for Fry. After pumping millions into King Valley, the club floundered, losing more than $1 million annually. Fry gave up on his golf dalliance and began looking for a buyer.

Thankfully, he found Simmonds and the newly created ClubLink. An accountant by trade, Simmonds never intended to enter the fairways-and-greens business. Sure, he liked to play, but his early career was focused more on the family's electronics business, A.C. Simmonds and Sons. In 1982, the firm bought the rechargeable-battery firm Dynacharge out of bankruptcy for $125,000. They retooled and refocused Dynacharge and sold it a decade later for $10 million.

During this time, Simmonds built a home that backed onto Cherry Downs, a relatively nondescript private golf course in Pickering, Ontario. In 1989, with the club struggling financially, Simmonds and his brothers bought the course.

"I wanted to build a house there," Simmonds says. "That's about the [amount of] thought that was put into it."

How hard could it be to run a golf course? Simmonds thought. Turns out it was much tougher than expected, and in no time Cherry Downs was losing $500,000 per year. A novice golf course owner at best, with no practical experience in the industry, Simmonds decided it was time for a change. He fired the course's management and took on the task himself.

Once he'd cleaned house, the problems became readily apparent. Cherry Downs had never been treated like a serious business. Internal controls and infrastructure were badly outdated, so Simmonds set himself the task of righting the listing ship. It took more than a year, but suddenly Cherry Downs turned a corner and became profitable.

Simmonds's epiphany came in 1992, while he was sitting on a beach in Florida. What if I took my experience at Cherry Downs and put it to work at other courses? Simmonds thought. And what if we acquired a handful of courses and linked them together, allowing members to patronize all of them? It was a concept largely unheard of in the golf industry.

Finding a unique concept that meets an interested audience is central to the success of any venture, but it is often hard to get financial backers to step up to support unprecedented ideas. That was exactly the issue Simmonds faced when he hit Bay Street in an attempt to raise the capital to launch ClubLink.

"I think Canada's tough on entrepreneurs," he says. "There are always a lot of naysayers. It is the Canadian way, I think. ClubLink is a pretty good example of that. There's no shortage of people who thought we'd go bankrupt. And even today, there are still people who don't believe it'll be successful."

It must have taken a lot of persistence in those early days.

"Yes, that's true," Simmonds says. "I wonder how many good companies die just because the owner doesn't have the personal self-confidence to make it. There's a lot of things you can't justify on a business plan. In the first few years of ClubLink, the numbers weren't justifying the plan. You just had to believe in it. And it was a long-term situation. You had to be patient."

His persistence paid off. Within a year of his daydreaming session on the beach, Simmonds raised $45 million through a public offering and acquired a handful of financially struggling courses, including King Valley.

But that's all history to Simmonds. We finish the eleventh hole—a deceptive par-4 that, at 330 yards, lulls players into a false sense of security—by both making par. Many believed that Simmonds put ClubLink behind him when he joined Minacs Worldwide about a year after leaving his golf business. The move seemed straightforward enough. Minacs, named after its founder, Elaine Minacs, had long been the leader in call-centre technology in Canada, having grown from a temporary employment agency into a call-centre business with more than five thousand employees by 1999 when it was taken onto the public markets. But the dot-com boom and the outsourcing bonanza that followed led Minacs to strain under competitive pressures. On top of all of this, the company's internal financial situation was in disarray, even though its annual revenue increased to $290 million. There was concern among Minacs's board that new legislation designed to promote corporate transparency after the high-profile failures of several U.S. businesses could come back to haunt the company, which had been fairly lax with its internal controls.

Simmonds is initially reluctant to delve into the Minacs situation, perhaps out of respect to the company's founder. But as we walk up the hill to the twelfth tee, the story starts to come out. "Elaine Minacs thought I'd be sympathetic because I'd worked in family-run businesses," he says, as we stand—a couple of holes clear of the group behind us—on the tee of the picture-postcard par-3, with its heroic tee shot over a large pond. "But that didn't turn out to be exactly the case."

He finishes his statement with a quick "God rest her soul." That's because one of the factors involved in the job offer was dealing with

Minacs herself, who had been diagnosed with terminal cancer. She died in May 2006.

We hit our tee shots—Simmonds's first ball comes up a few feet short and finds the water, while mine comes to rest pin-high—and start our descent back down the steep hill. It gives me ample time to ask what convinced him to take the job.

"It kind of intrigued me," Simmonds says, walking across the bridge that leads to the green. "But I told them there were two factors that they had to know up front: one, I wasn't going to give them a resumé, as I didn't have one, and two, I wasn't going to do any sort of psychological testing. I just don't believe in that stuff."

The company agreed to his demands and sent him to meet Minacs.

"I only ever met her twice, and once at her cottage in August before I started," he explains. "Even then she was in rough shape, and I went to see her for three hours. That's all she could do."

Simmonds took the job, starting in November 2005.

With the sun high in the mid-morning sky, he hits a high cut with his 3-wood down the left side of the thirteenth fairway, while my attempt to cut the right corner of the dogleg becomes ensnared in the trees and falls into the rough.

Simmonds thought he was being hired to straighten out the financial picture at the company and push forward with a fresh start. The company's financial situation wasn't dire, but it was a mess, with little focus being placed on corporate controls and accounting. He knew that if he didn't fix the situation right away, there would be significant problems later. The only issue was that Minacs wasn't thrilled with the decisions he was making.

"After I started, I delved into things that weren't sitting well at all," he says, putting down his bag next to his ball. "I think she wasn't prepared for how quickly I got into the business. She thought I'd take months to assess it and that I would be very reserved. But my attitude was I had one chance to clean it up. Because if I didn't, six months later it would be my problem and I'd own it. I think the board was pretty aware that there were things that needed to be addressed."

Minacs was a legendary Canadian businesswoman, I point out.

"And rightfully so. She was very successful. But she wasn't very sophisticated financially. She kind of flaunted corporate governance."

"Did she think she'd die before you got to it?" I ask as we walk to the green, where Simmonds's ball rests in the deep bunker left of the green.

"I don't know. I think she knew she was very ill, but probably didn't think she'd die at that point," he replies. "I wasn't that concerned, though, because I was doing what the board brought me in to do. Even though there was some dissension within the board, I knew I had their support."

That's when Minacs, from her deathbed but still holding 46 per cent of her company's stock, decided to go to war with the CEO she had hired only months before—and to oust the board that had approved his hiring and signed off on his decisions.

Simmonds is the sort of unflappable character who works well under these sorts of troubled circumstances, both on the course and in the boardroom. On the course, regardless of where he hits it, he tends to resign himself to his circumstance and attempt to extradite himself from whatever precarious situation he finds his ball in. There's little fuss made over any shot—good or bad—a mindset that works well in the game of golf, where one can't let a previous shot overshadow the next one. He plays quickly, not overanalyzing any situation, instead simply looking for the most obvious option and playing to it.

As our conversation about Minacs continues, he eyes his approach shot to the fourteenth green, situated in some flats and protected on the right by the unforgiving growth of bushes, wetlands, and trees. Simmonds pulls another fairway wood from his bag—his use of woods to replace his irons would make him the envy of any player on the LPGA Tour—and, with a quick swing, attempts to fly the ball to the green. But he's a touch too quick with the down-swing, and the club turns over, resulting in a low shot that hooks, coming to rest thirty yards from the green, in a grove of trees to the left of the putting surface. We walk briskly up the cart path towards our shots (my second rests in a group of trees just short of Simmonds's result).

The Minacs situation was Simmonds's second difficult corpo-rate fight in three years, following the attempted hostile takeover of ClubLink by real estate baron Rai Sahi in 2003.

"It was very awkward," he says of Minacs's attempt to wrest con-trol of her company. "I was taking a firm stand, as was a majority of the board. In the end, she said just put it up for sale, because she just didn't have the fight in her anymore. She didn't have the personal stamina and her health had gone downhill. So she said sell. And, frankly, I was probably a pretty good person to have there for that as well. I had a lot of experience at that."

It didn't take long for Simmonds to find a buyer. Only three months after Minacs's death, the company was sold to Indian-based Transworks for $125 million. Simmonds also knew that, with the sale, his time at Minacs would be limited. He signed a two-year agreement to stay onboard, but admits that Transwork isn't the type of environment in which he excels.

That doesn't mean it isn't without its perks. As we play the six-teenth, an intriguingly difficult par-3 with a green that falls hard to the front left, he talks about trips to India—playing golf at places like the Bombay Presidency Club in Mumbai, a club in the heart of a densely populated city that has eighteen holes compressed within eighty acres.

"The guy I report to likes to play golf, so it's been fun in that regard," Simmonds says, flipping my ball back to me after a failed putt.

Is there a big difference between running Minacs and ClubLink?

"Mostly, both jobs are about managing people and leading them in the right direction. It is coming up with the right offerings to meet the customers' requirements. Servicing them well. It is kind of the same thing. The big difference between the two businesses is that at ClubLink we had a distinct advantage. We were leaders in the marketplace. Now we're in a very, very competitive market. We have been a leader in Canada, but on a worldwide scale, we're well down the rung. It is more of a commoditized business. Price is a very big factor."

And what is he proudest of? Simmonds points to Glen Abbey, the annual home of the Canadian Open from 1976 to 2000, which ClubLink bought from the Royal Canadian Golf Association in 1998.

Buying the Abbey caught everyone unaware, I point out before walking to the left side of the par-4 seventeenth, a nasty, long two-shot hole with a downhill tee shot and a tricky green.

"We didn't chase it," Simmonds says after flipping his ball out of the bunker and onto the green. "It came to us. I would never have been so presumptuous as to approach them and ask them if it were for sale. It was a very popular opinion at the time that we'd over-paid."

And with a price tag of $40 million, likely the highest price ever paid for a golf course in Canada, isn't that exactly the case?

"People just didn't understand the transaction. Did we pay full price? We did. But has it worked out? Without a doubt. But we've taken $15 million real estate value out of it. So our net cost is about $25 million, and it makes over $4 million per year. Even under the RCGA, Glen Abbey was still making $2.5 million a year. At the time, Glen Abbey was the only golf course we'd ever bought that had positive cash flow right from the start. And it was clear that Glen Abbey was a far better-known brand name than ClubLink. I knew that right away. You can go anywhere in the world and people know Glen Abbey."

Anywhere? Mauritius?

"Okay—well, maybe not, but you know what I mean. It elevated ClubLink."

Elevated it, indeed. Following Glen Abbey, Simmonds expanded ClubLink rapidly, building courses like Rocky Crest in the Muskoka region of Ontario, and Glencairn in Milton, Ontario. The new courses were typically better than their predecessors, and they continue to make ClubLink an attractive proposition. The largest of its kind, the organization boasts more than sixteen thousand members throughout Ontario and Quebec.

"It's going to grow, that's for sure," Simmonds says, talking as if he still runs the burgeoning duffer's enterprise. "But in other ways, I think it'll be pretty much the same. The formula works."

Within a month of our match, Simmonds had worked himself out of a job—Minacs announced his departure, though he'd continue as an advisor. The news didn't surprise me; the only question in my mind was, what's next? Perhaps Simmonds gave me a clue as to where his heart was during our round, and even if it doesn't come to fruition, it was a sign of the difficulty a company's founder has in letting go of his baby.

"Would I love to have the chance to take ClubLink to the next level?" he said, preparing to hit a 7-iron into the amoeba-shaped eighteenth green that rests precariously behind a large pond. "You bet I would."

CHAPTER 11

Brad Pelletier
The Business of the Golf

"I will not rest until I have you holding a Coke, wearing your own shoe, playing a Sega game featuring you, while singing your own song in a new commercial, starring you, broadcast during the Super Bowl, in a game that you are winning, and I will not sleep until that happens."

—Jerry Maguire

THE CORPORATE SCRAMBLE is the bane of many.

These tournaments typically include people with no affinity for golf in the first place who are only there to network. That usually translates into a game played by those with no ability to do so. To duffers, hell might resemble six hours on a course in the sweltering summer, golfing with such people.

Of course, there are always a couple of beers—hopefully on your host's tab—to dull the pain or drown the sorrow, depending on your tolerance and your skill. But these aren't exhibitions of prowess as much as masochistic undertakings involving sticks, balls, and a lot of patience. And more beer.

That's why it was with some trepidation that I agreed to join Brad Pelletier for a scramble in Prince Edward Island as part of an event titled "Making the Connection—Legends of Golf." Sure, the title is a mouthful, but this year the match pits Canada's homegrown star, Mike Weir, against Vijay Singh, a scowling bomber of a golfer who hails from the golfing Mecca of Fiji. The scramble, with over a hundred corporate execs and salesmen from all over Canada, kicks off the two-day event. These suit-and-tie, office-bound types would spend the day hitting the occasional shot—and then take a shot from the passing beer cart. After that was all over, Weir and Singh would take to the course the following day to play a very different game—one that actually demonstrates a degree of skill.

Not that I give Pelletier any sign of these concerns when I finally get off the corporate bus that shuttles me on the rambling half-hour drive from my hotel to the Links at Crowbush Cove, where the events are being conducted. The Legends event is Pelletier's baby, something he dreamed up as the managing director of the International Management Group in Canada to promote golf in Prince Edward Island and attract lucrative corporate sponsorships. Not coincidentally, Weir and Singh are represented by IMG, which also produces the resulting telecast of the golf duel.

Mind you, my first worry is that we might need an ark before starting, given the torrential rains and hurricane-like winds that are battering the course as we move to our fleet of golf carts, all lined up neatly in preparation for the onslaught of golfers about to hit the links.

My mind is put at ease as soon as Pelletier announces that he has come to play. He's tall, with dark hair and sharp facial features that make him look younger than his forty years. And he's prepared for the weather, dressed in a heavy rainsuit, and puffing on a cigarette.

"I'm ready for the shamble," he says, mocking the tournament's format, which groups the players in fivesomes. Our quintet includes former "Crazy Canuck" Olympic skier Steve Podborski, now a marketing executive with communications company Telus, which sponsors another of IMG's big golf outings. He's accompanied by his wife, Kathy. It turns out Podborski is as unpredictable a golfer as he was a skier, but Kathy hits the ball short and straight—perfect for our needs. The final member of the group puts the pro in our pro-am: Greg McCullough is a slight, short-hitting fellow who paid his dues working at some of the country's highest-profile tracks, including Chateau Whistler, Fox Harb'r, and St. Andrews-by-the-Sea.

The concept of the scramble is simple enough. In a traditional game of golf, everyone plays each of their shots until they get it in the hole —or, as is more typical in the amateur game, they grow tired of being beaten by a stationary white ball, pick it up, and walk to the next hole. A scramble, on the other hand, is the preferred format of corporate outings because, usually, only one person has to have some handle on how the game is played. In this case, each person hits a tee shot. The best shot of the group is selected, and the next shot by each golfer is played from that point. Even if you can't hit anything but the occasional putt, you can feel as if you're contributing. I'm sure many see the scramble as great for "team-building," but more often it's really about seeing how much alcohol one can consume while not whiffing on the tee shot.

As the start of the event is signalled, we drive through the pounding rain and gloom to our starting hole—the ninth, as it turns out. The conditions are, frankly, more suited to synchronized swimming than golfing, but short of an act of God—which seems like a distinct possibility as the rain falls harder—nothing is going to keep this show from proceeding.

Sitting in the cart as Podborski attempts to limber up in the cool, wet weather, I ask Pelletier who I have to blame for my current predicament.

"Oh, pretty much everything here is my invention," he explains, referring to the Weir and Singh exhibition. "PEI called me two years ago and wondered what opportunities we had. And at the time, I'd just been watching [Jack] Nicklaus and [Tom] Watson on TV, playing their last British Open, and saw both guys in tears. I thought, 'This is it. This is about a story—it is more than just about golf.' I wanted Watson to turn to Jack and say, 'Remember that great shot you hit against me in '72?' To me, theme is everything."

So, Pelletier created the Legends event and had Nicklaus play Watson in a televised match. It was a commercial success that led to this year's show: two players who come from obscure countries and won the Masters.

"Everything is based on telling a story, on themes."

Fair enough. Now I know where to send my cleaning bill should I drown in the rain or fall on my ass trying to hit a driver on our first hole. The weather doesn't bother Pelletier too much, as he struggles to keep his smoke alight as he walks to the ninth tee—the hole playing laughably short, given the selection of tee box and the wind that is howling off the ocean and down the fairway.

Pelletier asks to borrow my driver—a recurring theme throughout the round, as three players develop iron envy and dip into my bag to grab my TaylorMades—and pounds one over the bunker that guards the right side of the fairway. The ball settles in the middle of the short grass, fifty yards from the green. It is yet another straight strike for Pelletier, one in a series that will occur throughout our round. It is also a pretty good analogy for Pelletier's career path since joining IMG.

To many, IMG is best known as the sort of monolithic sports management agency depicted at the beginning of the Tom Cruise movie *Jerry Maguire*. "Show me the money," the film's memorable catchphrase, seemed to encapsulate the morally precarious posturing and big-money deals associated with the industry, and it remains the easiest way to explain to outsiders what a firm like IMG does, even if it only makes up a small part of its current business. Cleveland lawyer Mark McCormack founded the company in 1960 to help develop business and endorsement deals for golfer Arnold Palmer. McCormack turned Palmer into one of the best-known pitchmen on television for the next four decades. Along the way, IMG grew into the largest sports representation company in the world. Over the years, it guided the careers of top basketball, baseball, and hockey players, as well as Olympic athletes, broadcasters, and even supermodels. In Canada, it represents the business interests of such names as Weir, Richard Zokol, Stephen Ames, and Lorie Kane, while its U.S. roster includes Tiger Woods and Roger Federer.

The agency's reputation as a sports powerhouse was well known, Pelletier says. Unfortunately, that could work to its detriment. "For a while, we thought that anyone could put the words 'IMG' on their business cards and they could nail down whatever meetings they wanted," Pelletier explains. "The problem was that once they went in with some big-name CEO, they shit their pants. They didn't know what to do."

Things started changing at the turn of the twenty-first century. Competition crept in, and the growing image of the greedy sports agent did few favours for IMG. The tumultuous time continued following McCormack's death in 2003. A year later, the firm was sold to Wall Street robber baron Ted Forstmann for a reported US$750 million. After Forstmann gained control, IMG began peeling back the layers of its massive business, determining which areas were central to its bottom line, which areas it could grow, and which were superfluous.

When the dust had settled, the company's Canadian operation emerged much smaller—with thirty employees, down from forty-five—and with a renewed focus on corporate development business, and, perhaps surprisingly, on golf. In the process, several high-profile executives, including former managing director Kevin Albrecht and golf agent Dan Cimorini, whose client list included Ames and Weir, left the firm.

During the transition, Pelletier emerged as the organization's rising star. Having grown up playing sports in Montreal, Pelletier attended the University of New Brunswick before heading to the London School of Economics to pursue a graduate business degree. He returned to Canada in 1992, intent on working in the lucrative world of business consulting. Instead, he was drawn into the sports industry, and at the age of twenty-six he began assisting in sales for the Canadian Tour's B.C. Open.

"I just worked my ass off selling," Pelletier explains as the rain slows and the skies brighten on our second hole. Not content with the status quo, he dreamed up new initiatives designed to promote the event.

"It was all about marketing. I convinced every professional B.C. player to come back from whatever tour they were on and play. I supplanted the market with these promotions."

The event was an astounding success, and Pelletier's marketing helped the B.C. Open draw crowds of thirty thousand, rivalling events on the much larger PGA Tour. He would later help build Nicklaus North Golf Club in Whistler and promote it through an event run by IMG called the Skins Game, a made-for-TV event where four golfers—with guaranteed paycheques—attempt to show some sort of competitive drive while battling for even more money in a match that doesn't actually mean anything. To Pelletier, the contrived nature of the match doesn't matter—it was a marketing venture that put Whistler's golf market on the map.

"It was magical," says Pelletier. "The whole market changed after that."

Following the Skins Game, IMG poached Pelletier from the Canadian Tour to start operations in western Canada. It didn't take long for his star to rise, as he landed sponsorship and event deals at a frantic pace. He did deals involving golf and figure skating, and even managed to sell a corporate package for Wayne Gretzky's charity golf tournament. When IMG needed someone to run its operations out of Toronto in 2005, Pelletier was the natural fit.

It isn't hard to determine what has made Pelletier such a successful businessman. On the course and off, he's affable and listens intently to what others have to say before responding. He's also clearly passionate about what he does—so much so that some might think he's less than genuine. Would he have made a good sports agent? Undoubtedly. But he appears to honestly believe that he's making a difference at IMG and can help those he's working for and with. The word "partner" is thrown around commonly in contemporary business, but one gathers Pelletier isn't just paying lip service when he talks about working closely with his athletes, corporations, and even governments—like Prince Edward Island's overlords, who have paid handsomely to host the Weir/Singh match.

IMG may have been the model for the company that fired Jerry Maguire, but Pelletier says that image is in the past.

"It has taken time, and I'm not sure we're totally there even now," he explains. "But it was never about telling people that IMG wasn't the same. It was about proving it. At this point, there should be nothing that is focused on the past. We're all about the future."

The weather starts to (finally) brighten as Pelletier talks about the problems that plagued IMG. PEI, after all, had a difficult time working with the organization when it ran a golf exhibition in the late 1990s. The goal was to change that perception when PEI was brave enough to try IMG a second time and called Pelletier, who became determined that the venture would demonstrate IMG's commitment to its clients—as opposed to merely showing them the money.

"We're not scared to stand behind what we're selling," he says. "There was a point where that wasn't the case, but I really believe in what we're putting out there, and I can justify it. In the past, we would have come in and dictated what was going to happen. But this is an absolute partnership.

"I'm prepared to sit down with a company and look at their objectives. And if we come to agreement on those, I'm prepared to say we'll guarantee it. I'm prepared to say that if we don't hit them, we'll have a backup or make good on other things. No one in the sports industry does it. I'm not scared to do it."

There are always a lot of balls in the air at IMG. Though the organization has done away with much of its traditional sports-representation business—selling its Calgary-based hockey agency, for example—the company still has interests in everything from snowboarding to figure skating to golf.

Pelletier's heart—and a lot of his background—is in the latter sport. He grew up in Montreal playing at Beaconsfield Golf Club, a smart private club with a classic course near the city's airport. Like most things he's attempted in life, Pelletier succeeded at golf, developing a smooth swing and a scratch game. Despite the weather—and his tendency to dip into my bag for unfamiliar clubs after deeming his rental set unsatisfactory—Pelletier plays sharp golf. These days, he plays a handful of times a year, but he often tips it up in interesting groups. Playing partners might include PGA Tour pros like Zokol or Weir, or, unfortunately on this day, a journalist, a short-hitting club pro, a former champion skier, and his wife. Of course, what we lack in skill we make up in charm. Or something like that.

Though he could easily have become a club pro, teaching lessons to trophy wives and folding shirts instead of running a sports agency, Pelletier says that was never in the cards.

"It was not something I ever considered," he says after hitting a short iron to the fringe of the petulant seventeenth green. "I was a good junior, but I never intended to play beyond that."

It is hard to say just how good a player Pelletier could be if he played more frequently. He still has a single-digit handicap, and the balance, poise, and judgment that only come from playing golf at a skilled level. He is clearly proud of his game, but is casual enough that he's fun to spend four—or in this case, five and a half—hours with on the golf course.

"That one caught more lip than Ron Jeremy," he says as our group desperately tries to make a putt on the first hole. The reference is, of course, to the famed porn star, and—well, you know.

Golf is still a big part of Pelletier's life, even if he ended up building his career around what goes on off the course as much as what transpires on its fairways and greens. For a spell, IMG was hired to try to sell the sponsorship for the Canadian Open, something Pelletier threw himself into with vigour and purpose. And he still loves to talk about the game, the business behind it, and the opportunities for Canadians in the sport. For a while, he worked as an agent for Zokol, and the Vancouver golfer still turns to Pelletier for advice. As Zokol says, Pelletier is a trustworthy guy in a business full of scoundrels.

Perhaps it is his ability to play that game, or his proximity to its biggest stars, that gives Pelletier empathy for what the best in the game experience. He's particularly fond of Weir, having taken a personal interest in the golfer's career since taking his role at the top of IMG. He understands the tremendous pressure Weir is under as the focus of a golf-mad nation that expects him to win regularly, especially after the left-hander took the Masters in 2003.

Golf is a solitary sport, Pelletier explains, munching a hot dog at the turn, and Canadians—and the media—often like to eat their own. "Did Mike Weir almost win the Canadian Open, or did he lose it?" he asks.

I have a feeling the question is rhetorical. Even though I have an opinion, for once I stay silent.

"He almost won it against a great player on a course he didn't like. But he gets criticized for losing or blowing the Canadian Open. That's golf. If [Toronto Maple Leafs' goalie] Andrew Raycroft has a bad day, no one blames just him. His teammates will say, 'It wasn't his fault—the fucking defence blew it.' That's not golf. There's so much focus on one guy. If this was the U.S., do you think they'd give him as much attention? No. Mike broke the barrier and now it is up to the rest of the guys to blow through it."

And when it comes to golf courses in Canada, it was Crowbush Cove that set the standard for public tracks. It was a pioneer in the attempt to create a destination that would prompt golf-mad players to jump on a plane and make a pilgrimage. PEI is putting a lot of effort into getting images of Crowbush out to the public through the IMG event because there are few courses in Canada that can rival its picturesque red sand dunes, its ruggedness as it nears the sea, and the way it presents a number of remarkable shots over ocean inlets. The brainchild of designer Tom McBroom, Crowbush has one of the most perfect natural settings for golf in Canada. Set hard against the ocean, and buttressed by an expanse of pine forest to the north, McBroom had a striking canvas on which to build his dream course.

Understanding that the sea could be used to tantalize throughout the round, he built two loops of nine, both of which at various stages in their routing involve the ocean. The best holes—like the par-3 eighth and the par-4 sixteenth—bring golfers to the edge of the world, with nothing but water in the distance. McBroom also used some old-world flair in these instances, running part of the back nine through wild sand dunes. If there's a better view in Canadian golf than the panorama of low-lying dunes and ocean that can be seen rising along the west of the course, I've yet to witness it.

However, that doesn't mean Crowbush is perfect. As the course was being built, special interest groups increasingly pressured the government not to forge too far into the dunes, and several "environmental areas" on the site were protected. While I'm convinced that "environmental area" is simply a euphemism for "ball-collection depot," the result was that a couple of holes—most notably the par-5 eleventh—are awkward. It is an unfortunate blight on an otherwise fine course.

Most people overlook these blemishes on what they perceive as the face of greatness. The course quickly put the island on the map, realizing the goal of the PEI government, which pumped millions into the project.

It worked—for a while. At a time when many geographic regions still hadn't discovered the lure of golf and its benefits to their local economies, Prince Edward Island had developed Crowbush Cove and Dundarave and reworked Mill Run. Tourists—and not just the standard Japanese pilgrims coming in search of Anne of Green Gables—began to flock to the small island to play a golf game that had spectacular visual elements, but was still priced within reason.

Over time, however, the product became diluted. Suddenly everyone in PEI with a farm decided they should enter the apparently lucrative golf industry. It went south fast, falling victim to the after-effects of 9/11, the rise of the Canadian dollar, and competition as more parts of the country discovered they, too, were golf destinations. The owner of one newly developed course went bankrupt, and later, in despair, took her own life.

Pelletier understands the change in the market.

"When PEI came on board, they were market leaders because they were strong, and they were organized and they were first out," he says. "Now, every area with a cluster of three courses is considered a golf destination. So, one of the things that has hurt them is they went from leaders to being one of many. Everyone is out there spending money in a co-ordinated way. And I think they need to be a leader, and there's a lot of competition."

To entertain those who have turned up for this corporate golf schmoozathon, IMG has flown in five-time world long-drive champion Jason Zuback. As we arrive at the tee, Zuback is pounding balls down the fairway for the group playing in front of us. Every scramble typically has some twist, and in this case Zuback will hit the tee shot for the group. They can then play his shot—or their own ball, if they want to be a hundred yards farther back on the fairway.

Zuback is a remarkable physical specimen. Though not particularly tall, he's built like a tank, with a narrow waist, muscular shoulders, and massive forearms. He immediately greets Pelletier— whom he knows from their time in Calgary, which the bomber calls home—and offers to hit one for us.

Watching Zuback smack a golf ball is like watching a spring overcoil to the point of breaking. When his backswing reaches its peak—with the clubhead pointing to the ground and travelling at a remarkable pace—it seems impossible that he'll ever manage to make it connect with the ball. But he does—with diamond-cutting precision. With a clubhead speed that tops 150 miles per hour, resulting in a golf ball that travels over 220 miles per hour, and with shots that often carry more than 360 yards—and that's in the air!— Zuback's "Golfzilla" moniker couldn't be more apt. Compared with the PGA Tour's longest hitters—guys like John Daly and Tiger Woods—he seems to be playing an entirely different game.

And in a way, he does. Zuback's only goal is to hit the ball off the planet, and that's just what he does for us. His first shot takes off high in the air and curls slightly, coming to rest 340 yards down the fairway, just inside the water hazard on the par-5 fifth. With a pond protecting the front of the green, for most players it is a three-shot hole. With Zuback's drive, golfers will hit short irons to the green.

Apparently, he didn't like his first smash, so he reloads and does it again. And again. And once more. Every time, the ball flies high in the air, coming to rest in the proximity of the fairway.

"I'll hit a good one for you yet," he says, taking another mighty hack. I'm not sure what "a good one," is—does he expect to hit the green in one?

As we take the long drive down the fairway in search of Zuback's "good" shot, it leaves me plenty of time to ask Pelletier about his plans. Having recently turned forty, he would seem to be an executive with places to go. He tells me the new, restructured IMG Canada is more successful than ever. But he's not planning to go anywhere—despite rumours of offers from within Canada's sports industry. Any decision is complicated by his young family.

"What's next for me? New York? Not with four kids. I don't see it," he says as our cart comes to rest a wedge shot away from the green. "My goal is to grow IMG in Canada as aggressively as I can."

He gets out and grabs a wedge from my bag.

"To walk away from IMG now—from the team I created—without knowing what we could achieve would bug the shit out of me."

Though I had Noah on speed dial and was preparing to get two of every animal when our round started, by the end the sun is out, as is the heat. It's steamy as we reach the eighth hole, a strong one-shot beast that plays more than 160 yards over an ocean enclave to a well-bunkered green. Pelletier and Podborski put their shots on the right side of the green, giving us a good one to pick from to complete our round. After four of us line up and miss the twenty-foot uphill putt, Podborski takes a full cut at it and rolls it into the centre of the cup. For a moment, all is silent. As a team, it is the first putt we've made all day.

"You're speechless," the skier says to Pelletier. "As long as I've known you, that's a first."

We end up at eleven under—not good enough to win anything. A year ago, Pelletier's group won the event. The prize was exactly what Pelletier, a guy with remarkable connections in the golf business, didn't need: another set of clubs.

Once Pelletier checks in with his staff to make certain everything is running smoothly, we reconvene on the balcony of the Rodd Hotel.

This evening, Weir and Singh, both fresh from playing the weekend at the Canadian Open in Toronto, will fly into PEI in their private jets. Tomorrow, IMG's team of event co-ordinators, public relations personnel, play agents, and others will come in to deal with the exhibition match. Everyone seems a little tense, since the weather forecast calls for rain, but Pelletier seems relaxed, sitting back in his chair, sunglasses on, beer in one hand, cigarette in the other, in front of a small glass table on a veranda that overlooks the fifth hole at Crowbush.

Last year, two of golf's greats—a focused Tom Watson, who still plays on professional golf's seniors' circuit, and the aging Golden Bear, Jack Nicklaus—played out Pelletier's dream match at Dundarave Golf Course on the east side of the island. Both players wore microphones and spoke to on-course commentators, meaning there was as much talking for the cameras as golfing. And sure, Nicklaus might have lost some of his legendary power and doesn't play regularly anymore, but the match had all the entertainment value of one of the pair's major championship shootouts, with Nicklaus winning on the seventeenth hole by shooting 68. For Pelletier, it was proof that his concept worked, and that he could sell events where the drama came from the story being told.

"I want to go places people haven't," he says, "and they love it. I just approached Jack about playing golf and telling a story and he loved it. It isn't about the competition. I don't care what they shot. I want them to open up and talk to the viewers. I want them to tell us what they were thinking on Amen Corner on Sunday. I want the story. If it is just about the golf, we're back where we started, and I'm not interested in it."

Does that make him more like a television producer than a sports agent?

"Maybe," Pelletier replies. "But that's what sport is about. I'm pushing our team all the time to take that approach."

It sounds a million miles away from Tom Cruise's Maguire and his silver screen battles with Cuba Gooding Jr.'s Rod Tidwell. No one is yelling about money or big contracts or massive sports franchises. Instead, Pelletier talks about competition, and new media, and the way sport can be integrated into emerging technologies. This is the modern-day sports agent. It is more about the business of relationships than negotiating multi-million dollar deals for the latest teen superstar.

"To stay ahead in our business, you have to be creative," Pelletier says. "To make impressions, you have to give people something they haven't experienced or didn't expect. What we bring are things that are done differently. Throughout my career, I've been trying to do things differently. Not quirky. Just classy and different. I'm a traditionalist."

CHAPTER 12

David McLean

The Insider

"Golf is a game kings and presidents play when they get tired of running countries."

—Charles Price, golf writer

IT SHOULDN'T TAKE TOO much longer than a couple of hours to drive from Kitsilano Beach in Vancouver to Nicklaus North Golf Club in Whistler. It's not a complex trip—a drive through Vancouver's downtown, past Stanley Park, across the Lions Gate Bridge, and up the vaunted Sea-to-Sky Highway. It's a straightforward excursion on most occasions, the type that's so direct it is hard to contemplate ever getting lost.

But, thanks to David McLean, the trip is longer now as the highway is ripped up in places, while rock has been blown out in pieces and moved by heavy equipment to expand the road. I count a half-dozen instances where massive construction equipment literally reshapes the mountain that runs along the east side of the highway.

Why is this David McLean's fault? Well, as the car I'm driving in gets stopped by yet another crew cleaning up the blasted rubble, I figure I've got to blame *someone*, and he is at least partially responsible. So, I've assigned it to him, even though I've never met the man. Okay, that may not exactly be fair, but like a great many things that go on in Vancouver, McLean was involved in Vancouver's 2010 Olympic bid as the federal government's committee representative.

Part of the pitch involved expanding the Sea-to-Sky Highway so that the busy stretch of road would be able to handle the increased traffic that would head to Whistler for many outdoor sports, from skiing to snowboarding. Of course, he was only one of ninety-six people on the board, so he's not solely to blame.

On the other hand, McLean is also my host for my round at Nicklaus North, so perhaps I won't let him know of my self-centred bitching. All the delays mean I arrive at the course with just enough time to hit a handful of balls on the range, which is a long cart ride down a bumpy path and across a set of railway tracks. By the time I get to the starter's hut near the first tee, there's only a few moments before my tee time. As I chat with the amiable Australian starter (Whistler is like the United Nations of Canada—everyone who works there is from somewhere else), I keep my eyes peeled for McLean, who is nowhere to be seen.

Suddenly, a golf cart steams up the sidewalk and onto the path near the first tee. The tall driver sports a wispy silver beard and wears a blue sweater. I immediately recognize McLean—not from his appearance, but from his bright blue golf hat emblazoned with the letters C and N. That's CN, as in Canadian National Railway, the company of which he is chairman.

Of course, that's only one of the things McLean does. The lawyer also runs his own company, the McLean Group, which includes Vancouver Film Studios, where television shows like *The X-Files* were shot, and he is the former chair of Vancouver's Board of Trade. Add to all this his involvement with the Olympics. And as if that weren't enough, he is also a backroom mover and shaker in the world of politics, a confidante to some of the country's richest and most powerful individuals, a man who casually punctuates his comments with references to names like Desmarais, Chrétien, and Tellier. If there's something or someone of national significance that David McLean *isn't* involved with, I haven't found it.

He steps out of his cart carrying a red CN golf cap, introduces himself, and offers the hat to me. Despite a moratorium imposed by my wife on new golf hats entering our home, I feel it would be ungracious not to accept, and I quickly swap it with the cap I'm wearing.

I give McLean the honours on the first tee and, without warming up, he takes a slow swing with a full shoulder turn and the ball heads right, finding the rough in front of the first fairway bunker, about 185 yards from the green. My fairway wood finds the centre of the fairway and we're off, heading up the cart path under grey skies.

CN has been part of McLean's life for more than two decades. A lifelong Liberal party insider, McLean was first appointed to the company's board in 1979, while Pierre Trudeau was in power. At the time, CN was a Crown corporation, but McLean's ties didn't help him during the rise of Conservative PM Brian Mulroney, and he left CN in 1986. At the time, he thought that would be the end of it, he says, walking across the wet fairway to play his ball. And, for a spell, it was. He focused his energy on running a series of businesses— from real estate, including the revitalization of Vancouver's historic Gastown district, to the purchase of Northstar International Studios, later renamed Vancouver Film Studios.

McLean's approach shot comes to rest just off the green, and a chip and a putt later, he's in with par. We grab a couple of irons and head to the second, a 180-yard par-3 over water that plays to an oblong green, which features a distinct plateau to the right which is perched in front of an expanse of sandy wasteland. It is an all-or-nothing hole that tells you a lot about the state of your game, the type that makes many clench their butt cheeks together. McLean's shot finds the front edge of the green, while my 6-iron takes off and tumbles into the back bunker.

McLean eyes his putt while I attempt a recovery from the sand. A few minutes later, we're both back on the green, and after he lags his putt near the hole and taps in for par, I ask why he came back to CN.

"Oh, Jean called and asked," he says.

I tuck my notepad into my back pocket and take a stab at my par putt, watching the ball drift left of the hole.

"Jean?" I repeat, tapping the ball into the cup.

"Chrétien," he answers. "He called and asked me to come back to CN. It was late in 1993, and he'd just come on as PM."

We walk back to our cart, and as we drive to the par-5 third—a short journey through a tunnel under a nearby road—McLean continues.

"I said no. It wasn't something I wanted to do and I had a lot of other things on the go. Going back to the board of a Crown corporation wasn't one of the things I wanted distracting me," he says. "But Chrétien wouldn't take no for an answer. 'Come and see me,' he said. So I flew to Ottawa and Chrétien said, 'I couldn't tell you this over the phone, but we're taking CN private.' I told him, '*Now* you've got my interest.'"

At the time, CN was being run by former civil servants Paul Tellier and Michael Sabia, who would later emerge as the head of BCE. McLean was interested in the transformation of the railway, and agreed to take a role at CN and help shepherd the business through its intended privatization.

It wasn't an easy process, he admits. In 1994, he travelled to the U.K. to investigate the privatization efforts that had been spearheaded by former prime minister Margaret Thatcher, and began considering the cultural and regulatory changes that would be needed to make the railway's public stock offering a success. Along the way, he ran headlong into then Transportation Minister Doug Young, whom McLean dismisses as "a weird guy who often got in the way.

"But when you have a relationship with the PM, you can get things done," he jokes as we leave the fourth green.

The success of the IPO clearly pleases McLean, who assumed the role of CN chairman, a position he continues to hold after Tellier and Sabia have left the company. The offering raised $2.2 billion, making it the most successful of its kind to that point. It solidified McLean's position as a well-connected man, the type that could get things done. It's a reputation that has served him well.

Like a lot of rich and powerful businessmen, early in his career McLean didn't have the time or inclination golf demands. There was always something in the way, he says, from his businesses to his work in politics and his family. His first love was, and is, basketball. He played while at the University of Alberta and still follows the game closely. In fact, for a couple of holes we discuss nothing but hoops, including his interest in Phoenix Suns guard Steve Nash, who grew up in Victoria.

"I'm a huge fan," he gushes. "Steve is one of those rare players that makes all of those around him on the court look good. If you want to learn to play the game of basketball, learn to play it like him."

By the time his two boys were grown, he found himself drawn to golf, and like everything he's involved with, once he took up the sport he did so with zest. Though he doesn't claim to be a great player—sporting a 23 handicap—he loves to play, and is a member of a handful of clubs, including the ultra-quiet Redtail Golf Club, hidden in rural southern Ontario, Shaughnessy in Vancouver, and The Boulders in Scottsdale, Arizona.

"My game is functional, nothing more," he explains. "As I've said to my kids, all you want to be able to do is play without embarrassing yourself."

In fact, McLean's self-deprecating comments on the matter downplay his ability. He may well be a relatively new player, but he's the type of high-handicapper one wants to be alongside in a match, especially since his high draw with a driver finds the fairway more often than not, and he hits the ball surprisingly far. His wealth and status in the business community mean he's played with his share of PGA Tour pros, from John Huston ("I chipped in for a par at a par-5 at the Air Canada Championship when we played with him. I got two strokes, so it was actually a net three. Huston turned to me and dismissively said, 'What was that?' I thought he was an ass.") to Mark O'Meara ("the kind of guy you'd want to play with every day. He just talked about fishing.").

While tales of playing with the pros are commonplace among Canada's business elite, McLean does impress me with a casual aside that he's trotted along the fairways of Domaine Laforest, the private golf course of the billionaire Desmarais family. Of course, this shouldn't surprise me: McLean's political connections ensure that he is well within six degrees of separation of Canada's best and brightest. In this instance, the connection is courtesy of his friendship with Chrétien, whose daughter France is married to André, the son of Power Corporation baron Paul Desmarais.

I've seen pictures of the course, I tell him, and Tom McBroom, the course's designer, has told me it is his best work, a place that rivals Augusta National for conditioning. McLean chuckles, affirming that what I've heard is all true. He makes it sound like some sort of golfing Xanadu, with fairways and greens unmarked by balls, since hardly anyone ever plays there.

"It's great fun playing there," he laughs. "You never see anyone else when you're on the course."

Generally, McLean doesn't take the game too seriously. A bad shot is easily put behind him, though like everyone, he enjoys the praise that comes with smacking one long and straight off the tee.

"It is hard to get your body to do what it is supposed to do," he says after a short, but straight tee ball on the seventh hole, whose expansive waste bunkers dominate the hole.

It was McLean's choice to play Nicklaus North. He joined because of its proximity to the home he keeps in Whistler. McLean's connection to the town involves more than just leisure, though: the McLean Group owns Blackcomb Helicopters, a company that flies charters for skiing and tourism out of the town.

McLean's link to Nicklaus North is more tangential and emotional. It is simply a course he enjoys playing—that's practically the sole reason he joined. Of course, there's some prestige attached to the course, but unlike some private retreat, Nicklaus North is open to the paying public. Its launch in 1995 was an attempt to rework the perception of Whistler from simply a winter destination for skiing into a four-season playground. Who better to entice the casual golfer than Jack Nicklaus, golfer and legend, winner of all four of the game's major titles? To give credit where it's due, Nicklaus understood the appeal of his "brand" before anyone even considered the notion of a pro athlete having one. He knew that his time as the game's best player would be fleeting. While his prime lasted longer than practically anyone's in the history of the sport, by the time he had shot and putted his way to his final Masters title in 1986, Nicklaus already had a backup plan. That plan involved creating golf courses and charging millions for his stamp of approval.

In most instances, Nicklaus's mark is limited to the promotional material for a course, usually involving photos of golf's greatest player hitting some shots during a grand opening affair with the club's owner, and maybe some reference to his "Bear" nickname in the title of the course. It's more direct at Nicklaus North, the only Canadian course to have the privilege of using the golfer's name, driving home the connection by utilizing miniature bears as tee box markers.

At Nicklaus North, one of the so-called "signature" designs for which he is paid more than $1.5 million, the Bear was handed a piece of property whose appeal was in its scenery as opposed to its topography. Over a flat piece of land surrounded by spectacular mountains, his team of designers crafted a course full of deep and expansive bunkers and greens that perplex the average player with their dips and swales.

Nicklaus did the best he could with what he was given. The problem with the course is that, like Whistler itself, it all feels slightly contrived. There's nothing natural about the engineered ponds that back onto multimillion-dollar condo retreats for the rich and famous. Like an aging Hollywood actress who's been under the knife so many times that her face is frozen in a permanent smile, there's something artificial about Nicklaus North.

None of this really matters to McLean, who isn't the type that really worries about what separates a great golf course from a good one. But his ties to the game itself run deep. His most recent dalliance is with a project called Sagebrush Golf and Sporting Club, a project pioneered by former PGA Tour pro and Vancouver native Richard Zokol. Located three hours from Vancouver on 380 acres of land in the Nicola Valley, Sagebrush is Zokol's attempt to create a course as majestic and private as the great retreats in other parts of the world, places like Sand Hills Golf Club in Nebraska and Friars Head in New York. At $200,000 for a slice of the pie, it is also among the most expensive private clubs developed in Canada.

Though Zokol won twice on the PGA Tour, he did so in an era before golf pros had multimillion-dollar endorsement deals and access to a private jet before they even won their first event. That meant that, like many entrepreneurs with a vision, he had to hit the road and sell his concept. Over four years of trying to raise money, pitching the ideas to wealthy businessmen in Vancouver and oil cowboys in Calgary and Edmonton, Zokol had a lot of doors slammed in his face before he ran into McLean.

"It is a good location for a course, but a tricky one because it is remote," McLean admits, eating a hot dog at the turn as we wait for the green of the par-3 tenth. "I told Dick to get the thing built, as it is hard to sell a dream."

So Zokol hired a designer and set about building the course he envisioned. It is scheduled to open in 2009, and McLean is convinced the idea has merit and that the club will be used by CN as a corporate retreat—a place to take clients, to lobby politicians, and hold meetings, away from the prying eyes of journalists and the public.

"CN was one of the first companies to buy into Sagebrush," he says, "because it works for a company like us."

In fact, these days golf works for CN, and McLean has played a big role in that. In 2005, the Canadian Open was at Shaughnessy, and, as a member of the club, McLean naturally attended the event. During the tournament, he got into a conversation about the potential demise of the Canadian Women's Open, which lacked a sponsor, had lost its status as a major LPGA tournament, and was thought to be on its last legs. McLean decided that the notion of CN becoming involved in the tournament had merit, and he mentioned it to the marketing executives at the railway. Within months, a deal was struck to brand the tournament the CN Canadian Women's Open.

"I get a lot of credit for it, but I think it is overblown," he says.

McLean takes a good cut with a 5-iron, and the ball sails over the green, coming to rest in a patch of rough between the left and back bunkers.

"I don't think it is all that complicated," he continues. "We wanted to give back to the community, give back to golf. But we all thought the women needed more help. It has worked out wonderfully. We've gotten a lot out of it."

In fact, the sponsorship was a stroke of good luck, starting just as a new era in women's golf emerged, led by new young superstars like Lorena Ochoa, Paula Creamer, and Morgan Pressel. Its image achieved even more exposure, if that's the right word, as the likes of Natalie Gulbis decided that shedding some of her golf attire and posing in a bikini might help her career. And, of course, the LPGA achieved headlines through the seemingly failed attempt by Hawaiian teenager Michelle Wie to play on the PGA Tour.

Someone once told me that CN sponsored the event not for the exposure, but for the fact that its trains derail in small Canadian towns every so often and the company needs the goodwill. McLean scoffs at the notion.

"It has nothing to do with that," he says flatly, as we leave the green and head back to our cart. It is all about marketing, he says, though it turns out several of the executives in the company are golf-mad. CEO Hunter Harrison played frequently in Chicago and Florida, before a recent back injury limited his play.

"Harrison loves golf. I love golf. Jim Foote, our VP of sales, loves golf. We really thought it was a good chance to expose the company to the country."

Golf aside, the esteem in which McLean holds Harrison becomes clear as soon as the subject of the company's gruff, self-made

CEO comes up. The son of a police officer turned preacher, Harrison is generally regarded as the force that has made CN one of the strongest and best-managed railways—and killer investments—in North America. He came as part of a deal by CN to crack the American market by purchasing the Illinois Central Railroad, which Harrison was running. A decade later, it appears that what CN actually acquired was a visionary CEO.

"Hunter is a great asset," McLean says with obvious admiration in his voice. "He may be the last of the truly great railroad men, the type who work their way up from the bottom. Let's hope he isn't the last, but it's hard to imagine anyone creating another Hunter Harrison. He's entirely unique."

By the time we hit the eleventh hole, a tricky par-5 with wetlands to the right and water to the left, our game has largely ground to a halt. Every shot becomes an exercise in patience, as we wait for the group in front to clear the fairway or green. The slow play doesn't seem to bother McLean, who relaxes in the cart, alternating the discussion to fit my questions, though it appears he'd probably prefer we just talked basketball.

While waiting for the threesome to putt out on the twelfth, a par-3 with a heroic tee shot over a vast pound to a green with enough sand to make the Sahara envious, I ask McLean about what he brings to CN more than a decade after he was appointed. Unlike Harrison, McLean never worked on a railway. He was a lawyer who didn't like practising law, I point out.

"Most of what I'm involved in just takes common sense," he says, staring at the green and leaning back in his seat. "You need to be able to stand back and see the big picture. A good board is involved in strategic planning and setting policy, not in implementing it. It is a chance for a good sober second thought. I mean 90 per cent of the job is communication—just talking through the issues."

The green finally clears and we head to the tee. With the hole playing strongly downwind, I loft a 9-iron that comes up short— just over the water, but in the front bunker. McLean, perhaps spooked by my shot, goes back to his bag and takes an extra club, rifling a shot that hits the green and spins down a swale, coming to rest in the front left corner.

Have his political instincts benefited him at CN? I ask. Just because he's comfortable running behind the scenes, hanging out with prime ministers, and "hunting and shooting" at the Desmarais's estate in Quebec, doesn't mean McLean is entirely engrossed in politics. At least, that's his perception.

"I don't like people thinking I'm some sort of political animal, because I'm not. I'm more of a businessman," he says. "But if you're a businessman and not involved in politics, then I think you're being foolish."

That sensibility extends to his job at CN, he continues.

"It is always important to understand the political climate surrounding business. That's why we have both Republicans and Democrats on our board."

When he's not focused on CN, he's spending time working with the McLean Group, which comes across as almost an afterthought in our discussion, though it's been hugely successful for McLean. As we hit the par-3 seventeenth—arguably the most visually challenging hole on Nicklaus North, with a green set two hundred yards away, jutting into the water, a moat of sand encompassing the left side—we're once again faced with a dawdling group of players in front of us. However, we are already resigned to a slow round, and McLean talks about the success he's had with his various enterprises—from the film studios, which are currently shooting television's *Battlestar Galactica* and just wrapped the movie *The Fantastic Four: The Rise of the Silver Surfer*, to telecommunications company Signal Systems—he admits the company has grown beyond his expectations.

"I see the payroll sometimes and it frightens me," he says, getting out of the cart and selecting a fairway wood for his shot. His sons, Jason and Sacha, both have executive roles in the company, and McLean expects their responsibilities to increase.

"You have to be careful you're not doing it just out of nepotism," he says, before adding proudly, "I'd hire both of my kids even if they weren't my family."

McLean's tee shot goes wide to the right, and he chips up, barely missing his par putt.

We hit the eighteenth, and McLean's drive flies to the right, coming to rest out of view in an area of wetlands. Our round has now passed five hours, and McLean mentions that he's being picked up in a helicopter and flown down to Vancouver for a party that night, returning to Whistler the next day. Perhaps worried that he's already late, especially with clouds darkening overhead, he quickly takes a drop outside the hazard and waits for the green to clear. With his annual election to CN's board all but assured until a mandatory retirement at age seventy-five, and his sons taking more and more control of the McLean Group, I ask what there is left to do. Not a great deal, he says, adding that he's begun turning down some offers in fear of overextending himself.

"That's a first for me, but I've got a lot to do as it is," he says. He lofts a 9-iron onto the green. Five minutes later, our game is over (I record a 78 to McLean's 93) and we grab a shuttle from the eighteenth green that runs up a path and through the parking lot of the nearby condos, stopping in front of the clubhouse just as McLean's wife, Brenda, pulls up in the couple's SUV.

McLean thanks me for the round, tosses his clubs in the back of the vehicle, and gets in the passenger side. The car quickly pulls out of the parking lot.

His helicopter awaits, and with so many elements in play, so many businesses to run, and so many balls in the air, so to speak, David McLean has no time to spare.

CHAPTER 13

Peter Schwartz

Taking His Shot

"Dream golf is simply played on another course."

—John Updike

PETER SCHWARTZ IS ONE OF those intriguing, often electric, personalities you only meet on a handful of occasions over a lifetime. And yes, this sort of personality is often polarizing, leaving those in their wake often astounded—sometimes positively, occasionally negatively. Either way, these individuals are usually easy to spot. They command attention, and that's the case with Schwartz. I suspect that wherever he goes and regardless of the environment—be it in the cufflinks-and-tie culture of the boardroom, or a place like Westmount Golf and Country Club—heads turn.

Clearly, there's an aspect of the man that enjoys it. Otherwise, it is hard to imagine why one would show up at an illustrious, and curmudgeonly, old private golf club like Westmount dressed in a bright yellow, form-fitting golf shirt and green shorts with a yellow checked pattern. Schwartz's longish dark hair is parted neatly in the middle, and he sports a visor and golf sunglasses. He exudes self-confidence.

Schwartz emerges on the range as I'm hitting balls as a warm-up. A golf bag slung over his shoulder is boldly emblazoned down its side with the word "Öviinbyrd," the name of the club in Ontario's cottage country that Schwartz created. I ask about his outfit, which is only slightly this side of outlandish. Is this how forty-year-old business executives dress on the course?

"What this?" he says, shrugging as he warmly shakes my hand. "Oh, my wife picked this out for me."

Then, coolly, without any sign of self-consciousness at my biting remark, Schwartz takes out an iron and hits a few soft wedges. His three-quarter swing is a model of control and calculation—indeed, Schwartz seems to consider his every move, both on the course and in the office. Which is probably why he's such a strong golfer: it's a game that appreciates those who can develop a plan and follow it through to its conclusion.

Schwartz is the product of the dot-com boom, a time when young entrepreneurs could take an idea, develop it, float it on the public markets, and walk away with millions, all in a few years. He started his career fresh out of the University of Western Ontario's business school, and in 1989 began working for a Waterloo, Ontario, company that handled logistics planning for Pepsi. Schwartz recognized the company's potential, and as the Internet rose to prominence, he moved the business, now called Descartes Systems Group, into Web logistics. In essence, he helped create a computer network that linked the various delivery mechanisms often used by large companies. He was CEO at twenty-eight. Descartes went public two years later and was listed on the Nasdaq by the time Schwartz was thirty-one. But like many young executives in the accelerated world of the Internet, it was all over by 2003, when, with Descartes in the midst of a financial mess, Schwartz lost a power struggle for control of the company and resigned. He was thirty-six.

"The passion I had at Descartes wasn't so much about the product and what it did," he says, soon after we tee off on the first hole at Westmount, a lengthy par-5 with a large dip in the fairway that offers a speed slope for well-hit drives. "It was about the people I did it with. It is exhilarating being around intelligent people that have a common goal."

He wouldn't have admitted it at the time, but Schwartz found running a public company challenging. A classic entrepreneur, he loved the game of building and constructing a company out of hard work and a good idea.

He steps up and hits a hard 3-iron fifty yards short of the green.

"I saw a business opportunity. I enjoyed building the company and I enjoyed the building stage of the company," he says. "I certainly wouldn't change any of that. But there's a point where you build the company—where you grow it to the stage where you don't know the people you're working with every day, and the kinds of things you are doing aren't the things you necessarily enjoy.

"You begin to realize that just because you recognize a business opportunity and get along well with the people you built the business with, doesn't mean that you necessarily enjoy the business."

Somewhere in the process, Descartes became a monster, a product of Internet hype that was never sustainable. Schwartz suddenly found his little logistics company in the midst of the Web revolution. The business's stock price surged to more than $130. It was never a sustainable rise, and few were surprised when it cratered.

The failure of Descartes left Schwartz uncharacteristically defensive. He isn't the type used to failure, let alone having investors and pundits blame him for the millions in losses that occurred as Descartes's stock rocketed to earth. He'd made his fortune off Descartes, but was left without a job and with a lot of explaining to do. The problem was that no one wanted to listen to what he had to say.

His inability to have anyone consider his side of the story, of how he was put on the sidelines and then forced out of the business before its downfall, has long bothered Schwartz. He hits a high draw up the hill of the second hole and, as we stride up the fairway, he says the most troublesome element of the Descartes meltdown is that people—many of whom he's never met—will judge him on the basis of the failure.

Following Schwartz's departure, things went from bad to worse at Descartes. Eventually, the executive who forced Schwartz out was fired himself, accused of doctoring numbers to improve results. The company's once high-flying stock fell to $1.37. It didn't matter that Schwartz wasn't with the business when it collapsed. To many, he still bore the brunt of the blame for the disaster.

"It is frustrating to know that people will always be educated by other people about who I am and what I am," he says, carving an iron into the right front bunker. "We set out to build a really exciting technology company. At the time, there was no sign of Nasdaq hitting five thousand on the horizon. It wasn't about that. But, frankly, no one will ever know that. I'll just be known as some flash-in-the-pan Internet guy. That's disappointing."

He finishes the last sentence with a tone of resignation. But in typical Schwartz fashion, he flashes a smile, puts it behind him, and strides down the fairway.

We finish the hole—Schwartz makes par to my bogey—and walk behind Westmount's clubhouse to the long, par-3 third hole that plays over a pond to a green that runs away. It is just another strong hole on a course that is a remarkably consistent, and occasionally fantastic, an example of the brilliance of Stanley Thompson, the fabled Canadian golf designer and *bon vivant*. Thompson, who died in 1953, is responsible for the inherent genius of half a dozen of the best courses in this country. He started work on Westmount in 1929 at the behest of a handful of disgruntled golfers from another nearby club. The club spent a total of $49,679 to create what has become one of the cornerstones of Canadian golf, a course that has forced golfers to be creative and thoughtful for more than seven decades.

Created using horse-drawn plows and hard work, the land at Westmount was the canvas for Thompson's aesthetic vision, and it has remained largely faithful to his concept. Fairways still dip and plunge with the random movement of the land, creating a wonderfully natural playing surface and a few uniquely quirky aspects. The designer had tremendous trees to pick from in routing this masterpiece, and many of those remain on the course today as a testament to the longevity and brilliance of Thompson's vision.

While it was once 224 acres of farmland, these days Westmount is located in a suburban area of Waterloo, surrounded by subdivisions and winding community roads. Despite the changing surroundings, even today, in the era of cannon-like drivers forged out of space-age metals and golf balls that fire like missiles, Westmount is no pushover. Perhaps the only surprise about Westmount is that a solitary Canadian Open—in 1957—was ever held at the course.

Schwartz joined Westmount after leaving Descartes. He wasn't yet forty, but many had already written him off. I've known Schwartz since I was a cub reporter covering Descartes at the height of the Internet bubble; at the time, I doubted he would stay down for long. But his next move remained a mystery.

There were likely options, but given the publicity surrounding his departure from Descartes, there were probably fewer than he would have liked. However, Schwartz's impetuous personality and focus make him hard to keep down. He's the type that is able to pitch sand to the Bedouin and make it convincing. When he speaks, he's able to conjure a passionate pitch that demonstrates his commitment to whatever he's flogging. It takes a certain type of charisma to pull that off, and Schwartz has it in spades.

When he left Descartes, he decided his next move would be different. It would involve something he loved and could develop through his mix of intuition and business skills. Thankfully, despite the meltdown at Descartes, Schwartz was well heeled, with the resources to test his entrepreneurial mettle.

"The older I got, I kept thinking, 'Wouldn't it be nice to do exactly what I want to do?'" he says. "And I realized that if I had the chance to do something again, it would have to be something I was passionate about."

Schwartz's snappy swing lets him down on the third hole, and his flared tee shot finds the trees on the right, well short of the hole. We find the ball resting in a grove of large trees. To most, the hole would be a disaster. But that's not how it appears to Schwartz.

There's still opportunity to be had; one just has to look a little more deeply and closely for the options. Golf, like business, often comes down to looking at the risks and weighing them against the possible reward. Schwartz does this well, gripping down on a 7-iron and punching the ball around a tree trunk, where it comes to rest next to the green.

"An entrepreneur is not an inventor," he continues. "He's someone who recognizes a good idea and does all kinds of unnatural acts with it to turn it into a business."

Schwartz's next unnatural act involved one of the loves of his life: golf.

His idea was relatively simple, but the business world is littered with simple ideas—especially in the golf industry. Schwartz wanted to build a golf course. It didn't matter that he had no experience in the business—he felt he could succeed where others had failed.

Usually, when someone announces they want to build a golf course, it coincides with the sound of dollars being sucked from their wallet. Far too often, golf courses are a testament to one's ego, built by individuals who made their fortunes creating widgets and who feel that success could easily translate to the golf industry. More often than not, they fail, leaving floundering courses worth tens of millions on the verge of bankruptcy.

Schwartz, whose golf experience was limited to playing good courses during his tenure as CEO of Descartes, often at customer events, was aware of this trend. But he still felt his idea had merit. He wanted to devise a product—in this case, a golf course—that matched the needs and interests of a potential market.

The resulting course—named Öviinbyrd, a play on the little oven birds initially found on the property—opened in Port Carling, Ontario, in Muskoka's cottage country, in 2004. Despite all the pessimism, it was an immediate success.

If the point of any strong business is to have a focus that appeals to the customer, then Schwartz's course was a straight shot down the fairway. If Öviinbyrd was a company, it would be an old-world

Fortune 500 business, one that's reliable, presents consumers with what they want, and has a timeless quality. Designed by Thomas McBroom, whom Schwartz met due to the relative proximity of their respective summer homes, Öviinbyrd is a course that is uniquely Canadian. Utilizing the rugged landscape of the Canadian Shield, the course's rocky outcroppings are mixed with huge deciduous forests and matched with greens that are devilish in their simplicity. The combination makes for a course that is different from its rivals both aesthetically and functionally. As pretty as a postcard, Öviinbyrd lulls players into a false sense of security before snatching away the scores of those overconfident enough to test the course's limits. It is a remarkable course, one of the best in the country.

Schwartz knew that the course would help sell the club, but that it was only one factor. First and foremost, the club would have to satisfy Schwartz. If it passed that test, then it would likely impress his friends as well.

"Marketing 101?" I ask.

"Exactly," he replies as we lug our clubs up the blind fairway on the fourth hole, a par-4 that bends to the left. "I looked at what was missing in Muskoka. I stopped and said to myself, 'What is the most important thing in a golf course?' I thought to myself, 'Access—that's the most important thing to me.' That's not what market research would tell you. It would say you needed a big clubhouse, fancy staircases, massive gates, good course. I looked at all of that and threw it out—it was about access. Far be it for me to say I figured this out and no one else could. I just started with what I really enjoyed. Then I shared it with people like me, and the answer was obvious."

The idea was to take the concept of high-end private retreats, like Magna Golf Club and other palatial golfing clubs, keep what mattered to members, and strip away the costly features that Schwartz felt didn't add to the experience.

"I sometimes think the best way to build a business plan is to think not about what it should be, but to think about what it should not be," Schwartz says. "What things really bother people about their experiences? Until you ask them, sometimes they don't even know or recognize it."

And what about all of the courses that have faltered and failed to find an audience? Did he want to prove the naysayers wrong?

"That didn't motivate me. It confused me. I wondered why they hadn't figured it out for themselves. What is so wrong with their business models? The reason they thought that is they couldn't see the opportunity. They didn't look backwards and say, 'What is the hallmark of this club? What matters to people? And can they get it anywhere else?'"

Schwartz was only eleven when his father died, and while he grew up comfortably, he was never part of the upper crust, nor did he belong to a ritzy country club. Even these days, he is more interested in the golf than the stuck-up culture that often surrounds a private club. At Öviinbyrd, Schwartz displaced old-world ideas of how a country club should be run. Gone was the notion that men had to wear dress pants and collared shirts in the clubhouse. In was a more casual style, a less regimented approach where shorts and flip-flops were acceptable. It was all part of Schwartz's vision.

"If you grew up second- or third-generation money, then you're used to 'mister this' and 'mister that.' But this isn't that kind of club. This is something different."

His concept struck a chord, and the course—and the real estate component that came with it—was a success out of the gate. While other golf projects launched at the same time struggled to find members and those willing to flip out their credit cards for a round, Schwartz's Öviinbyrd flourished. Real estate was easy to move, and the club was filled with members willing to shell out tens of thousands to belong. It all came relatively naturally to Schwartz, who spent a lot of time working on developing the course after leaving Descartes.

"I thought it was reasonably easy to figure out the business model for a golf course. I'm surprised other people have had the same issues. Maybe I had the determination—and balls, since I can't think of a better word for that—to figure out a way to build a business. I look at market research and look for missing opportunities. I never felt I was taking a risk with any of this."

It isn't that Schwartz is risk-averse. That much is clear as we walk to the eighth hole, a tidy, drivable par-4 with out-of-bounds on the left and trees and rough to the right. It is a classic illustration of the risk/reward ratio: a short two-shot hole, one that can be reached with a precise blast from the tee. But only the best shot will find the green, and a yawning greenside bunker is more likely to swallow anything but the truest shot.

That doesn't seem to matter to Schwartz. His evenly paced, smooth swing typically offers both precision and power, and has allowed him to play near scratch for most of the previous decade, even though he rarely has much time to practise. In this instance his short swing is a hair too fast, resulting in a high hook that disappears into the trees before being spit out like an olive pit into the rough about fifty yards from the green.

Schwartz mutters about not hitting the ball well and does a slow jog up the fairway. As we launch the search for his ball, I ask Schwartz whether his business philosophy changed after creating Öviinbyrd.

"Sure it did," he says, after locating his ball. "It was where my artistic side met with my knowledge of how to build a business."

He chips a low wedge into the opening of the green, throws his clubs on his back, and continues: "For me, creating something like Öviinbyrd is a demonstration of where your artistic side meets your ability to figure a business out. To me, that's euphoria—when you take something you really enjoy, your creative side, and put it together with your knowledge of how to run a business. Anyone who has an artistic side would love to do just that, but they can't always make a living at it. For me, I've been lucky, I guess."

Schwartz took that luck and the experience of Öviinbyrd—as well as some of the millions he made at Descartes—and decided he would try the real estate business. It would become a big component of Schwartz's post-Descartes business, the Laurence Group, named after his late father.

"When I travel around the world, I like to go to a city centre and look at the shops and piazzas and courtyards. And there's none of that here. It is just strip malls. For me, it was bringing the ideas I'd seen elsewhere and bringing them to the core. Finding people's desires to have nice accommodations, and their desire to have character in their lives. That was the goal."

His first real estate project—an ambitious loft condo/commercial development in his hometown of Waterloo—was a hit, leading Schwartz to follow his nose into other real estate concepts.

"I'll do one at a time," he says, walking down the undulating fairway of the eleventh hole. "Anything more than that would be work. And what fun would that be?"

Schwartz's golf game re-emerges on the back nine, where he makes a series of pars and birdies in rapid succession. Despite complaining that his game was hurt by two years of "playing tour guide" at Öviinbyrd, it is rock solid, with a deft touch around the greens. It doesn't hurt that Schwartz works with Brian Mogg, a PGA Tour instructor he befriended, who makes regular visits in the summer to Öviinbyrd. Proof positive that a golf game can be turned around, Schwartz is eyeing a score in the mid-70s even after a rocky start. He's optimistic throughout—even when the ball starts to go a little bit sideways.

Despite his success, Schwartz has his detractors—holdovers among investors and those in the business community who blame him for Descartes's failures and who resent the success he's had since leaving the company. I often wonder if these people are really resentful of the fact his success came at such a young age, and involved a new business paradigm, one they barely comprehend.

We both hit the green on the short par-3 seventeenth hole, and I ask Schwartz if his image can recover from the tarnishing it received at Descartes.

"I don't know if it ever will," he says.

"That must be troublesome," I answer.

"I don't know if I'd say I'm disappointed," he says, lining up his putt. "There are some things I'd have liked to have done differently, no question about it."

So, it's like a golf game—you recount the experience and think about where you could get some strokes back?

"I suppose it is. One thing is for sure, I'm not running a popularity contest in my life. My level of happiness is directly related to how many days I get to be myself. And if who I am offends someone, then there's nothing I can do about that. But if you know me well, I don't think you'll find I'm a bad guy. If there's someone out there who knows me well and doesn't have a high regard for me, I want to know why they feel that way."

He lags his putt and taps it in for par.

"People draw conclusions when the story doesn't make perfect sense to them. They like to fill in the blanks themselves. And if they don't know me, they didn't get the truth. I tend not to create opinions about others, especially if I don't know them. It isn't what I do. I'm not an easy guy to figure out from the outside. And if they are forced to draw conclusions, they'll probably get it wrong."

As for Schwartz, he says he'll continue trying to look on the brighter side of business. His experience hasn't left him cynical, though no one would be surprised if it had.

"I trust in people until I know otherwise," he says standing on the eighteenth tee, as dark storm clouds loom overhead. "I've been screwed by five guys in my business life. Five guys. And I've dealt with thousands that I had good relationships with. So I'm not going to change the way I think. But I know who I'm dealing with—people who are largely skeptical."

We hit our drives—mine to the left side of the fairway, Schwartz's farther to the right—and begin our walk up the final hole, a 380-yard par-4 that plays to the edge of Westmount's clubhouse. One thing is clear: Schwartz isn't going to be running another public company anytime soon. That's just fine with him. Between his real estate work, another golf course on the horizon, and further development of his Laurence Group project, which sees him working on financing arrangements for entrepreneurs, his plate is full. These days, he's focused solely not on what is expected of him, but on what he wants to do.

"I've never really thought about the fact that I take what I love and turn it into a business," he says as we shake hands on the final green. "You're right. I bet that's what's driving me subliminally.

"Working with entrepreneurs is exhilarating. These people are like me—they're doing what they love, and doing it with people they love. Its infectious, and I can't get enough of watching people live their dreams."

And Schwartz insists he's not through living out his dreams.

"If someone could rip my brain apart and look at the things I love the most, then they'd see opportunities," he says. "I've been lucky enough to figure out how to make a business out of three or four of them."

As we walk back to our cars in the parking lot, with a thunderstorm quickly descending on the unsuspecting players out on the course, I can't help but think it is only a matter of time before Schwartz looks to another of his passions and finds a way to make megabucks out of it.

And that makes him a lucky man indeed.

CHAPTER 14

Gerry Barad
Cocaine for the New Millennium

"Every rock 'n' roll band I know—guys with long hair and tattoos—
play golf now."

—Alice Cooper

"I'M A GAMBLER," Gerry Barad says as we step onto the first tee at
Scarboro Golf and Country Club. "I gamble that people are willing
to buy more tickets for a tour than we paid for that tour. That's the
essence of what I do."

You might not recognize Barad's name, but you've likely seen his
handiwork. For three decades since he was a struggling university
student in Vancouver trying to figure out whether he had the goods
to get into law school, Barad has booked concerts. It started with
now-obscure punk bands in small dives, the places where loud
bands played for a handful of those willing to pay the cover charge.
Thirty years later, Barad's stable includes the biggest musical acts
in the world—like the Police, Van Halen, David Bowie, and even others whom you might not consider to be musicians, like J. Lo.

While his head is in the music, his heart and passion are elsewhere. Barad is a golf freak. He loves the game. Specifically, he loves
golf courses. He's fascinated by the nuances and tiny differences that
make some courses great and some average. And while some prefer
fine wine or fine cars, Barad prefers golf. He's an eclectic connois-
seur of the best the game has to offer, having played the top courses

in the world regularly since he first reintroduced himself to the game in 1995. Courses like Chicago Golf Club, arguably the most exclusive club in the world—Barad has played it a half-dozen times this year, though he's not a member. Or Sand Hills, which may be the most remarkable course built in the past five decades. It is located in rural Nebraska in a place that even Google Earth can't find. Barad and some buddies took a private jet down to play for a weekend. What about Myopia Hunt Club, the throwback that held three of the first ten U.S. Opens? He went out for a round and then took everyone—caddies included—back to Fenway Park to watch the Rolling Stones.

None of this is to suggest he's a snob, but he's been known to turn up his nose at famed courses that don't fit his vision of what a golf course should be. Barad discusses golf in the same way an aficionado of fine wine would describe a great bottle. The best wine is about taste, smell, sight, and feel, but is ultimately about character. Barad talks about great golf courses in the same way, dismissing those that don't measure up and taking apart the elements that make others exceptional.

Take, for example, a recent trip to St. Louis. Barad was there to check in with a tour he'd booked for Rush, the Canadian prog-rock band known for its twenty-minute drum solos, mystical lyrics, and fanatical fan base. The band's guitarist, Alex Lifeson, is a known golf head, and when Barad came to check in, the pair decided to use a spare afternoon before a show to rock around one of the best Gateway to the West had to offer.

"Alex wanted to play Bellerive," Barad breathlessly blurts. "I told him, '*FUCK BELLERIVE!*' If I'm coming to St. Louis, we're playing St. Louis Country Club. It's a Macdonald–Raynor from 1914, and the second hole, with its Biarritz green, is fucking remarkable. The third hole, a long Eden, is even *fucking* better!"

If you need that translated from Barad-ese, it goes something like this: "Alex wanted to play a course that held the 1965 U.S. Open, one of the most fabled of all golf tournaments. But I don't consider Bellerive much of a course, and I don't get to St. Louis all that often.

So if I'm going to play in the city, I'll get us a round at St. Louis Country Club, designed by C.B. Macdonald, who built the first courses in the U.S., and later renovated by Seth Raynor. Built in 1914, its second hole has a green that plunges in the middle, only to rise to a back tier. And as good as *that* is, the next hole, a replica of the eleventh hole at St. Andrews, is superior still."

Or something like that. You get the point.

Either way, it is reflective of a typical Gerry Barad conversation about golf. Spoken in a code known only to hardcore golfers, or that extreme group of nerds and shut-ins who find studying the design of golf courses to be of paramount importance, Barad remembers every great golf experience he's ever had.

I know this first-hand, as Barad, dressed entirely in black ("My Gary Player look," he explains, though it could be more reminiscent of Johnny Cash), recounts plenty of them over the course of our round at Scarboro. But he never comes across as pretentious about his fascination. After all, the best courses are, he says, "a bit quirky. And I'm attracted to them because I'm a bit quirky," he adds. Which is indeed the case.

In fact, he's just offbeat enough to love places like Scarboro, even though he's a member at the ultra-difficult National Golf Club of Canada north of Toronto. But the National was undergoing a major renovation when we were scheduled to play, and since Barad has long been a fan of Scarboro's small greens and short fours, he figured it would be the next best option for our match.

Sandwiched in a strange enclave between large, modern homes and subsidized high-rise apartments, Scarboro is actually one of the country's oldest and most intriguing private clubs. The only remaining course in Canada created by A.W. Tillinghast, the master architect behind such famed layouts as Winged Foot (the course that held the 2006 U.S. Open) and San Francisco Golf Club, Scarboro is a throwback to another era, when the game was played with hickory clubs and Haskell balls. Though it was created in 1912, likely with a routing by George Cumming, a Scottish golf pro who moved to

Toronto at the turn of the century, it was later given an extensive facelift by Tillinghast. It is his vision of the course that largely survives today, spread out over 144 acres by a river valley that now sits in suburban Toronto.

It is charming and unusual, with small, severely canted greens, and one hole (the eighteenth) where you must hit your tee shot over a busy road to a fairway that sprawls up the hill beside the clubhouse. The ghosts of great golfers walk the hallways of its mansion-like Victorian clubhouse. Four Canadian Opens were contested on its lay-of-the-land fairways—including the 1940 tournament, in which a good 'ol boy called Sam Snead bettered the aptly named Jug McSpadden. It may now be too short to hold a modern version of the tournament, but that doesn't mean Scarboro lacks the qualities that make for an intriguing golf round.

Indeed, it is easy to see why someone like Barad would be attracted to a course like Scarboro, a track that has not changed all that much in nearly a hundred years. Scarboro is full of blind shots and strange rolls. The course's eccentricities match Barad's personality.

Giving up on the notion of heading to law school, Barad started his career running a record store and putting on the occasional punk or new wave show as a twenty-year-old in the late 1970s. He graduated to bigger shows, getting deals to promote concerts by up-and-comers like the Police.

"I put on the first show in North America by the Clash," he explains, walking up to the green on the short but sporty third hole, with its treacherous green. "I put on the first U2 show in Vancouver. They played the Commodore Ballroom and had to play 'I Will Follow' twice because they didn't have enough songs. I think that was a 'Cheap Thrills' night—we charged $3 per ticket."

By 1985, he'd hooked up with Concert Productions International, led by, among others, Michael Cohl, who at eighteen spent a brief period of time running an Ottawa strip club. But Cohl had his eye on bigger things than the next girl on the pole, and eventually came to control much of the Canadian concert business at places like the Canadian National Exhibition and Maple Leaf Gardens. In 1988 Cohl placed a huge bet by acquiring the Rolling Stones' *Steel Wheels* tour, one of the most successful tours ever staged, and came out the other side by largely reinventing the music touring business.

By the time Cohl and his partners eyed Vancouver, Barad was already established as the go-to guy for concerts in the city. They acquired Barad's expertise and then turned his boundless energy loose on Europe, where he championed tours by Pink Floyd and Prince, and helped run Brockum, the merchandising offshoot of Cohl's empire.

"I should have gone to law school, but instead I was hawking merchandise for Pink Floyd all over the world," he recalls as we make the walk up the hill to the ninth hole, a par-4 that looks easier than it plays.

Eventually, Labatt's acquired CPI. By 1995, Barad was in the tax haven of Bermuda at the centre of Cohl's new business—The Next Adventure (T 'n' A—get it?). His job was to determine the best way to route and book a tour. Should the band's gear be taken by train or by truck? Should the group play Europe in the middle of the tour and then return to North America? What happens if a band's show in a market doesn't sell? Barad may be a fast talker, but his real job is finding where each musical act fits on the supply/demand curve.

"Someone once asked me, 'Gerry, how many dates at the Gardens can U2 sell out?' I told them I don't want to find out," he says, as we take a pause to grab a Gatorade at the halfway house. "You'll only find out when you don't sell out that last show. You don't want to find out on the nineteenth show that they can't sell out twenty. It is all about managing expectations."

These days, Barad is the advance man for the biggest musical acts as the chief operating officer of touring for the massive Live Nation, which produces more than 28,000 shows annually, playing to more than 60 million people.

Barad's role means he considers all the options surrounding a tour—the number of shows, which countries and cities to play in—and then determines where he can book an act and what he can charge for a ticket. While it sounds like an incredibly complex process, Barad has been at it for years and understands all the subtleties and issues that can arise. He even has regulars he works with. Bands like U2 and Coldplay, and singers like Roger Waters and Madonna, all come to Barad and Live Nation when they want to book a tour. In turn, Barad develops long-standing relationships with the acts and management.

"There's no auditioning for us," he explains. "Either you want to work with us—and in turn we want to work for you—or you find someone else."

Though booking a modern tour, with its private jets, organic chefs, and mobile gyms, might sound miles removed from the sex, drugs, and rock 'n' roll days of Led Zeppelin groupies and a mud shark, as we trudge up to the tee of the par-5 tenth, Barad says there's still a (legal) high about a great rock spectacle.

"You go to a show—say, the last U2 show at the Air Canada Centre. There's twenty thousand people getting off that night, having a great time, and you know you had something to do with that. Forget the money and the accolades and the private planes and all that other bullshit—the buzz at that show means something to me."

Given his gregarious and occasionally outrageous personality, it stands to reason that Barad is one of the more unusual, and unusually engaging, golf partners one will find. There's never a dull moment, as he lurches from topic to topic, including favourite golf expressions—"What's an Osama bin Laden?" he asks as we tread up the seventh fairway. "I know where it went, but I can't find it."—to the best restaurants to eat at on Long Island. But ask him for the best concert he's ever seen, and even the loquacious, effervescent Barad becomes quiet. Apparently, this is a tough question.

"It could be Lena Horne in 1980," he says, pausing to think. "It could also be Captain Beefheart. I did seventeen shows in 1981. I was at the last show he ever played—the Golden Bear in Huntington Beach on January 31, 1981. Final song was 'Kandy Korn'—a twenty-nine-minute version for the encore. That was as good as it gets. That was it. If anyone else tells you they've ever played since, they're lying."

And how, exactly, does he remember that?

"I've got a photographic memory and an addictive personality," he shrugs. "What more can I say?"

Given what he does, it isn't altogether surprising to hear Barad speak in itineraries. He starts, and doesn't finish until he's listed all the events he undertook in a certain period of time, including the plans that fell through. It could be a list of venues and transportation for a major concert tour, but more often than not it is a machine-gun run-through of some golf-related trip from which he's just returned. His recollections are frenetic, entertaining, and sometimes exhausting. He can recite nuances most people overlook or don't consider worthwhile mentioning, specifically when it comes to golf holes he's played on some recent jaunt to Long Island, or California, or the Midwestern U.S.

Standing on the thirteenth hole at Scarboro, and with his game heating up, Barad is in fine form. He provides me with what I've come to refer to as a "Barad Catalogue," detailing his previous weekend in Pittsburgh.

"Well, I flew in to Pittsburgh on Friday—commercial, Robert, which you know I don't do. On Saturday, we played Longue Vue, which is a great club—almost unknown, but Tillinghast, you know, like this place," he explains breathlessly, referring to Scarboro's designer. "And man, it is a great club. Longue Vue was tremendous, but it isn't one of those obvious places you'd play. It is what I call 'mid-Tillie.' Those clubs are underrated. Longue Vue, Baltimore, Scarboro—I'd take them over the big ones. They are all a lot better than they get credit for. Most of those well-known ones are frauds. Well, maybe not frauds, but you know where I'm coming from."

Now he's getting away from the list and into editorial territory. But we're still waiting for the green to clear on the hole ahead, and it doesn't take Barad long to get his focus back.

"So we went to dinner at Capital Grille, then we didn't even bother to go out for drinks because you know where I'm off to on Sunday: *OAKMONT, BABY!* So we played Oakmont on Sunday—and man, I'm hitting it sideways off the tee. I have no idea where it is going. Sometimes it is left, sometimes it is right. But I'm rolling them in from everywhere. The caddy just says, 'Die it here,' and I'd hit that putt and it would go in. The guys I was playing with said they'd never seen putting like that. And the greens...the *greens.* They are stimping like fifteen. They were faster than the U.S. fucking Open. Like putting on pavement. Incredible—*incredible!*

"So we finish at one, and the guys in my group ask if I want to catch the second half of the Steelers game. But I told them I didn't care, that I'd rather head home, so I went to the airport and flew back to Toronto. Oakmont was great—GREAT, I tell you. Maybe the *best ever.* I'm thinking that might just be the case."

And that's all in one breath. It's sometimes surprising he doesn't pass out from his exuberance. But that's also probably exactly what made him good at hyping punk rock shows in his youth and what makes him better still at putting together the Police's reunion tour.

Of course, Barad does have a pedigree that can't be acquired, regardless of how much money one has. Though he only holds three memberships—the National in Toronto, Olympia Fields in Chicago, and Atlantic City Country Club in New Jersey—Barad has found his way onto almost all of the world's best. That's either because his contacts in the music industry—the people who run or own stadiums and arenas—are only too pleased to provide a kind word that opens the gates to the best golf in North America, or because members of these clubs are only too anxious to invite the chatty and amiable Barad for a match in return for the chance to meet Mick and Keith.

"I have a certain currency that is useful," he says.

His connections have amazed even the toppermost of the pop-permost.

"Irving said I was the most connected golf guy in North America," Barad says, referring to an occasional golfing buddy, Van Halen manager and music legend Irving Azoff, before adding, "but Irving's a buddy, so maybe he's just saying that."

And even as sales of compact discs drop amid widespread sharing of music over the Internet, people still want to get access to the best seats for the best shows. And there's no one better equipped than Barad to provide them.

Throughout it all—the fancy golf courses, the massive stadium shows, the jets, and the jet-set lifestyle—Barad says his goal was to never grow up. "I still consider myself, in many ways, an adolescent," he says. "I'm still a teenager at heart."

A tired and road-weary teenager, apparently, because by the seventeenth hole, a downhill par-4 that winds to the left, Barad asks if there are any more questions.

"I'm bankrupt," he says. "I got nothing more."

"Morally, or mentally?" I ask.

Barad just grins.

Reason Number 226 to love Scarboro Golf and Country Club: it has a nineteenth hole.

And not just any short betting hole. Nope. This one is a nasty 135-yard one-shot bastard with a green that runs downhill as fast as a rabbit with sore feet.

Famed Mexican-American swashbuckler Lee Trevino once spoke about a particularly difficult course as having greens that were like "stopping a 5-iron on the hood of a car." He was actually recalling a round at the TPC at Sawgrass, but he could have just as easily been speaking about Scarboro's nineteenth. Its difficulty is doubled by the fact it is played in front of the clubhouse's veranda, which is inevitably packed with people enjoying a post-round beverage or three.

To Barad, this odd feature just adds to the allure of the course. It doesn't hurt that he smacks a low 7-iron just short of the green and chips up for par, while I hood a 9-iron and rattle it off the nearby paved cart path, narrowly avoiding a couple of older gents watching nearby, en route to writing down an "X" on my card. Barad, despite shooting 46 on the front, cards an 86 overall. I come in with an 81.

Still red-faced from the embarrassment of my wonderfully awful final shot, I pull my hat a touch lower and head to the patio for a quick pint, knowing that, regardless of how badly struck the ball was, everyone will have seen a worse shot. It is a truism of golf, and one of the great facets of the game.

Settling in on the patio of Scarboro's remarkably picturesque clubhouse, Barad sits down and begins pontificating about the state of his industry. Battered and bloodied by downloading of music from the Internet and changes to its business model, the music business is in a distinct state of transition, and Barad, Live Nation, and TNA are taking front-row-centre seats as the carnage settles. Despite the industry's plight, fans, many of whom aren't willing to drop $15 for a CD, are still willing to kick out $200 for Madonna or U2 tickets. With the company's stable of heritage acts and superstars, Barad continues to book the biggest bands in the world. He's just helped line up a tour for the revamped Van Halen (and, you guessed it, golf is part of that equation for Barad as well), and at fifty he can still appear genuinely excited about the business's possibilities.

With the signing of Madonna to a deal with Live Nation worth more than $120 million, it appears Barad could be central to the emergence of a newly structured music industry.

"I think there's going to be some new blood, for sure," he says, sipping on his beer. "The model is broken and bands are going to take more control. The future is someone like us buying all-encompassing rights. You'd take over all aspects of their career. You'd do the record, managing, some publishing and merchandising, and their television. There's still a model for records that sell—especially the download business.

"Are we capable of doing all those things? Sure we are. Cohl put out the DVD for the Stones's *Four Flicks*. He just did a distribution deal. He did it all. There are models that work. But why are you paying for some big record company's overhead? Sure, there are record companies that are going to try to get into the promoting business as well. It is easier for us to do what they do than for a record company to get into the promotion business. They've tried it—it didn't work."

While he's part of the musical revolution, at least in the backrooms anyway, Barad will still keep hitting the links, using his unusual personality and remarkable connections to play the best the game has to offer.

After all, and with apologies to the Rolling Stones, it's only golf, but Barad likes it.

"I don't want to go to a gym or work with a trainer. I can't be bothered. What I want to do is walk around a course a few dozen times a year with a twenty-five-pound bag on my back. I want to play golf and carry my clubs. I'll say this—golf is the cocaine for the new millennium."

CHAPTER 15

Peter Viner
Escaping the Glare

"I think they need to look at their own lives before they use that pen.
I'm sure a lot of those guys in the media don't have perfect lives."

—John Daly

THERE'S A DELICATE AND nebulous protocol that accompanies playing golf with your boss. Do you let him win? Do you try to win to show him your mettle? Do you demonstrate your focus by staying cool at all times, or your passion through a mild display of agitation at a bad shot?

Maybe the best bet is not to play with the boss at all. But what if you end up teeing it up with your boss's boss's boss? Now, *that* takes a certain degree of delicacy and diplomacy. Sort of like Henry Kissinger in China, except armed with a set of Titleist blades. You get the picture.

This is why I've got a mild case of anxiety as I drive up the lane, past the driving range and clubhouse, and into the gravel parking lot of Mad River Golf Club just south of Collingwood, Ontario, to meet with Peter Viner.

As a columnist at the *National Post*, I have never directly dealt with Viner. He was always several well-spaced rungs up the food chain in the CanWest Global media empire from my role as a filler of white space between the paper's ads. But for a time, particularly when I was writing my golf and business series, he was the publisher.

He'd often stride past my veal-fattening pen to ask about whom I'd teed it up with as of late. Then he'd goodnaturedly chastise me for using the paper's money to play golf and be off in an instant for whatever meeting he was expected at.

Four years later, I approached Viner about playing golf with me. By this time, his stint at the *Post* was long in the past; he had been elevated to the role of CEO of CanWest MediaWorks, the holding company that controls the media empire's sixty-five newspapers, a couple of television networks, specialty TV channels, and a bunch of Internet properties. I'd switched roles as well, now holding down a slot as the paper's underappreciated golf columnist. Asking Viner to take an afternoon away from conquering the Canadian media landscape to play golf was the equivalent of a junior staffer in the dusty backrooms of some obscure ministry dialling up the prime minister and inquiring about whether he'd be up for a game and a few beers. In other words, it was unlikely.

For a while, I couldn't get Viner to actually just say no to the round. The problem was he didn't say yes, either. Through a dozen emails, we bounced possible times and dates back and forth, with Viner finally agreeing to play, but always unable to nail down a spot on his calendar. Finally, he picked a day for our game and... promptly announced his retirement from CanWest after almost three decades of working for the company. Of course, he still has the home phone number of Leonard Asper, the CEO of CanWest, and I still write a column for the paper, so there's always the need for some degree of sophisticated delicacy in our game.

"I'm not a good golfer," he told me by email. I assured him it didn't matter. He wasn't heading out on the PGA Tour, just hacking it about with me and talking about his role in the rise of the CanWest juggernaut.

I meet Viner in the club's pro shop. Now over sixty, Viner presents an air of self-confidence as soon as you meet him. It likely comes from being a salesman for a large part of his career. He's dressed casually in a yellow golf shirt, khaki pants, and a blue ball cap. He extends his hand and suggests we head to the range, where he'll introduce me to our playing partners for the day.

It turns out it'll be all CanWest all the time, as we're joined by two of Viner's longtime pals from the television side of the business: Doug Bonar, a former big muckety-muck in broadcast technology, and Ken Johnson, who ran sales on the television side before sliding ratings led to a 2005 purge. After the group smacks a few on the range in the late summer heat, and once everyone is sufficiently dripping with sweat, we proceed across the laneway that leads to the first tee.

The first hole, which slides casually towards out-of-bounds on the right, with the fairway flanked by high golden fescue on the left, pretty much sets the tone for the game. Bonar hits a high slice that lands in the left rough, while Johnson, sporting a bad back that forces him to lash at the ball with his arms as opposed to turning his shoulders, hits a worm burner that finds the fescue. Viner steps up to the tee. The hole isn't overly long—only 486 yards—and Viner doesn't seem too worried, despite the unfortunate results of those playing in front of him.

He fiddles with his stance, waggles the club a couple of times, and takes a slow, loose cut at the ball. His swing collapses at the top, with the club almost falling on Viner's shoulders, but he manages to right it on the way down. The ball takes off down the centre of the fairway.

"Oh, don't go too far that way, Pete," Viner says aloud as his ball slices to the right. It eventually finds the safe ground of the fairway, 220 yards from the tee. I follow with a hybrid that lands in front of Viner's ball and rolls to the right edge of the short grass.

Viner hits a mid-iron lay-up, but pushes the ball too far to the right and finds his view of the green partially obscured by a large tree. My second shot from the fairway with my trusty hybrid soars high and lands on the front of the green. Our playing partners struggle along behind us, but they catch up a couple of shots later and we reconvene on the first green. Perched at the crest of a hill, the hole provides a panoramic vision of the surrounding landscape and golf course. Viner chips from off the green, but fails to make the putt for par. Not that it seems to bother him. Retirement—or at least cutting back his hours to a couple of days a week—seems to agree with him, I point out.

"I've been working in the television business for a long time," he says, plunking his wedge and putter in his bag on the back of the cart before sitting down. "I have some things I want to do before I can't do them anymore. As my wife says, the cannibals were circling, and I wanted to get out before the water came to a boil."

Since escaping the media hordes, Viner has kept himself distracted by, among other things, playing golf at Mad River. Not that Mad River is exactly a relaxing course. Living up to its name, it has plenty of frustrating, confounding, and downright annoying elements, like the false front on the second green, a putting surface that's about as large as a quarter, or the fourth, which is about as tight as a pair of skinny jeans on John Daly after his fourth Big Mac and twentieth Diet Coke.

The course was the creation of Bob Cupp, who had formerly worked for Jack Nicklaus before setting out on his own once the Golden Bear decided to make his design business a family affair. Cupp, a former club pro with a penchant for all things artistic—writing, drawing, and painting—quickly demonstrated a vision for courses with a high degree of strategy that often had quirky, unusual facets that could perplex both the high-handicap player and the scratch player alike.

Mad River, which is hidden among the rolling hills of Creemore, a rural Ontario town not far from Georgian Bay, contains all of Cupp's mad concepts, including postage-stamp greens with slopes that would make a downhill skier envious, fairways that bleed into cavernous bunkers, and hazards that lie hidden like a snake in long grass.

Viner's attraction to the course isn't as much about its layout or design as it is the fact that most of its members paid tens of thousands on an initiation to play the course on weekends only. That means Viner, in his newly retired state, can hack the ball around on weekdays with his wife, Kathie, without worrying that a round will eclipse four hours.

"There's just no one here," he says. "It looks like the place was abandoned sometimes."

Rarely has Viner had a chance to slow down the pace of his life since he entered into the television business in his mid-twenties, when he landed a sales job at the new network created by Global Communications. The network—which was really just a single Toronto station whose signal was beamed throughout southern Ontario—immediately struggled to find both an audience and advertisers willing to fork over cash to a station without viewers. The whole thing collapsed in a matter of months, as millions in losses mounted. Others fled the sinking ship, but Viner stayed on.

Eventually, two investors bailed out the network: Global Ventures Holdings and iwc Communications. Both companies were led by controversial visionaries. Izzy Asper, a lawyer turned politician turned businessman, helmed Global. The other partner in the venture, running iwc, was Allan Slaight, a businessman obsessed with magic, both of the broadcasting and the hocus-pocus kind.

Slaight, who bought 45 per cent of the television network, would later say he had to be absolutely ruthless to be certain the network would survive. How did Viner avoid the hatchet in such an environment? I ask as we search for my tee shot in the rough to the left of the second fairway.

"I was only twenty-eight when Allan Slaight came and asked why I was still there," says Viner, the brim of his blue ball cap pulled low. "I told him I was there because I was the only one still willing to do the job with everything that had gone on. I told Al that I'd stay on in the role with the condition that if he didn't like what I did, he could fire me at any time, no questions asked."

That must have been a risky play, I point out after we decide my ball is lost forever. I hit a wedge onto the right fringe of the bunker and Viner continues.

"I figured if it worked, I'd dine out on it forever, and if it didn't...well, oh well. Who the hell else was going to make me a sales director at a television network at twenty-eight otherwise? Eventually, he made me vp."

Though he's sitting pretty after hitting a strong tee shot down the middle, Viner's approach shot is fat, with sod flying nearly as far as the ball itself. His third is hardly better, catching the slippery front edge of the green and trickling down the front until it comes to rest twenty yards in front of the hole. He sighs and chips the ball again with more force. He has better luck this time, and the ball comes to rest ten feet to the left of the flag. He quickly walks up and marks it with a coin, perhaps worried that gravity will somehow take hold and deposit it once more on the fairway.

I'll give Viner credit. Aside from an "ah, damn," as the ball rolls off the green, he's hardly flustered by the failed execution. His ability to stay calm as all hell breaks loose around him probably goes a long way towards explaining his lengthy stint at CanWest, an organization seemingly built on turmoil and led by Asper, a chain-smoking deal-maker from Winnipeg who was bold, brash, relentless, and hugely successful.

Viner's rise mirrored that of the network itself. Asper eventually bought out Slaight and built the network with U.S. television programs and hard sales pitches. Though the two men could not have had more diverse personalities, Viner found his greatest supporter in Asper.

"He was a one-off," says Viner after finding the green of the par-3 third with an iron approach. "They won't make another one like him, but that can be said of others—guys like Conrad Black and Ted Rogers. I think Izzy was different, where some of those guys are just obsessed. Izzy was obsessed *and* super smart."

Viner also liked Asper's autocratic rule, which made it entirely clear under whose direction the organization was running.

"With him, you always knew who was running the show," he says, walking off the green after recording his first par, one of only two he'll make on the day. "Izzy used to say to me, 'It is your job to give me advice, Viner, but given what I do, I don't have to take it.'"

We play a couple of holes without much discussion, largely because Viner struggles with the par-5 fourth hole—not surprising, given that its fairway is about as wide as a bowling lane. The fifth isn't much better, as he makes double bogey while I make my second birdie of the day.

By the time we reach the par-4 sixth, a sporty, short hole that is reachable with a blast down the middle, our conversation returns to Viner's career. Happy with his performance in Toronto, in 1980 Asper sent Viner to Vancouver to fix CKVU-TV, a station in which CanWest owned a stake. By all accounts, Viner was responsible for a startling transition, sharpening the station's focus while CanWest battled to gain control. Eventually, Viner came to loggerheads with Asper's ownership partner and found himself out on the street, literally. Being fired was something Viner didn't expect, but Asper told him it would only be a matter of time before CanWest owned the station outright.

"Izzy said stay around for six months, hang out at the beach, and we'll figure this thing out," he says. "But I just couldn't do that."

The 270-yard sixth has the appearance of an easy hole. Golfers can be easily lulled into a false sense of security because, aside from a tree down the left and some deep bunkers, there's little keeping them from a good score. But its miniscule green, with a deep swale that propels all but the best shots off the back and into wispy fescue, is the great equalizer.

My tee shot with my driver flies over the green, coming to rest in knee-deep grass. Viner's shot, with an iron, sits near a large oak on the left side of the fairway. While I recover and make par, Viner's approach comes up short and rolls back onto the fairway in front of the green. Two putts later, he strides back to our cart to record a bogey to my par.

Unwilling to wait for Asper's promise of a new job, Viner left CanWest and took over as the top executive in charge of Telemedia's eighteen radio properties in Toronto. It wasn't long before he was back in the fold, first to run its four western television stations and then Australia's Network Ten. The latter network was struggling through a receivership when, in 1990, Viner was sent to investigate what opportunities there might be for CanWest.

"The CEO had a jet and his own chauffeur, even though the place was bleeding money," Viner says. "It wasn't hard to figure out what needed to be done."

Three of four tee shots find the green on the downhill par-3 seventh, a hole with a deceptive green that falls off steeply at the back. We drive down the hill, and park the cart, all the while talking about Viner's trip Down Under.

Asper invested in Ten and put Viner in charge of the project. The new assignment worked well for him. Even though he took over more than a decade ago, he is animated when he talks about the station. Asper left him alone to rectify the problems, he says.

"Izzy was a deal-maker, not an operator. The results were good very quickly, so there was no micromanaging going on."

Viner's first putt from the back of the green slows too quickly, leaving him a lengthy par attempt that fails to find the bottom of the cup. He flips the ball into his hand and walks back to the cart.

Ten became a huge turnaround success, but Viner grew restless and wanted to move on to something new.

"The problem with Australia is there was nowhere to go and I was out of party tricks," he says. He hits a slicing drive off the eighth tee that finds the fairway, about 150 yards from the green. "Izzy called up and said, 'Can you come to Winnipeg and help get the boys ready to take over the company?' He said he was going to retire—which was a lot of BS, of course."

Like the heads of most family businesses, Izzy Asper knew there would come a time in the not-so-distant future when he wouldn't be around to run the media empire he'd forged on the strength of his personality, determination, and ability to recognize a good deal. He had three children: Gail, David, and Leonard. All three were lawyers, and Asper wanted Viner to show the two boys the ropes of the television business. He made Viner CEO of CanWest Global and said he was preparing to retire.

"He said he was getting ready to turn the company over to them," Viner says, lowering his sunglasses as we drive into the sun on the ninth hole. "Of course, that wasn't exactly the case. At the time, he said the boys would never run CanWest, but it was my job to make them better owners."

It turned out the sales pitch was better than the actual deal. Though he was nearing seventy, Asper wasn't prepared to disengage from the media giant he'd created. And Viner, whose expertise was in operations, was uncomfortable in Asper's world of smoky boardrooms full of deal-makers.

"Izzy's idea of a meeting was to sit around a table with a bunch of lawyers and financial engineers and dream up deals. That just wasn't me."

Two years after landing in Winnipeg, Viner was sent back to Toronto as the company's vice-chair, a position without a specific role or purpose.

We park our cart near Mad River's clubhouse, a building styled like a country home in keeping with the club's rustic nature. We head into the open dining room to refill bottles of water and grab some sandwiches.

"I was considering my next act when we bought the newspapers from Hollinger," he says, walking down the steps to our cart.

After spending $2.2 billion to acquire a large part of Conrad Black's media portfolio in 2000, the Aspers found their newly minted flagship paper—the *National Post*—hemorrhaging millions each month with no end in sight. Assured he could count on his honest assessment of the paper, Izzy turned again to Viner.

"He really wanted me to go and try to save the *Post*," says Viner between bites of a sandwich on the tenth hole, a short par-4 with a raised green tucked in a hillside over a marshy hazard.

The fact that Viner had no experience in the print world wasn't viewed as a shortcoming, because at the time neither did the Aspers. He turned out to be a quick study.

"I loved the people, and since I'd fixed problems with Izzy my entire career, I think he felt it just made sense," Viner says, sipping from a bottle of water. He takes off his sunglasses and continues, "To a lot of people, running newspapers and running television stations looks the same, but it isn't. They aren't even close to being similar."

We play out the hole, with Viner lipping out a long putt, resigning himself to a bogey, and he drives the cart to the par-3 eleventh, a relatively plain one-shot hole with a green dissected by a nasty ridge-line. Viner's tee shot is nearly perfect, coming to rest pin-high, eight feet to the right of the cup.

Did he enjoy the *Post*? I ask.

"It was an amazing experience," he says, stopping the cart near the green. "There was so much to learn, and you don't usually get that experience at the stage of your career that I was in. It was like going back to university."

By 2003, Viner had reached a crossroads at the paper. The Aspers had installed Rick Camilleri, a former music industry executive, as the head of its media operations. Viner makes it clear he had little time for Camilleri.

"He wasn't a leader," Viner says as we ride down the hill on the par-3 fourteenth. "His idea of leadership was to go into his office and close the door behind him."

We walk down a slope towards the large green that rolls from the fairway, building to a back edge situated in front of a creek. While Johnson's ball finds the expansive putting surface, Bonar, Viner, and I are left with chips to a tricky pin tucked in the far back corner. None of the three finesse shots works out, but once we're all lining up putts I ask why Camilleri got the job. Why, if he didn't display leadership, would the Aspers trust him with part of their media empire?

At once, all three answer: "No comment."

I laugh. The lack of discussion on the matter speaks volumes.

Though Viner was at loggerheads with Camilleri, he still had to determine what should be done with the *National Post*.

"I told them they had two options," he says bluntly, standing in the rough on the par-5 fifteenth with a wood in his hands. "They could either shut it down and pin it on Black or be prepared for ten years of losses."

How did the Aspers take the news?

"David wanted to [keep it running], Leonard less so," he replies. In the end, with the loss cut to millions—as opposed to tens of millions—the Aspers decided to keep the paper open. Viner was shuffled off to run a nascent radio station business for CanWest, but in practice his career with the company appeared finished.

Our round ends abruptly on the fifteenth hole after my drive sails inside the right tree line and comes to rest on the fairway; a thunderclap rings out through the valley and lightning strikes close enough to the south to make me quickly toss my driver into the bag. As we proceed down the hill, acorn-sized raindrops begin hammering the ground. We make a hasty run for the parking lot—at least as hasty as a slow-moving golf cart will allow—and Peter suggests I follow him back to his home for a post-round respite.

We drive south from Creemore along rolling country roads until we come to Peter's tasteful house perched on the top of the hill overlooking a large pond. By the time we arrive, the rain has retreated and the sun has returned.

We sit down in his living room, joined by his wife, and he brings me a Coke.

I ask him why he didn't retire after the end of his tenure at the *Post*. Viner says that was his intent. He was "winding it down," especially after the death of Izzy Asper in October 2003. At the same time, CanWest's television side was struggling and the newspaper operation was not running smoothly, despite a planned ipo to take that part of the business onto the markets as an income trust.

"Leonard called and said, 'We're going to make a management change, and we'd like you to come in and run the Canadian operations,'" says Viner, leaning back on his couch. "They were about to put it into trust and they didn't want to make the move after doing that."

I ask Viner if he thinks that being the children of such a successful figure puts too much pressure on David and Leonard Asper. He nods.

"The kids are in a tough position," he says. "If you do well, it is because the old man set it up that way. If you don't, it is because you didn't have the skills or talent. The fact of the matter is Izzy Asper, Ted Rogers, and Conrad Black are one-offs. You don't see their type all that often. You look at the Asper kids on paper, and they are clearly three smart kids, all with law degrees. Any parent would consider them successful. But did they start a billion-dollar corporation from scratch? No."

Viner took over and ran the IPO. He also dropped some of Camilleri's more ambitious concepts, like *Dose*, the free youth-oriented magazine launched just prior to taking over the role. But the federal government's decision to tax income trusts in October 2006 limited the options available to the company, and by 2007 the plan was to take CanWest MediaWorks back as a private business.

"I was going to leave in June, but they were going to take the company private and didn't want my announcement to complicate that," Viner says. "About six months before my contract was over, Len said would I extend it and I said no. I have things I want to do."

"And the cannibals were circling?" I ask.

Viner laughs.

"I think I was keeping them at bay," he jokes as I thank him for his hospitality and head to the door.

Maybe the kettle hadn't heated up yet, or maybe the flesh-eaters were hiding in the bushes. But if there's anything Viner learned in his three decades in the dog-eat-dog world of media, it is that it's always better to exit on your own terms, as opposed to being chased out the door while looking over your shoulder.

CHAPTER 16

Stephen Bebis
The Salesman

"By all means, screw their women and drink their booze, but never write one word about their bloody awful golf courses."

—Henry Longhurst, journalist

THERE'S NO OTHER WAY to describe it: Magna Golf Club is ostentatious. The course is perched vibrantly out of the grasp of all but the lucky few, those fortunate enough to have six figures' worth of disposable cash to drop down to play golf. Until recently, when its position was usurped by a couple of even more private upstart clubs, Magna held the crown as the most expensive to join in the country.

And it shows—from the gates that guard the entrance to the driveway that winds its way up between holes, leading to the entrance of the massive clubhouse. It costs more than $13,000 annually to belong, and even at that rate rumour has it the club loses money. That's not particularly surprising once you wander into the clubhouse—a misnomer if there ever was one. There's nothing particularly clubby or intimate about it. It is more akin to a grand European estate home, with high ceilings and an incredible main dining room buttressed by giant hearths. There's no two ways about it—Magna's clubhouse is a testament to wealth, power, and influence.

All this is to be expected, considering the club was created by auto parts baron Frank Stronach, a man not known for his subtle gestures. Over many decades, Stronach, who started in the tool-and-die business, built an auto parts empire in Aurora, Ontario, a town about a forty-five-minute drive north of Toronto. His is a classic Horatio Alger story of the boy who immigrated to Canada, dreamed big dreams, and ended up running a $20 billion business that employs thousands.

Of course, Stronach is also known for the particular brand of capitalism that has led to his astounding wealth. He made $33 million one year, and when his detractors called it excessive, he replied that he should have been paid more. He's the emperor of the Magna kingdom, its corporate headquarters stretching out around the golf course like a gothic village.

Magna is a club that is home to many of Bay Street's most affluent and successful, with a smattering of NHL hockey players—many of whom work out in the club's gym in the off-season—thrown into the mix. Former Maple Leafs right wing Tie Domi plays out of the club—he has, after all, been linked to Stronach's daughter, Belinda—and its fairways are often home to such politicians as former Ontario premier Mike Harris, or Magna board member and former Liberal cabinet minister Ed Lumley.

I pull up to the front of the clubhouse to be met by staff ready to valet-park my car. On this day, as I watch my Ford Focus driven to the lot, I wonder if it'll be lonely among the Ferraris, BMWs, and Jaguars. Maybe there will be a lowly Lexus thrown into the mix, but mine will be the only four-door North American hatchback on the premises.

One of these exotic cars probably belongs to Stephen Bebis, an American by birth, but an entrepreneur who found most of his success north of the forty-ninth parallel. He's my playing partner on an overcast, windy, cool August day. Since we've not selected a spot at the club to meet, I go in search of him.

"Mr. Bebis is in the pro shop," says the attendant as I walk through the doors. Not that I asked. The information was simply volunteered, my identity being confirmed when I checked in with security at the main gates. The intrusive nature of the club's service personnel takes some getting used to, even if one is a regular at a more traditional private golf club. You can hardly walk five feet without someone on the club's staff asking if they can help you with something. Hold your bag, sir? Clean that club, sir? Do you need a towel, sir? After a while, it gets a touch overbearing for my taste— while stopping to grab an apple from a bowl sitting near the locker room, I'm afraid the staff will want to help me with that as well. Help chewing your apple, sir?

Thankfully, before it comes to that I run into Bebis, chatting amiably with the pro shop staff in the lower level of the clubhouse, and we wander out the shop's doors and to our cart. At the driving range while we warm up, Bebis pulls out a brand-new set of Ping golf irons.

"Not even on the market yet," he remarks, his accent giving away his Connecticut upbringing.

Bebis owes much of his success, and a large part of his net worth, to people willing to participate in a pastime that principally involves hitting a little white ball, finding it, and hitting it again, over and over. That's due to Bebis's invention of a chain of big-box retail outlets called, aptly, Golf Town, which he launched in 1999. At the time, hardly anyone expected the concept to fly. After all, naysayers said there would never be enough consumer interest to keep afloat a 21,000-square-foot store full of golf gloves, golf balls, clubs, clothes, and instructional aids.

"People said it would never work because it was a different concept and Canadians would never shop there," says Bebis, handing off his iron to the range attendant to have its grooves cleaned. "And I'd heard that before starting Golf Town. But it was a gamble. It was a huge part of my net worth. My wife and I had bought a small house, drove a plain car, and worked seven days a week to make it work."

Bebis had faced his share of detractors before, he says, hopping into our cart and touring down around the clubhouse to the first tee. When he left the U.S. to come to Canada, he owned little aside from some big ideas. He'd worked at The Home Depot for the better part of the 1980s before coming north to try to launch the concept—a chain of big-box home-improvement stores—here. Under the Aikenheads banner, the new chain, backed by the financial power of Molson Companies, utilized the best of what Home Depot offered south of the border. They say that imitation is the sincerest form of flattery, and that must be the case because Aikenheads so closely approximated The Home Depot that Bebis's former bosses bought it. Though he'd been in Canada for almost a decade, Bebis returned to the U.S. (to Florida, to be exact) and joined a chain of sports equipment franchises. When that ended in 1998, he became determined to return to Canada.

"I called Mickey Cohen, who was my boss at Molson when I was with Home Depot, and said I wanted to come back to Toronto," Bebis says as we search for his tee shot in the rough to the right off the first fairway. "I loved Canada and I missed it. All my friends were here, as were my wife's friends. We loved the diversity—we loved it. I told him that if he saw any opportunities to please let me know."

Cohen told Bebis to go to Minneapolis and take a look at a store called Golf Galaxy, which was to golf what Victoria's Secret is to lingerie. It was massive and contained all the latest and greatest in golf gear. "I went to see it and I liked it. We took their idea and changed it and modified it for the Canadian market. We decided to build a store that we would like to shop at as golfers. So that's what we did."

Bebis pauses and searches his bag for his laser rangefinder before teeing off on the second hole, a 157-yard par-3 over a large pond. When he can't find it, he grabs his cellphone and dials Magna's pro shop, asking if the valet can grab his rangefinder out of his car. Oh, the wonders of the full-service club. Not knowing the exact yardage doesn't hurt Bebis's shot, which lands just right of the pin and runs down a slight slope to the front of the green. Two putts later, he's made par—not bad for a man who didn't play the game until 1993.

The Golf Galaxy concept appealed to Bebis because he was in the throes of the game at that point, as a new player willing to try anything new to improve. He understood the lure of new golf gear and the way shiny new clubs can hypnotize avid players the way head-lights do deer, leaving them more than willing to fork over their cash in exchange for the promise of shaving a stroke off their handicaps.

By 1998, Bebis was fully involved in developing the idea, working with partner Murray Bozniak to find financing. The pair worked a seemingly endless number of hours, Bebis explains, parking our cart on the wide third fairway.

"We put everything we had into it," he says, "but we found time to play golf. We played at the old Gormley Green—you know, the public course that became Station Creek. We played first off at 6:30 in the morning, and had to play fast because we had to be back at work by 9:30. The great thing was that if you played enough rounds there, you got a break on your green fees."

There's a palpable sense of irony as we sit in the middle of a club whose membership consists of multimillionaires and the Golf Town founder is discussing how to save five bucks by becoming a frequent player at a downmarket public course. But it has been my experience that for many entrepreneurs, the struggle to create their vision is almost as invigorating to them as seeing its eventual success. That appears to be the case, as Bebis regales me with tales of the early days of Golf Town for most of the front nine. He often speaks passion-ately about the industry and retailing in general, especially how it differs between Canada and the U.S.

Even though he was determined to make the concept of a big-box golf store work, it was not immediately embraced. Bebis's timing was poor. He was out pounding the pavement trying to con-vince investors to pour money into a retail concept at the same time as the dot-com bubble was puffing up like an overinflated balloon. He knocked on more than thirty doors without garnering any inter-est, before the investment wing of insurance giant Manulife agreed to put some cash into the venture.

With no one around us on the course, Bebis stops the cart next to the tee box of the seventh hole, a par-5 with bunkers protecting a fall-off area on the right side and thick forest on the left.

"All I was asked the whole time I was trying to raise money was what our Internet strategy was," he says. "One guy, honest to goodness, told us our concept was outdated because retail wouldn't exist in ten years. It was so crazy, we thought maybe we should go out and hire an Internet strategist or consultant to tell us what we should do."

Bebis grabs his driver, wanders up to the tee, and smacks a low cut that comes to rest just above the right bunkers.

"Thank God we didn't do that," he says, smiling. "Those guys are all out of business now."

Though he was fascinated by the game when he launched Golf Town, Bebis wasn't much more than a weekend hack when it came to his abilities. He started as a 36 handicap—the maximum allowable in the rules of golf, though lots of people don't even play that well—but being ambitious and having a tolerance for hard work, Bebis managed to cut down a stroke or two a year. He's now a 15 handicap who plays relatively frequently.

"You never want to embarrass yourself," he says. "You want to give some indication you can play."

The end result is that Bebis *isn't* embarrassing himself on the course—and his choice in golf courses is only bound to add to the appeal for anyone lucky enough to be invited out with him.

Magna's golf course is as big and bold as its surroundings. The scale is massive—large rolling hills, wide fairways, huge bunkers, and greens that run as fast as Ben Johnson on steroids. With a maintenance budget that eclipses the GDP of many small African nations, Magna always appears freshly scrubbed. It is as if the grounds crew regularly get down on their hands and knees to inspect each individual blade of grass for fear one might be out of place. And I can't say for certain they don't.

Golf is supposed to be a game that resides comfortably within its natural environment. There's nothing that feels natural on this course at all. It all seems like someone's contrived notion of how a golf course would appear if you had an unlimited budget—which is practically the case. But to those not looking to critique its nuances, it appears perfect.

The opening holes run alongside Stronach's compound, which functions as a corporate headquarters, its large, grey buildings looming over the second and third holes. The course changes slightly and becomes more expansive as it moves into an area of newly constructed multimillion-dollar homes before heading back to the clubhouse at the turn. From there, its sprawling fairways run over rising hills, plunging to the final holes in a low-lying area, before emerging in front of the balcony of the club's palatial headquarters.

The course was designed by Toronto's Doug Carrick, a quiet, unassuming man whose personality contrasts drastically with the exacting nature of his designs, where strategic options must be carefully examined on almost every shot. Magna was Carrick's second course for Stronach's auto empire, following an earlier project in Austria that has hosted several European Tour events. It is an odd pairing—Stronach's bombast and bluster versus Carrick's shy, almost aloof, nature. The arrangement between the auto magnate and the golf architect is made all the stranger by the fact that Stronach doesn't even play golf, spending more of his time with his racehorses at the track. He's a regular patron of the club's dining room, so much so the Caesar salad retains his name, but he hardly ever sets foot on the club's fairways. Nor, apparently, does Belinda, his daughter and hand-picked successor. However, his mark is left on the course's scorecard—with each hole named for one of his horses. Stronach may not partake in his golf playground, but its success in attracting some of the richest Canadians as members surely strokes his ego.

The course, which opened in 2000, is a great attraction for Bebis's clients, he admits. While he plays golf at Magna on weekdays with customers and suppliers, his personal time is more likely restricted to playing Bigwin Island Golf Club (another exceptional Carrick design), which rests next to his cottage a few hours north of Toronto.

Many who watched Golf Town open in 1999 would be surprised to see it not only operating, but expanding and growing. Bebis is well aware of this, and when I tell him at the turn that I was among those who were skeptical, he doesn't blink.

"Our competitors said we wouldn't last," he explains. "The rumours spread right away that we were going out of business."

As we tackle the par-5 twelfth, where Bebis records a fine par after yanking his tee shot into the fescue short of the fairway bunker, he explains that Golf Town tapped into the game's popularity, which grew after Tiger Woods erupted onto the international scene in 1997. Woods became the new Michael Jordan—the world's most famous athlete—and Bebis understood the game of golf would expand its player base from the country club warriors who had been its foundation to include more casual participants. The one thing they all had in common? They would all need equipment, and many would pay for the best in the hope it would magically improve their games. When that failed, they'd simply ante up for another $500 driver designed to correct their slice.

"This is a game," he starts. "This is a hobby and people spend their money accordingly. No one needs to golf, but it is a passionate sport. If you look at really wealthy guys who are passionate about sailing, they spend millions on their boats and more on a crew. They sail all over the world. They do crazy things. They hire guides and climb Mount Everest. They spend tons doing it. Golf? You buy a putter. When you think of it that way, golf is not that crazy."

Not that crazy, indeed, especially when you consider the alternatives.

"Oh, exactly," Bebis says. "A friend of mine has two Ferraris. He has a racing team and races all over North America. It is costing him big bucks. Another friend has a yacht. It costs him $1 million per year to maintain it. Everyone has their deal. Golf is the deal for a lot of others."

Bebis also brought a decidedly American approach to customer service and management. This has led some to find him arrogant, a characterization that Bebis shrugs away when I raise it as we come off the fourteenth green. His focus was always on bringing a unique degree of touch, to borrow a favourite term of the industry, to his customers.

"I told people when we launched Golf Town that we were going to make love to our customers. They all laughed at me—but I meant it."

The remainder of our round is played in a friendly fashion, like two old colleagues getting together for eighteen holes and a couple of beers. We gossip about the industry, with Bebis asking questions and telling stories about his decade in the golf business. Of course, with his connections in the business he's also gone through the rite of passage that seems to be the preserve of ultra-successful execs: he's played with Tiger.

"Oh yeah, I played with him in Orlando at a Nike event," Bebis says following a birdie on the seventeenth. "We got three holes with him. He was charming and friendly. It was called 'A Day with Tiger.' He came up and teed up my ball for me. He worked like a teaching pro, talking about our swings. On one of the par-5s, it took me two shots to get to his tee ball. On another, I had a chip and he came over and asked me about what I was going to do, where I wanted to land the ball, and where I wanted it to finish. He told me I was on the right track, and the chip finished about a foot from the hole. 'Great chip,' he said. I mean, Tiger Woods saying you've made a great chip—how good is that?"

Good indeed, as is Bebis's game on a windy, overcast day. Flying around in a golf cart, and never encountering another group during our round, we finish in just under three hours, with Bebis carding an 83 to my 75.

We head to the locker room after the round so Bebis can drop off his golf jacket and we both can tidy up before heading to the dining room. While handing his shoes off to the attendant for cleaning, Bebis runs into Kris Draper of the Detroit Red Wings, half-dressed, apparently recently emerged from a shower.

It always stuns me that business people—many of whom are rich enough to own their own sports franchises and have had no small degree of success themselves—get so slobbery over professional athletes. Bebis quickly introduces me to Draper—whom I recognize only in passing—and then attempts, in an awkward fashion, to engage the muscular thirtysomething centre in a discussion. Bebis mentions they've met on a handful of occasions, but it is clear that Draper has no recollection of those encounters and lets the conversation die quickly.

We wander up to the dining room, where Bebis asks the staff if, at 11:30, it is too early to have lunch. No one is certain, but given the six-figure initiation fee, I'm not surprised when the waitress tells us we can order whatever we'd like.

Bebis can afford it. His big-box gamble struck gold. It turns out that people really do think it is easier to buy expensive golf equipment than to hit the range and really learn to play. The first stores made $16 million in revenue within a year of opening, but by 2004 the company was making $166 million in sales, and raking in $17 million in profit. Golf Town had grown to include twenty-one stores, and Bebis had big plans. In order to fulfill those plans, he needed more money. The next step was clear—to head onto the public markets.

"How does a small company of $200 million go public?" he asks as our omelettes arrive. "To go public, we wouldn't have been on the radar screen; there would have been a lack of liquidity on the stock. I don't even know whether we'd have gotten on the TSX."

Instead, he focused on turning Golf Town into an income trust, raising $102 million in the process.

"And as a trust we could easily make acquisitions. We were selling at a high multiple, so we could raise money and raise debt. We could make accretive transactions. Ultimately, we made the right decision. If you bought it when we went public in 2004, you've had a return of over 30 per cent per year. It is hard to beat that in any investment in the past couple of years."

Who'd have thought there was so much money in selling golf drivers at the retail level? No one—which is why Bebis ended up stealing a large hunk of the Canadian market. The only problem was, Bebis explains between bites of his omelette, "after that the gates opened and everyone wanted to become a trust."

And thus, two years after Bebis went to the public markets, the federal Conservative government turned on Golf Town. Well, not just Bebis's company, but all income trusts in Canada, companies that essentially avoided paying taxes by giving away their profits through disbursements.

"I was in shock," he says, putting down his fork. "We were preparing to make an acquisition—and it just shut us right down. I called my banker and just told him that was it. I was very angry at the Conservatives for a very long time. They probably made the right decision going forward, especially with BCE and Telus looking to become trusts. But we spent a lot of time and effort to go public. To say they were going to pull it from us was unfair. They should have given us ten years or grandfathered it in.

"The banks were looking at it. That's what scared them. But why hurt a little guy like me?"

The government decision caught Bebis in a catch 22. He wanted to expand the chain, but downward pressure on the company's income trust units all but eliminated that option. Just a week before our game, the situation changed again, when the pension fund of the Ontario Municipal Employees Retirement System found the fairway with a $214 million acquisition offer. It was too good for Bebis to refuse—and Golf Town suddenly had new owners.

Would he be in the situation if the markets hadn't turned suddenly sour following the government's decision?

"It is hard to say—a what if, could if. We didn't have any plans to sell until OMERS knocked on the door."

As he wipes his face with a Magna-branded napkin, Bebis makes it clear that he's not going anywhere. The company's new owners wanted to be certain Bebis would stick around, and he's reinvested some of his proceeds from the sale back into the new company.

"What job could I have where I get to play great golf as part of my occupation?" he asks, a quizzical smile running across his face. "The investors who just bought Golf Town all wanted to know whether I was staying. 'Stephen, what assurances do we have that you're going to stick to this?' I told them, 'At what other job can I play at Pebble Beach with Callaway or in Mexico with TaylorMade? What other job lets me do that?'"

None that I can think of, which is why Stephen Bebis will likely be holding Golf Town board meetings on courses for years to come.

CHAPTER 17

Thomas McBroom
The Architecture of Business

"Golf architecture is the art and science of designing and building golf courses, and it involves much knowledge of landscape, soils, grasses, water drainage, engineering, and sometimes—I feel—black magic."

—Alistair Cooke, journalist

"Twenty years ago, people weren't aware of [golf design] as a profession.... Now the first question in the marketing is, 'Who designed this course?'"

—Tom Doak, golf architect

DO YOU SEE HIM?

That guy walking down the fairway in front of you at your next game, the one with the smooth, flowing swing, who sort of ambles along, always chatting and appearing to be having a good time, the one who flew in on the private jet or parked his BMW in the parking lot before grabbing his clubs and heading to the men's locker room.

There's a good chance that, if the club you're playing is in Canada and is worth the green fee you paid, the lanky chap with the slightly shaggy grey hair, one Tom McBroom, designed it. Golf is his business and his obsession. He just doesn't create playing fields for the game, he also craves it, playing more than four dozen times this summer alone—a lot for a guy so busy.

He is at the top of a profession that doesn't sound like it should be a profession at all. Even a child with a pencil can draw a golf hole. Pretty much every Sunday-morning hacker has said to himself, "I could do this" while double-bogeying the opening hole. After all, how hard can it be to turn a fine piece of property into a stunning golf retreat, full of dangerously placed bunkers, greens that run like ice on a freshly surfaced rink on a cool January day, and hazards that make you certain you'll be reaching for another Pro V1 soon enough?

Harder than you think, and McBroom, born at the height of the postwar boom in the 1950s, has spent the last two decades demonstrating that there's more to building great golf courses than simply knowing the appropriate type of sand to use in the bunkers. He's so good at it that he's earned more in his career of wandering around muddy fields conceptualizing golf holes than the grand poobahs of most companies make in their lives.

No one would have guessed this result when McBroom started his enterprise. At that point, he was simply viewed as crazy. Off his rocker. A bit thick in the head. However you want to put it, that was the perception most had during his high school and college days, when McBroom announced he was going to pursue a career designing golf courses, he explains, holding an umbrella as the light rain continues to fall as we stand on the first fairway of St. George's Golf and Country Club in Toronto's west end.

"Everyone thought I was always the black sheep, the odd duck in the family, who wanted to be a golf course architect," he says. "My family wasn't even a golf family—Dad was a doctor. He was chief of medicine in Mississauga for thirty years. It was like saying you wanted to be a writer or a painter. It was like, 'Why would you want to do that?'"

McBroom's interest in creating golf holes may not have made a lot of sense to those around him, but he was following his heart.

Now standing on the first hole of the best golf course in the country (Tom's words, not mine, though we agree on the fact), where he's been a member since 1996, wearing a blue shirt emblazoned with "Granite Club" (one of McBroom's fifty-plus golf designs—he can't ever be criticized for missing an opportunity to market his products), one could be forgiven for sizing McBroom up as one of the executives and bluebloods for whom he's spent his career dreaming up and building playgrounds of golf.

All kinds of golf, in fact: Muskoka golf, like Rocky Crest, with its huge expanses of exposed bedrock that accentuate the fairways as a frame does a picture; or parkland golf, like Heron Point near Hamilton, with its rolling fairways and heroic tee shots. Private golf: hidden courses worth millions, built for some of the biggest names in Canadian business—Peter Munk, Paul Desmarais, Jean Monty, and others. Or public golf: courses where someone can plunk down their credit card and test themselves against McBroom's imagination. Or courses created with golf pros—people like Tom Lehman (Lora Bay in Collingwood, Ontario) or Annika Sorenstam (forthcoming, in the West Kootenays region of British Columbia.)

And while he once created courses for the thrill and a small paycheque, he now drives a fancy SUV and commands up to $500,000 for every design.

Walking down the opening hole ("I prefer to walk—I hate carts," he says), bag slung over his shoulder (crested with the logo for Öviinbyrd, another of his designs), McBroom appears to have it all. Articulate. Smart. Wealthy. And with a good swing and a sharp short game to boot. Hell, I'd hire him to run my company if I didn't know he's too busy marking off a bunker somewhere with a can of spray paint and determining whether the fourth hole should feature a tee shot that favours a draw or something that demands a bit of a power cut.

But it wasn't always that easy, he admits as we walk towards the second fairway, after McBroom picks up a five-footer without putting ("I don't make six on opening holes," he explains).

"Oh, I've said for some time that my timing has been a big break," he says, striding briskly to the tee of the massive par-4 second, certainly among the best holes not only in Canada, but the world.

That break may only be a drive east across the city of Toronto from St. George's, but McBroom's first project, Oakridge Golf Club, seems light years away from the opulent clubhouse at St. George's and his current career that has him hanging out with former Masters winner Seve Ballasteros in Florida or jetting to Europe to work on a project for some billionaire. Lost amongst a sea of other public courses that one can buy one's way onto with two twenties and a nod of the head is Oakridge. McBroom designed the course in 1987, and it opened two years later.

For that first course, a sporty layout on a relatively unassuming site for golf, McBroom claims he can't exactly remember the amount he was paid. Fifty thousand? Less? "It sure wasn't six figures, I'll tell you that," he says.

That's all changed in the last two decades. Now he's feted by the rich and famous as the Canadian golf designer to the stars—or at least to those corporate types who made a boatload during the tech boom of the late 1990s and were smart enough to hang on to the tens of millions needed to build their own private golf oases.

Golf Design Tips Learned from Tom McBroom While Playing St. George's

1) Great owners make great golf courses

In his inimitable style, where he makes remarks that might sound arrogant coming from anyone else, McBroom explains that he simply puts more into his work than his peers. He thinks strategy on and off the golf course.

"Here's where I think I'm good: I connect clients to the market," he says, on the fifth hole, a spectacular downhill par-4 that rises to a green perched on the far side of a valley.

Always good to highlight your strongest point. Now continue.

"I talk about more than aesthetics and bunker style to them—I talk to them about the business. What are we trying to achieve? How can we make this venture successful in the market? Those are the kinds of conversations I try to have with my clients," he says, pausing in the landing area near a large fairway bunker as our playing partners hit their shots.

What if it is a course like the one he built on the estate of Paul Desmarais? Yes—*that* Paul Desmarais. The one who holds parties attended by Bill Clinton and Leo DiCaprio at his palatial estate. The same man whom Peter C. Newman, chronicler of the rich and famous, once called "a giant because he has used his power to gain unprecedented political influence, not for any demonstrable financial gain, mind you, but simply because he enjoys playing politics as much as he likes making money." In a similar fashion, Desmarais has the cash—because of the $100 billion Power Corporation conglomerate—to build a golf course as a plaything. In my mind, that's the definition of affluence—having the money to build a golf course just because you can.

No one plays the course, called Domaine Laforest, so I ask McBroom how exactly one develops a business plan for it.

McBroom isn't even fazed. "Even if it is just a fun course like the one I did for Desmarais, you want to know who is going to be playing it and how they are going to get enjoyment out of it," he says, pulling an umbrella from his bag as the rain begins to fall more steadily.

And if no one plays it?

Well, then, no one really knows whether it is great. Either way, the legend of its great greens and majestic fairways that rival Augusta National's carpets grows exponentially with every reference.

Even if no one sees it, building Domaine Laforest was the experience of a lifetime, McBroom says. And it can't hurt when those lucky enough to know the secret handshake to gain access to the Desmarais family estate call Domaine Laforest the best golf experience ever. Not that these accolades surprise McBroom.

"If you know anything about the Desmarais family, you know there's a style that they live. It is a style that is incomprehensible to most Canadians. But it is known as the Desmarais style in Quebec. If they touch something, they do it beyond imagination. It is incomparable in style and scope. It is like what a king would do in England five hundred years ago. It is that kind of a thing. And he felt he needed golf on his fifty-thousand-acre estate."

While Paul Desmarais may love a huge tract of land, it turns out he knew "absolutely nothing about golf," McBroom continues. "But he loved the construction and he loved the art of banging together a golf course in the middle of the woods in Quebec. He just loved that. He has a great mind and would become fascinated by the artistic details. He also became fascinated by the elements that made up a bunker, though he knew nothing about it. He also became fascinated by the irrigation system. He designed the pumphouse himself. I was shocked by it—but then I came to understand his mind a bit and understood that he grabs onto things. It is how he's come to be where he is. He has an amazing mind for detail."

McBroom's ability to forge lasting ties with some of Canada's power brokers, from the Desmarais clan to former BCE chief executive Jean Monty, through to his regular work for corporate golf giant ClubLink, has been as much a key to his success as his ability to create a daunting tee shot.

It is something of which McBroom is very aware.

"I put huge value on relationships," he says.

More than on creating great designs?

"Let's put it this way—I have to like the people I work with. That's very important to me, Rob. A site is hugely important, but at this point I want to work with people I really enjoy. There's a special bond with some of these guys."

Given all of this, you can be forgiven for thinking McBroom's love of a good deal eclipses his interest in creating a good green. That's not the case, he says, but sometimes it appears that way. When he talks about the business of golf, as opposed to his business within golf, that's when his eyes light up and his passion really shows through.

"I like to have broad-based discussions about what will make a course successful. And there's always the question of what is success. It is probably more than a great-looking course and strategic bunkers. Sure, that's part of it. But that's just one of many elements. I really work with these guys and we work to make it successful. I haven't had any projects even remotely close to failing."

He'll later clarify that last remark, noting one of his recent private courses has struggled to attract members. But even though that course may not have been a resounding financial success, at least it won an award, he notes.

2) **Building exclusive private golf clubs creates mystique. Mystique leads to more designs.**
You'd think the best way to become a success in the golf business is to have your courses played by as many people as possible. That's not always the case.

As we take the short walk to the back tee on the tenth hole, the designer puts aside the score card for our round and stops calculating side bets just long enough to explain that in golf, sometimes having fewer people see your courses is better.

Take, for instance, Öviinbyrd, a sporty, smart design crafted on a fascinating natural canvas in Muskoka by McBroom for a membership of tech entrepreneurs and hockey players like Paul Coffey. It might only have 180 members and be open four and a half months a year, but those who see it and play it might just have a few million lying around to pay for their own course. At least that's McBroom's working theory.

"Öviinbyrd will be a great project for me, over time, because of the network that plays there and the quality of that experience," he says. "Oh, and it is private—that's a big factor."

His most recent retreat for the jet set is called Club de Golf Memphrémagog, a little course he dreamed up for Paul Desmarais Jr., the scion of the ultra-rich, ultra-private family, and partner Jean Monty. And yes, it is McBroom's second design for the Desmarais family. This course should actually get some play from its members, those with connections to the Desmaraises, like Geoff Beattie, who runs the Thomson family's $24 billion empire. Maybe there are more courses in the works—McBroom didn't mention whether Desmarais's daughters, Sophie and Louise, are looking for their own. Everything in its own time, I guess.

And the fact the hoi polloi will never get to see these amazing golf courses? That's not an issue to McBroom. "I don't do this to be loved by the masses—I don't care," he says emphatically. "Memphrémagog will be discovered over time because it is a great golf course. Six or seven years ago, I sat down with Monty and Desmarais and we worked out what that course would be, and then we built it."

What's it cost to join? If you have to ask, you don't belong, the designer says.

"If you have to justify $25,000 in annual dues, then you can't afford to join," he says frankly.

3) **Even when you're working for the filthy rich, don't forget your place.**

Working with the Desmarais family, or other rich golf barons like Öviinbyrd owner Peter Schwartz, is a lot of fun, McBroom admits. Sure it is, I respond—those guys always have the biggest budgets. And, unless the market drops off the table, they can always pay—another key factor in golf design.

McBroom chuckles as he chunks a shot just short of the creek on the treacherous downhill par-4 fourteenth. If you enter the world of the ultra-rich long enough, it is easy to find comfort in the surroundings, he admits.

"I'm just natural in that environment. I can play golf with you and then talk to Desmarais. It is a skill," he adds. "You do it as well."

The difference is that I only come in for a golf game or an article, whereas McBroom might be around for a couple of years, or whatever the gestation period is for a particular course. In the end, regardless of the length of time he's about, it always ends the same way.

"It is a different world they live in," he says. "You will always be an outsider. You are a service person. They bring you into their world as a service provider. But are you ever one of them? No. I'm someone they brag about—'You know, our course is designed by Tom McBroom.'"

That's right, I can see it now—my Tom McBroom course is better than your Graham Cooke course. Or something like that.

It is interesting that McBroom decided our game should be held at St. George's, considering there are at least a dozen of his creations within a relatively short drive of Toronto. Maybe he made the decision because it is where he's comfortable—away from the details of his designs that may not have been implemented in exactly the fashion he wanted. Or maybe McBroom picked St. George's because, to most, it is the pinnacle of golf in Canada. It is the best of the best, the one against which his top designs are judged. Though there are courses that rival it, most are just pretenders to the genius demonstrated within St. George's plunging fairways and devilish greens.

Built as a collaboration between developer Robert Home Smith and Canadian Pacific Railway chief Sir Edward Beatty, the course opened in 1929 as the Royal York Golf Club. The pair hired Stanley Thompson, an eccentric dreamer, drinker, and golf designer, to craft their project. In turn, Thompson, who also created the likes of Banff Springs Golf Course and the course at Jasper Park Lodge, worked the valleys that wander the land, designing a parkland layout that is near perfection. More than seven decades after it opened, it is typically considered the best course in Canada. Its masterful clubhouse—which used to be home to overnight rooms that are now offices—is a testament to a bygone era when legendary golfer (and dandy) Walter Hagen tackled its meandering greens. It has been host to Canadian Opens and royalty (Prince Andrew wore jeans to play, despite the protests of some members). These days, it is home to several hundred members and has been lovingly restored to its appearance from the days when Stanley Thompson toured the property, with a bottle in his pocket and a notepad in his hand.

McBroom has had a long-lasting attachment to the course. He came with his father to the Canadian Open when it was last held on St. George's pristine fairways in 1968. As we walk the start of the final stretch of holes, McBroom explains the connection to St. George's is based partly on a boy's passion for the game.

"I was right at the landing area on eighteen where Bob Charles hit his drive," McBroom says with a look that's somewhere between a smile and a smirk. "I watched him hit his 7-iron tight from there to beat Nicklaus."

Which leads to another key point in understanding Thomas McBroom: he loves competition, both on and off the course. His comments on golf courses are often punctuated with biting, sharp, and typically dead-accurate remarks aimed at his competitors in the business—architects like Doug Carrick, who once worked with McBroom before heading out to follow his own successful path in the business.

Certainly, one of McBroom's great skills is salesmanship and his generally affable nature, which makes him fun to spend time with. And unlike many who work within the game of golf, he isn't jaded by the business that surrounds the sport. He genuinely loves to play and challenge himself, this time in a match paired with me against two others—Jason Logan, the editor of *ScoreGolf* magazine, who sports a short backswing and a lot of game; and Mark Teskey, who sells concrete for a living (not personally, of course—he owns construction firm Teskey Concrete) but has a feel for golf that comes from a lifetime of hanging around St. George's, one that demonstrates he's spent a lot of time on the links when he's not pouring basements. Like a Vegas gambler, McBroom keeps track of the bets and side bets, and games within games. Frankly, when it is all over I have no idea how the final tally was decided. But McBroom pegs us as taking the entire Nassau—front, back, and overall—both of us carding an identical score of 82, even though we're dripping from a downpour at the end of the round. No one questions McBroom's math—after all, if you can't trust your golf architect, who can you trust?

Trying to get McBroom to pick the favourite of his golf designs is nearly impossible. Sitting at a table after our round, sipping a draft beer and a scotch ("Any scotch, I don't care what it is," he instructs the waiter) in the comfortable confines of St. George's bar, he simply won't buckle and admit to having a course that personally stands out over his career.

Robert Trent Jones Sr., the man who made a brand out of golf design, once said, "Golf courses are like children. I have no favourite." But we all know that's a fallacy. Parents might love all of their children equally, but that doesn't mean they don't have a particular fondness for one that might outshine another. McBroom isn't biting, though, no matter how many different ways I pose the question.

"Come on, Robert," he says, scotch in hand, with the scorecard from the round laid out in front of him. "Not going there.

"I'll never tell you. I just won't," he says, putting on his best poker face, one that features a slight smirk. "Sure, some turn out better than others for different reasons. But I won't tell you which—it is a matter of principle. You give it your best shot every time out, despite the client, despite the site, despite the budget."

Like a corporate exec who finds success in different fields, McBroom has consistently changed his vision for what makes a course intriguing, for what brings people back time and again. Though many won't recognize the subtle details that have changed in his vision over time, McBroom is keenly aware of every little alteration in his style. It may seem contrived to some, but for the designer it is what keeps him coming back.

"I think most artists change. I think most artists would be frustrated if they did the same thing over and over again," he starts. "Last month I went to see a Picasso exhibit in Vancouver. Talk about an artist morphing drastically from one thing to another. He was never the same."

So McBroom's career follows that of an artist who went from cubism to surrealism, who fathered numerous illegitimate children, and who died at a dinner party?

"Well, maybe not that last part," he admits.

So, when someone reflects back on his career, what is McBroom hoping for? Immortality through the construction of sloping greens?

"I think people will say I've created an amazing variety of work. And that would make me happy," he says. "I think if you look at the greats in the past, there was no one style of work. The routing was the skeleton and the bunkering was the flesh, and that changes over time. Some guys, like Robert Trent Jones, did the same thing time after time. But in my work it is an evolution, a morphing of styles and an improvement of ideas over time."

But it isn't the need for change that keeps him going, and he says it isn't the need for another bigger-budget course and six-figure contract, either. It is something more basic.

"It is the kick of doing a new golf course. It never gets old. It is a huge kick. You probably understand that—it is a buzz. You don't get tired of it."

It may be the thrill he's after, but he has been paid millions to get his buzz on. With dozens of designs in play, and more coming every year, there's no end in sight for McBroom, no retirement age to target. Freedom 55 means taking work in Europe for bullion billionaire

Peter Munk, or chasing down a new project in Provence with Sorenstam. There's simply no time to ratchet back his workload and start playing golf full time like most successful retirees. When most people retire, their desire is to play more golf; for McBroom, his retirement will involve fewer projects that are more carefully selected. It might be legacy-building to some; to Tom McBroom, it is just good business.

All of which is a huge leap from his meagre start—in terms of both notoriety and finances. He is no longer considered the black sheep—he now hobnobs with the establishment, building courses for the rich and famous, and in turn, he has captured some of that wealth and fame for himself.

"Oh, I've gone well past my dad," he says, speaking on the phone the day after our round. "I could retire right now if I wanted to. But this is too much fun."

Not even a great architect could have designed a life this well.

CHAPTER 18

Norm Keevil
Dreaming Quietly

"Golf is a lot like life. When you make a decision, stick with it."
—Byron Nelson

FIVE BILLION, SEVEN HUNDRED million dollars is an astoundingly large figure.

Most of the time when you're wandering around the golf course, you might be talking about a $5 Nassau or a $1-per-skin game. If the stakes really get high, as they do at clubs like Woodbridge, Ontario's National Golf Club of Canada, and a handful of other courses across the country, figures reaching into the thousands might occasionally come up, and at the end of a match money clips will come out and bills will be peeled off. What the taxman doesn't know won't hurt him.

But that's not the kind of money I'm discussing with Norm Keevil, as we walk off the back nine of Vancouver's prestigious Shaughnessy Golf and Country Club. Nope. We're talking billions, though thankfully it isn't part of a wager, because no book advance would cover that kind of loss.

Rather, I'm talking to Keevil, a geophysicist and the longtime brain behind mining giant Teck Cominco, about trying to raise $5.7 billion overnight, the largest proposed stock offering in Canada's history.

Think about the figure for a moment. It's a smaller number than the total number of hamburgers sold by McDonald's (well over 100 billion), but bigger than the estimated gross domestic product of Barbados ($3.4 billion). It is almost incomprehensible, something I point out to Keevil as he wanders to the left of the tenth fairway (our first hole of the day) to play his stray tee shot from near the tree line.

Yet it was the amount of money Keevil and Teck Cominco tried to round up overnight in August 2006 as part of a "Hail Mary" plan to buy nickel miner Inco, which was valued at $20 billion (which is more than the GDP of Uruguay, for the benefit of those keeping score at home).

In the midst of a battle for control of Inco with two other suitors—both foreign companies interested in acquiring the Toronto-based miner—Teck had one last chance. In order to make its offer more attractive, it had to raise more cash. In order to raise more cash, it had to sell a lot of its stock to institutional shareholders—and it had to do it in a matter of hours to stay in the game.

"The Hail Mary pass worked for Doug Flutie in Miami because he had an A-list of receivers," Keevil jokes as we walk down the slope towards the treacherous tenth green. "But we were dealing with Bay Street in August. That's when the B-team is covering holidays."

He pauses for a moment, then quickly pulls a wedge and hits it a touch fat; the ball comes to rest with a thud in the muddy collar of the green. I chip my ball past the flag and we both walk briskly towards the hole.

"We called one of our investment banks and told them of the deal," says Keevil, putting down his bag and pulling out his putter. "But the guy we usually deal with was on holiday in Spain. We were speaking to the fellow in Toronto late in the day, and he said he had to call his boss in Spain, but that it would be awfully late there."

Keevil chuckles, a thin smile crossing a face punctuated by character lines representing each of his sixty-eight years.

"I think he was afraid he'd wake up his boss," Keevil continues. "So he calls and his boss picks up and immediately says, 'Do you know what time it is?' It is clear that he woke him up. And the guy tells his boss of our plan. But being so late, the banker says, 'Tell them no.' The next day, after the boss has had time to think about it, he called us back. By that time, it was too late."

With that, the Hail Mary was fumbled. Unable to raise the cash, Keevil and Teck's CEO, Don Lindsay, decided it would be best if the company dropped its multibillion takeout offer. Along the way, pundits criticized his company for not being aggressive enough. The notion was that if Teck had been an American enterprise, it would have found a way to make the deal.

It is this final notion that raises Keevil's hackles. He putts his ball from the fringe and it takes the slope of the notoriously tricky green, sliding past the hole. He fails to make his comebacker, and cards a double bogey. As we walk to Shaughnessy's eleventh tee, it is clear Keevil is annoyed. But I've played golf with him before, and recognize it isn't with his play or with me. He's bothered by the idea that someone would call him a conservative businessman because he's spent most of his adult life as a deal-maker, someone who could put together ventures worth millions.

That doesn't mean Norm Keevil is aggressive or particularly outspoken. He's easily likable, with the sort of "aw-shucks" personality that means he comes across as humble even when making big pronouncements, which he's prone to do on occasion. But I don't think he makes the comments to draw attention to himself. He makes bold statements because he believes them to be true. He may be the controlling shareholder of one of the larger mining companies in the world, but he's quiet and understated. On the golf course, he almost comes across as shy, especially since he's not quick to blurt out just any comment, his thoughts masked by a slight grin that shows up regularly.

There's little small talk with Norm, at least not at first. He appears to give careful consideration to his choice of words, though he appears more studied than timid. To me, it looks as though he wants to give each subject a certain gravitas before voicing his take on it, making him circumspect as opposed to reticent or evasive. He has a doctorate in geophysics, after all. He may not be a rocket scientist, but he's probably as smart as one.

"You don't build a company for forty years and bet it on one hand," he says in regards to the stinging criticism dished out after the Inco affair. "That would just be ridiculous, don't you think?"

Yes, indeed it would, I reply. But not everyone agrees. Newspaper pundits and corporate critics lined up to take shots at Teck after the failure to acquire Inco, I point out.

"Peter Munk and Eric Reguly said Canadian companies lack the balls to pull off the big deals," he replies, referring to the founder of Barrick Gold and a columnist for the *Globe and Mail*. The use of the word "balls" is as close as Keevil gets to a real make-your-mother-blush four-letter word as I'll hear during the three hours we spend walking around Shaughnessy. "They are just dead wrong. Our play for Inco was a good idea, especially if we'd managed to make it work. And it was certainly as aggressive as anyone had ever done. It was entrepreneurial."

Could he have done the deal some other way, I ask? Simply hit up the banks for the cash?

"For sure we could have loaded up on debt," he says. "We did that in the 1970s—loaded up on loans from the big banks. Thank God they never called them in—it would have been a disaster. I mean, you've got to make mistakes every once in a while. But these days, if you make two or three of them, your company no longer exists."

One of the reasons the Inco takeover became so important was because it occurred at a time when Canadian resources companies were being eyed by foreign enterprises looking for takeover opportunities. That made it a political hot potato, drenched in rhetoric about the need for Canada to carefully consider the ramifications of selling its non-renewable resources to foreign interests. Even Keevil became involved, saying Inco CEO Scott Hand "sold out Canada for his own purposes" by spurning Teck's offer to create a "Canadian mining powerhouse" and instead sell to a foreign company. His strident perspective on the matter and his harsh remarks seem contrary to the typical considered approach of the man. I can only imagine Keevil said them in a very even tone.

"I'd have like to have kept Inco in Canada, but that's more of a personal matter than a political one," he explains.

Are we going to see more takeovers like Inco?

"There's no doubt about it, there's more coming."

Is it a bad thing?

This question makes Keevil pause. He considers it for a moment before answering.

"No, I don't think it necessarily is," he says. "There's been a lot made of it, but it opens up opportunities for other people to come up with ideas and concepts."

I suspect Keevil wouldn't be typically drawn into such conversation on the golf course. He'd rather chat about the PGA Tour pros he's played with (former Masters champ Fred Couples gets a big thumbs up, as does the affable Fred Funk) or his recent time spent playing his Hawaiian home course (the Plantation at Kapalua, host site for the PGA Tour's annual Mercedes Championship) than dig into the nuances of his business. I can't really say I blame him, and for a couple of holes we just play golf, like two men who just happened to come to the first tee at the same time and decided to pair up and venture out on the course together.

As we walk to the fourteenth hole, our fifth of the day, our conversation compensates for the fact that neither of us is playing well. With the course saturated by May rains, my game hobbles along, the victim of having left my clubs in the closet all winter. Keevil, who sports a 16 handicap, struggles as well, perhaps due to the soggy course conditions. Thankfully, neither of us is so involved with our game that it obscures a magnificent sunny day on a fine golf course.

Frankly, it doesn't appear that Keevil attaches that much significance to his play. In golf, there tends to be two ways to play holes: well or badly. How you distinguish between the two depends on your personal expectations. A bad hole for one type of player can be good for another. Keevil doesn't seem to worry about this at all, with a personality that allows him to distance himself equally from highs and lows. Even when he struggles mightily, as he does on occasion, he doesn't seem frustrated by the experience. Its a good thing he's so level-headed, considering that Shaughnessy is so wet that we both hit a couple of wayward shots—we know the directions of the shots, but no amount of searching results in finding them, likely because they are plugged a few inches into the drenched turf.

Keevil has long been a member at Shaughnessy, but he rarely plays at the club, he explains as we cut from the eighteenth green around the clubhouse to the first tee.

"The problem with being a member that plays infrequently and is getting old is that you only remember how you used to play the holes. You don't know how you play them anymore," he explains in reference to shots from his younger days.

Aside from having a high level of disposable income that allows for membership at a fine club like Shaughnessy, there's nothing outward that would indicate that Keevil is a golfer. Balding, with a thin strip of white hair running along the edges of his head, Keevil doesn't appear particularly athletic. Still, he takes the game seriously—walking quickly, rather than riding in a cart, despite the fact he's nearing seventy. Like everything he does, Keevil's passion for the game is quiet but assured. He plays frequently if inconsistently, which explains his 16 handicap.

"I grew up playing with a 5-iron as a boy at a great spot about a quarter-mile from our home outside Port Credit," he says as we wait for the fairway on the short par-5 opener to clear. "Then I played three times in fifteen years before coming back to the game."

Thankfully, golf is one of those games that hooks players, regardless of ability. One good shot is all it takes to draw one back into the fold, and Keevil has been hooked since he reacquainted himself with golf in the early 1970s. So much so that he's also a member of the Royal and Ancient, the governing body for the game based in Scotland, and makes annual pilgrimages to the Old World for the club's annual matches.

"Everyone needs a sense of humility," Keevil says. "Golf gives it to me."

Knowing how to move one's golf ball around Shaughnessy is key to any success one might expect to have on the course, especially given the devilish nature of its putting surfaces. Greens are the defining characteristic of any great golf course, often providing the finishing touch to a masterpiece. Nowhere is that more clearly the case than at Shaughnessy. The land, despite being perched next to the Pacific Ocean, appears unspectacular at first, offering subtle rolls. While it doesn't offer the astounding views of Vancouver, as Capilano Golf and Country Club does, it does provide a challenge on the greens that are almost without peer in Canadian golf. Like a good mystery, Shaughnessy reveals itself over the course of a round.

I'm sure that was the intent of Arthur Vernon Macan, better known as A.V., who created the course, the second he'd built for the club. The accomplished amateur golfer arrived in British Columbia from his native Ireland in 1912. Within a year of landing in North America, Macan created what would become Royal Colwood in Victoria, and was developing a conceptual philosophy for designing golf courses. A huge fan of the Old Course at St. Andrews, he loved wide fairways and greens with plenty of pitch.

Like his courses, Macan had plenty of character. Though at thirty-three years of age he could likely have skirted World War I, Macan enlisted. Trained as a machine gunner, his left foot was struck by a shell at the notorious assault on Vimy Ridge, resulting in the amputation of his left leg from the knee down. When he recovered, Macan returned to British Columbia and to golf. He remained a top amateur, and quickly became a sought-after golf course designer, responsible for clubs like Vancouver's Marine Drive.

He built the first course for the club, called Shaughnessy Heights, for a group of businessmen on land leased from the Canadian Pacific Railway. It remained in its original location from 1912 until 1960, when the lease with CP expired. Though he was nearly eighty years old, Macan was recalled to build a new course, in a more modern style on land leased from the Musqueam Indian

Band. The course opened only four years before Macan's death, but was immediately deemed of championship quality, and it hosted the 1966 Canadian Open. Canada's national championship would take almost forty years to return to Shaughnessy. By that time, its remarkable setting, with several holes looking out towards Iona Park and the Pacific Ocean, had distinguished Shaughnessy as one of the best golf courses in the country.

Just as Shaughnessy has played an important role in the development of golf in Canada, so has Teck Cominco been at the forefront when it comes to mining. Once separate businesses—Teck started as Teck-Hughes Gold Mines in 1913, while Cominco sprang to life in 1906 as the Consolidated Mining and Smelting Company of Canada—the association between the two businesses began decades later in 1986. They officially merged in 2001 in a deal orchestrated by Keevil.

It was Keevil's father (also Norman Bell Keevil) who laid the foundations for the current business. Armed with a doctorate in geophysics from Harvard, Keevil's father took over Teck in the 1950s following his discovery of a high-grade copper deposit in the Lake Temagami region of Ontario. Considered a pioneer in mining exploration, he expanded Teck to include mines across Canada until he died in 1989.

The son followed in his father's footsteps. Born in the U.S. while his dad was studying at Harvard, Keevil joined his father's business straight out of school in the 1960s, rising to the role of CEO by 1981. There was nothing sexy at the time about mining, a sector that was viewed as either staid and dull or full of swindlers and prospectors trying to make a buck before they were discovered.

"For years, metal prices were declining," Keevil says. "Then you've seen the trade wars spring up, and suddenly commodities like metals are important again."

And, in turn, Teck Cominco has become arguably the most important mining company in the country and the largest supplier of zinc in the world. Zinc isn't a sexy metal. It isn't gold or copper, though Teck mines for those as well. But with the economic explosion in China, zinc is a hot commodity, and Teck's fortunes have soared with the demand.

While the high demand is likely to continue, there's a problem facing Teck Cominco and other companies like it, a problem of which Keevil is acutely aware: miners are getting old. And though established companies can be run by lawyers and bankers, creating new mining businesses—the next Teck Cominco, so to speak—is the challenge, one typically undertaken by engineers. Keevil has had to confront the age issue head-on in recent years. Former Teck CEO David Thompson was sixty-five when he stepped down from the role, leaving the company scrambling to find a replacement.

Keevil smiles mischievously. "I'd have taken the job if I were twenty years younger."

As we trudge through the wet ground towards the third hole, a fascinating par-3 with a fallaway green that runs next to a slight creek, I ask about the current CEO, Don Lindsay, a former banker. Keevil tells me to hold that thought and makes a lurching swing, hitting a low ball that comes to rest with a splat in a muddy patch twenty yards short of the green.

"Don's not just a banker, he's also a mining engineer," Keevil points out after making a bogey. We walk up a short incline to reach the fourth hole, a terrifically difficult dogleg left that measures 403 yards from our tees. "We talked to a lot of people. Some came close, but they weren't quite right. Maybe they would have worked if we hadn't focused on Don."

Lindsay was an interesting choice. A mining engineer by training, he'd spent two decades working in banking, eventually rising to the position of president of CIBC World Markets. But he's not the type of showy executive who likes to flaunt his success or wealth. He still drives the first car he ever purchased. It is the type of practical personality that appeals to Keevil.

"I'd known Don for some years," he says. "We hadn't dealt with him directly, but a light bulb came on and we thought he'd be right. And he had to decide whether he wanted to spend the rest of his life at the bank. It turned out that he didn't, so it just happened to fit."

Beyond setting the current executive structure of the company, Keevil seems uncertain what role his family will play at Teck in the long term. It is an issue that faces many family businesses in Canada, one for which there is no easy solution, he acknowledges after hitting a long iron into our final hole, the ninth, a 390-yard par-4 with a small raised green that slopes hard from the back.

"I don't know what will happen, actually," he says. He's quiet for a minute, clearly thinking through his answer. We walk to the green in silence.

"One of my sons is a director," he says as we reach the hole, referring to the third generation of Norman B. Keevils to play a role at Teck. "But I don't know what we'll do, really."

We finish our round with two feeble scores—my 88 to Keevil's 93—and walk towards Shaughnessy's understated clubhouse. Clubs are left with the attendant, and we walk into the men's locker room, jettisoning muddy shoes and wind shirts, and proceed into the lounge that looks out onto the eighteenth hole, where a group of golfers are lining up their putts.

Keevil pours us coffee and sits down in a low chair at a nearby table.

He's content to continue working at his own pace, he explains, helping guide the company when he thinks it needs a helping hand, leaving Lindsay to run the operations.

"That way I can do the things that most interest me," he says. "Which is sort of what I've always done."

He still keenly follows what's going on in the Canadian market, and is especially dismayed at the rise of private equity and hedge funds. Entrepreneurialism needs to be fostered for Canada to stay at the forefront of business, he says, but private equity has little interest in helping create a climate where new business ideas and models can be developed.

"Private equity just isn't accountable to anyone but their investors, which is crazy," he says. "Take someone like Joe Hussein at Intrawest—he's the victim of these hedge funds."

The Vancouver resort operator that created Whistler was taken out by a private equity group in 2006. With low interest rates and easy access to pools of capital, hedge funds have swooped in and picked off several great Canadian companies, Keevil adds.

"When Hussein was taken out, the country lost a really good entrepreneur. Do you think the hedge funds will be as good as he was at developing new ideas? Of course not."

One of the questions Keevil faces these days is the future of Teck. Born in 1938, he now spends plenty of Vancouver's cool months in Hawaii with his wife. Though he still checks in with his office frequently, he's years removed from running the daily operations of the company. But he controls the company, holding on to a majority of the voting shares, though the company has other sizable shareholders, including Japan's Sumitomo Metal Mining and Quebec's Caisse de dépôt et placement.

Teck's involvement with Sumitomo is intriguing, considering Keevil's comments about Inco and foreign ownership. It is conveniently not discussed, though Keevil does talk about his involvement with Sumitomo's Japanese executives. There are many cultural differences between the two companies, he admits, but they have one thing in common: golf. In fact, the Srixon driver Keevil uses throughout our round is a gift from the CEO of Sumitomo.

"Koichi Fukushima, the CEO at Sumitomo, came over and played Bear Mountain with me and gave me the driver as a present," Keevil says, admitting the choice of a Srixon driver perplexed him at first, at least until he found out the golf equipment maker was one of the businesses Sumitomo owned.

"I didn't know the company's connection to golf," he says. "But out of politeness I felt compelled to use it. I kind of like it now."

In fact, the mutual love of golf remains a constant between the company's executives.

"The Japanese have a game called 'Olympics' that we play when I'm with the guys from Sumitomo," he says. "If the person with the furthest putt from the hole makes it they get gold, right through to the third-closest getting bronze. But in a foursome you need something else. For our benefit, they decided fourth place would be zinc."

As he stirs his coffee, staring down at the table, I ask him about the biggest change he's witnessed during his decades at the helm of Teck Cominco.

He lifts his head, smiling broadly. "We were only a $20 million company thirty years ago," he says. "Now we're $20 *billion*. Not bad, is it?"

CHAPTER 19

Ralph Klein
The Myopia of Politics

"What a shame to waste those great shots on the practice tee. I'd be afraid of finding out what I was doing wrong."

—Walter Hagen

OVERLOOKING A HIGHWAY, not far from Calgary's busy airport, sits the Elks Lodge and Golf Course. It isn't an elite golf club like Calgary Golf and Country Club, with its twenty-year waiting list and blue-blood membership with pockets full of old money. And it doesn't have the exposure or prestige of new-money clubs like Glencoe, which resides on the outskirts of the city and is home to those who have made their fortunes in the oil boom that hit this western city in the last two decades. It doesn't even receive the same recognition as Heritage Pointe, a high-end public facility that houses many of the city's corporate outings.

In fact, the Elks isn't in the league of any of those courses—at least not to those that only give it a passing glance. Its weathered and battered clubhouse is sadly out of date—and style. Its involvement with the Elks Lodge, a group whose mandate is to "inculcate the principles of charity, justice, brotherly love, and fidelity," also positions it in its own unique space in the golf market. After all, how many clubs can say their basis included a mandate to "enhance the happiness of its members" while also perpetuating itself as "a fraternal organization"?

Yes, there's something joyfully anachronistic about the Elks Club, right down to its cart, which lugs people up and down the hill from the clubhouse to its tiny range. Striding into the clubhouse, with its antiquated bar and bunker-like pro shop, is like stepping back in time—to about 1963, in fact.

Not surprisingly, no legendary designer laid out this course. Though the course opened in 1923, no one seems to know who built it. Surely the fabled Donald Ross never stepped off a train here to dream up the course on the back of a napkin, as he did elsewhere. A.W. Tillinghast never had a couple of drinks while making an appearance, and apparently Canada's best designer, Stanley Thompson was busy elsewhere.

Thankfully, it doesn't really matter who designed the course—no one who plays it has spent one instant worrying about such details. What matters is the course, and the club got lucky there, ending up with an understated design that utilizes the big hills and rolling swales, some flashed bunkering, and the occasional pond. Nothing fancy—it is a working-class hackers' course through and through. The people who play the Elks just want to golf. They aren't worried about the social trappings or how membership at the club will be perceived by their neighbours. And though most people outside of Calgary have never heard of the Elks—you won't find the club promoting itself in travel magazines or glossy golf publications—it is an intriguing and smart course that's unpretentious and welcoming.

And while it may not be as regal as the private clubs, the Elks is where I'm expected to meet the former king of Alberta. He may have passed his crown and throne to his successor, but many still perceive Ralph Klein as the ruling monarch of this oil-rich province. And like a courtier waiting to see a king distracted by sycophants and others in the court, I apparently shouldn't hold my breath waiting for King Ralph to arrive.

"He's at some building dedication for a Native band," says Rich Jones, who was a Calgary emissary for Klein when he was premier. It is Jones who has made the arrangements for the round as a member of the Elks. "I hear he's on the road and we should just start our game and he'll catch up."

No one, regardless of position or stature, should ever hold up a golf game. Therefore, while Klein is cruising with his driver/body-guard on the highway outside of the city, we tee off, joined on the day by Elks Club pro Jason Plosz.

It doesn't take long to recognize that Plosz is the player in the group, a straight-hitting club pro from the flat plains of Saskatchewan, where golf balls roll a long way and sand greens were once prominent. He's a smooth swinger, having played college golf in the U.S. His ability makes up for the inadequacies of both Jones and myself—both of us are, well, less straight.

Here's an example: Ever had the first-hole jitters, where you can't get comfortable and a tee shot just doesn't set up to your eye? That's exactly what happens as I stand amongst a gathering of anxious golfers, all waiting to tee off after our group leaves. I'm sure they're thinking it'll be a long round after my cold block goes a mile right, nearly landing on the green of a corresponding hole. Jones fares only slightly better, hitting a low runner that escapes the long fescue grass but finds the bluegrass rough.

We continue to ham-and-egg our way around the first four holes of the course, with Plosz hitting fairways and greens and making pars. I, too, hit fairways—just not the ones I'm usually playing. Jones, a mid-handicapper, keeps the ball in play, racking up bogeys.

That's when King Ralph presents himself to the court. He comes flying out onto the course at the fifth hole on a golf cart. Only he doesn't look very regal. In fact, he looks like he just came back from a beach vacation for aging seniors—maybe not Miami, but something not far from it.

He's decked out in a red golf shirt emblazoned over the left breast with the Fox Harb'r logo (a memento from a recent trip to Ron Joyce's golf escape) and blue shorts with white socks that run halfway up to his knee. The entire affair is topped off by sandals he's wearing over the socks, a fashion faux pas that probably wouldn't have been allowed to pass even thirty-five years ago, when fashion crimes in golf were common.

Though it's only been three years since we first played golf together—incidentally, also at Elks Lodge—Klein looks older, heavier, and tired. Never a tall man or an imposing figure, Klein looks worn out. And he's complaining that his stomach is bothering him before he even gets out of the cart—perhaps something he ate at the dedication ceremony isn't sitting well.

Regardless, he lumbers out of the cart, shakes my hand, grabs a club, and makes a few light passes. He's caught up to us on a short hole, only 370 yards from the tees we're playing, with a fairway that swings to the right around a pond. It isn't exactly a difficult hole, but it does require a certain degree of precision. From my previous experience playing with Klein, I know that accuracy isn't his strong suit.

We let Klein hit last.

"Why bother practising? You just waste all of your good shots anyway," he says, waggling his club.

He hits the ball low and left, coming to rest just short of the pond. We drive up the fairway in our cart, stopping near his ball. He half-apologizes for being late.

"I'm busier now than ever," he explains. "But that's what you're supposed to do, isn't it?"

Klein had been invited to a ribbon-cutting for the Blackfoot tribe. One might have thought these ceremonial duties would have ended for Klein when he stepped away from politics only months earlier. Apparently not.

"Ralph is one of the great Native advocates in Canada," Jones tells me at the start of our round. "He's the one politician in this country who gets the situation, and [the Natives] trust him as well."

Who knew? From an Ontario perspective, Klein is defined more for what he's against than what he favours. He's against gay marriage. He's against the Kyoto accord. He isn't apparently a big advocate for the homeless. He is characterized more as a hard-drinking, intolerant redneck from western Canada.

He may well be many of these things, but he's also a big supporter of the Blackfoot tribe. It seems inconsistent with his hardline stance on many issues, but Klein says that's not the case. He even speaks some Blackfoot, and his wife, Colleen, is Métis.

"Ordering and shopping Blackfoot?" I ask as we approach the green.

That's when the laugh emerges. It is a hearty laugh, coming deep from within him, but it also sounds calculated, as though he doesn't sincerely see the humour but is too polite to say so. Imagine Jabba the Hutt in the third *Star Wars* movie, and you'll have some sense of the tone.

"HO. HA. HA. HA."

He stops for a second and turns back to me.

"Yeah, that's it," he says. "HO. HA. HA. HA."

"Seriously, though," I ask, "there must be something more to it." Klein says there is. He only had a peripheral interest in Native issues until the 1977 Berger Report, the result of a government inquiry into land usage for the Mackenzie Valley oil pipeline. At the time, Klein was a civic-affairs reporter for Calgary television station CFCN. When the station made what Klein calls "an outrageous slander" on the Natives involved in the Berger Report, the station was ordered by the government to do a documentary on Native issues as a means apologizing for its actions. Klein was handed the assignment.

He came away with an appreciation for the Blackfoot, and for Native issues in general, he says. And even though he's not premier, apparently the First Nations people still think fondly of Klein, which is why he was late for our game.

These days, Klein has more time for ribbon-cuttings, especially since stepping down as premier in late 2006, after fourteen years in the position. It was hardly a highlight of his career. Klein was forced to vacate his post by a party unwilling to allow him to take his own time and exit in his own way.

"Oh, yes, I made a mistake announcing it," he says, referring to his decision in March 2006 to say he planned to exit his position a year later. "I wanted another year, but once you announce you're leaving, you're a lame duck. That was all there was to it."

With that, the most popular—and controversial—premier in Alberta's history was history. By the end of 2006, Ed Stelmach held the premier's seat and Klein, a polarizing and challenging figure, was looking for a job.

He wasn't out of work long, and his new job at a Calgary law firm apparently hasn't been kind to his golf game. Since leaving office and joining Borden Ladner Gervais as a "business advisor," he hasn't had time to golf as frequently. There's a certain irony in joining a law firm and playing less golf than one did as premier. As a golfer, Klein is, well, a fine politician. His game is about what you'd expect from someone who took it up relatively late in life and who apparently considers practising to be a character flaw. He played frequently as premier, sometimes three or four dozen times a summer—often in Edmonton and at the Glencoe, where he's a member—and has played with the most powerful leaders in Canada, including Jean Chrétien and Paul Martin. Of course, he also recounts rounds at Fox Harb'r and other spots that make one wonder if he isn't keeping an accurate count.

Despite it all, he is persistent and doggedly determined. He has no ego tied up in the way he approaches the game. If everyone else is hitting a wedge on a hole, as happens on the downwind par-3 sixth, a hole protected front and back by daunting bunkers, and Klein needs a wood to reach the green, he'll pull out his 5-wood and give it a rap. He doesn't hit the ball far on any occasion—two hundred yards is a relatively long shot with a driver—but that's not surprising for a man who now officially qualifies for a senior's discount. Though he appears to make few considerations in putting, it is clearly the one part of the game that comes naturally to him. Hunched over, with his paunch hanging over his belt, he hits the ball with a wrist stroke that appears ripped from some Arnold Palmer instruction manual from the 1960s. No matter what it looks like, it works, and Klein makes a disproportionate number of long putts during our round. And, of course, there's always the politician's discount, a time-honoured tradition among political types that allows him to pick up a bunch of three-footers without being worried about finishing.

Unfortunately, none of this makes him an engaging playing partner. One wants to be dazzled by the populist appeal and casual manner that made him premier for more than a decade. For me, however, that Ralph Klein never materializes.

After our first game, which came when Klein was at the height of his political powers, I came away confused by the man and his popularity. One on one, Klein came across as especially reserved and somewhat distant. He sucked on a Diet Pepsi—a "Mormon beer," he'd later tell me—and was quiet, rarely making conversation unless asked a direct question. None of the legendary Klein charisma, that quirk of his public personality that made him so popular amongst the everyman of Alberta, came across during that initial foray around the course.

I often wonder if my experience would have been different had I played with the boozy, larger-than-life figure that Klein was prior to going cold turkey in 2001. Would he have made outrageous remarks after a couple of brown pops? Would he have been looser, and given less consideration to his remarks?

As mayor of Calgary in the 1980s, Klein used to check the pulse of his constituents by retreating to a local watering hole most afternoons and downing a few (or more) with those who frequented the establishment. But that man appears to have disappeared, replaced by an older, weathered model that takes antacids for an upset stomach and sips water in his golf cart.

There were issues he wanted to deal with before retiring, he tells me as we approach the halfway mark of the round. Two final initiatives—a new cancer treatment facility in the province and an integrated energy plan—are "sufficiently pregnant to go," he says.

He's probably right. After all, one of Klein's great skills is his ability to determine, usually ahead of the curve, the issues and aspirations that will resonate with the public. He understood that when he helped land the 1988 Winter Olympics, and he had enough insight to move away from the Liberal party and towards the Conservatives when he made the move into provincial politics.

Gauging public opinion is apparently easier than determining the distance over the pond to the tenth green. Klein stops talking just long enough to slice a 6-iron into the watery abyss.

"I hate water," he says as the ball splashes.

"I always got out with the people," he explains, casually tossing his iron back into his bag on the back of the cart and taking a seat for the ride to the green. "I always wanted to know how things resonated with Martha and Henry. I wanted to know what Miss Grundy thought. That way, you find out which way the parade is headed and try to get out in front of it."

Martha and Henry and Miss Grundy. They populate many of Klein's remarks. Average Albertans always appreciated Klein's populist perspective, so much so that they were willing to forgive his transgressions—like the time he drunkenly flipped a handful of change at a homeless man and berated him for being at a shelter.

"Thirty per cent of people didn't like my politics," he admits. "That's pretty much normal. Actually, it is quite good."

He pauses and breaks into a long laugh.

"Ho. Ha. Ha. Ha. If you get 30 per cent pissed off at you, that's not all bad. Just as long as you satisfy the other 70 per cent! Ho. Ha. Ha. Ha."

We reach the par-4 twelfth, one of the more intriguing holes at the Elks. With a wetland along the length of the left side of the fairway, and a green obscured by reeds and other plants, the short 303-yard two-shot hole can be reached in one by those willing to take a bold, 260-yard approach directly to the flag.

Klein's game isn't such that he can take advantage of it, and just as he easily gauged public opinion, he recognizes there's no reward in assuming this risk. Instead, he grabs his 3-wood and takes a cut that lashes the ball out to the right, well away from the hazard.

Of course, not everything he did was popular. That 30 per cent he talks about kept their backs up—and shouted loudly and often carried placards—throughout his time as premier. As popular as Klein was with some, he was equally unpopular with others.

"My average day wasn't complete until there was some sort of protest," he says, shielding his eyes from the sun. "But the average person—Martha and Henry—said I was doing the right thing. The point was to get the government out of business and to offer them some leadership. That's what they wanted."

"They" being Martha and Henry? Or Miss Grundy?

"Exactly," he says.

As we approach the long par-5 fourteenth and the two monster par-4s that follow, Klein appears to be fading. His game deserts him on the par-5, where a hoseled tee shot into long rough is never found.

Leadership meant listening to Martha and Henry, especially when it came to social issues. He opposed gay marriage, for instance, when a bill recognizing non-traditional unions was making its way through the federal parliament. Did he do it because he disliked gays?

With his game already sputtering, this clearly isn't a conversation Klein hoped to have.

"I don't hate gay people," he says defensively. "I don't dislike them. I have friends who are gay. As I told two reporters, I like you and I like you. I just won't marry the two of you. But this idea that I dislike gay people is wrong. I know a lot of gay people. They're nice people."

I ask him to size up his time as premier, and Klein smiles. He began his time as the province's leader saddled with a $3.5 billion budget shortfall. By the time he left, Albertans were swimming in oil and were handed an annual surplus of $8.7 billion. Sure, Klein's rise mirrored the resurgence of Alberta's prosperous oil patch, but he is still regarded as one of the most successful politicians in the country's history.

Not that he accomplished all of his goals, he says.

"The one issue—and it is a big issue—that I failed to resolve was health care. People have the impression it is free."

Who thinks it's free? Martha and Henry again?

"Exactly. Or Miss Grundy. They think it is free, but it costs $12 billion a year. And unions and raging grannies, well, they put the fear of God in Martha and Henry every time the issue of health care is raised. It is the number one issue facing Stephen today."

Stephen Harper?

"Exactly. The environment? It isn't nearly as big an issue as health care financing is to Canadians today. It is just the issue *du jour*."

So, he opposed the Kyoto accord because he didn't think the environment was a pressing issue?

"No, that's not the case. I opposed Kyoto, but that's not because I didn't want a reduction in greenhouse gases. I just thought it was just poorly considered and would cost Martha and Henry a lot. There were better options."

Though he's clearly struggling to finish, Klein can be counted on for his determination. On the seventeenth hole, a 180-yard par-3 that plays to a green fronted by a large pond, Klein grabs his 5-wood and fires away, with a wild, flailing swing that delivers a low, sharply hit ball that quickly finds the middle of the pond. But almost before it has found the drink, Klein has another on a tee; he hits this one to the right, short of the pond and near a small tree. He attempts an all-or-nothing recovery, but it isn't clear that it makes it over the water. After making the walk down the path to the semi-island green and searching for the ball for a few minutes, it is clear it is lost. Klein doesn't bother dropping another.

With storm clouds rolling in, we finish on a par-4 that slides to the right, braced by a ridge line on the far side of the fairway and a line of trees on the near side. Though this hole was more likely found than constructed, its nasty green, falling hard to the front, makes for a fine hole to finish a round on—and a tough par.

"Any regrets?" I ask.

"Nope," he says. "Just wish I'd retired sooner."

So, what does the future hold? Klein is already talking of retiring, leaving the cozy confines of his job with the law firm. Is he planning on buying an RV and heading for Florida?

"Oh, I don't think I'd do that," he says. "Ho. Ha. Ha. Ha."

What, then?

"You know the saying—you get old too soon and smart too late…"

He doesn't finish the sentence, instead trudging up to the tee and smacking the ball to the right into the rough, near the trees that guard the right of the fairway.

My attempt finds the short grass and we drive to Klein's ball. I pull a wedge and my putter from my bag, and take a look at King Ralph, who looks spent.

Does he ever miss the days of carousing, sitting in bars and just talking to people? Does he ever wish he could turn back the clock?

"Sometimes," he says quietly. He then burps and hangs his head in his hands before concluding, "but I feel a lot better in the morning now."

Evidently.

I walk into the fairway to play my shot, leaving Klein to flail in the rough in an attempt to advance his ball.

In the first round we played, Klein holed a dramatic, thirty-foot putt to salvage his bogey. It was a fitting end to his round and made a nice conclusion to my story. This time, as I walk up to the green, Klein is nowhere to be seen. Apparently, somewhere in the right rough he simply gave up and drove his cart to the nearby halfway house to use the facilities. As he doesn't reappear, Jones, Plosz, and I putt out.

It doesn't matter whether he finishes the game or not—and Klein knows it. His successes are in the past, where he was among the best to play the game. That game has changed, and now no one bothers to keep score.

CHAPTER 20

Ron Joyce

From Timbits to Tee Shots

"They don't build courses for people—they build monuments to themselves."

—George Archer, professional golfer

RON JOYCE MISSES THE BEST part of coming to Fox Harb'r.

That's my take anyway. Joyce, fuelled by his billion-plus donut dollars, simply takes his Challenger into the remote location on the Nova Scotia coastline, dashing over the shore before touching down on the five-thousand-foot runway, where his jet pulls up alongside his waiting Mercedes. He then ambles down the jet's steps and takes a short ride up a laneway, passing the immaculately maintained gardens, before stopping in front of the clubhouse or driving a little farther through his pristine golf course, coming to rest in the driveway of his palatial home, located on a rocky crest perched over the water.

That's a trip, to be sure, but it isn't the one I'm on.

Instead, I'm bombing in my rental car along a two-lane highway that twists its way along the coast with all the directional consistency of an insect in high wind. From Moncton, which contains the nearest airport of any merit, Fox Harb'r is a two-hour drive east along a remarkably picturesque stretch of the Sunrise Trail Scenic Route, through small Maritime towns that were once fishing villages, over bridges that span ocean inlets, and down near the Northumberland

Strait, where Prince Edward Island can be seen perched across the whitecaps.

Along the way, you pass by the full gamut of Canadian society, from the downtrodden seaside homes that sit unpainted and often derelict, to upscale cottages that one imagines to be holiday retreats for well-heeled easterners. The road dips, passing Pugwash's invigoratingly rugged Northumberland Links golf course and singer Anne Murray's nearby home, before bending south over some hilly terrain, eventually emerging next to the body of water that provided Joyce with the name for his resort. The road winds along a splendid peninsula and past a beautiful field on the right. The club's large iron gates come into view, and I pull the car alongside the intercom. After quickly announcing that I'm not an interloper, and in fact have come to see Ron, I drive along a road that winds through the golf course, past the runway and the accompanying sign that reads, "Attention: Watch for Approaching Aircraft." Then I park my car in the visitors' lot behind the clubhouse and walk past the first hole to the patio and pro shop.

That's where I find Ron Joyce, the billionaire who created a Canadian institution when he established Tim Hortons as the preeminent restaurant chain in the country. He is sitting at a long table, sipping a glass of water and holding court over an early lunch with a large group of men all decked out in typical golf attire—collared shirts and khaki shorts.

Joyce sees me immediately.

"Robert, come and join us," he says, gesturing to a nearby chair, a broad smile spreading over his face.

He introduces me to the group, which consists of the senior management of television and Internet giant Shaw Communications, as well as a handful of investment bankers from TD Bank. They've come to Fox Harb'r for a corporate retreat, but one never knows whom you might run into at the resort—from world leaders like Bill Clinton and George H.W. Bush to Wayne Gretzky (who was there a few weeks prior to my visit) or Tim Hortons franchisees, who often use the location for charity golf outings. Since my golf clubs and luggage somehow failed to arrive with me in Moncton, I've shown up at the resort with nothing but a briefcase, tape recorder, notebook, and pen. No clubs, shoes, or golf balls, though I assume (rightly) that there will be little trouble securing temporary playing paraphernalia at the resort.

In an effort to offer full disclosure, I've known Joyce—or RJ, as friends refer to him—for several years since first playing golf with him in 2002. Though you can get a great sense of someone's character while playing on the golf course, you really understand what makes them tick—both the good and the bad—when you write their autobiography, as I did with Ron for a year starting in late 2004. The book took nearly a year to complete, and during that time I regularly worked in the seclusion of Fox Harb'r and Joyce's home off the thirteenth fairway, occasionally heading out to the course under the late-afternoon sun to bat the ball around the holes that run along the ocean. Ron would rarely join me on these occasions, taking the time to check with his financial advisors, call his office in Oakville, Ontario, or return emails. That meant I usually played the course without another soul on it, which isn't uncommon at Fox Harb'r, given that only about three thousand golfers test its perfectly conditioned greens each year.

Playing a golf course alone, without any distraction, is a unique experience. With Fox Harb'r hidden behind iron gates and fencing, and well removed from intrusions, you become lost in your own thoughts. It is easy to see why the land, with its low cliffs running along the ocean and mix of forests and dramatic rock formations, so appealed to Joyce when he first saw it two decades ago.

Fox Harb'r has been Joyce's pet project for almost ten years, though he actually acquired the land in 1987. He loves entertaining at the facility, and it is common for friends and business associates to visit, play golf, and have a few drinks with their host, which explains why I find Joyce sitting next to Jim Shaw, the burly son of the founder of Shaw Communications and the company's current

CEO. Joyce sits on Shaw's board of directors, and the company is using Fox Harb'r for a retreat, away from the prying eyes of Bay Street and hidden from the media. Make that most of the media— no one appears to have expected me to materialize.

Lunch is soon over, and Joyce gets up from the table, excuses himself from his guests, and suggests we go for a drive around the resort, so he can show off his latest alterations to his dream. Having worked so closely together, I have a certain comfort level with the burly former cop, something that was built up over time. Though he ran a restaurant empire that spanned more than two thousand Tim Hortons at one point, Joyce can be quiet, even insular. And I quickly learned there was no point in filling up the silence. Beyond the occasional, "So, how are you doing?," Joyce has never been big on introductory pleasantries, so I'm not surprised that little is said as we get into his silver Mercedes, parked in front of the clubhouse entrance. He puts the car in drive and skirts around the clubhouse, slowly and silently taking a back road past the spa and towards a recently cleared area that will become the location of new amenities for the resort.

He stops and rolls down the window.

"I had a budget of $20 million when I started," he says through a whispery growl, staring off at the mud where trees used to stand. "But I bet I've spent six times that much. It is a piece of art to me, and it is my legacy in many ways. It all makes sense, because I'm more of a builder than I am a user."

And considering its location—well removed from any large urban centres, but only a short drive from Joyce's hometown of Tatamagouche, where he was raised by his mother in a small two-room house—it is surprising that Fox Harb'r even exists. It is hard to imagine that anyone would advise creating a world-class golf resort in such a remote location. If it weren't for Joyce's love of the land, and his desire to build something that would appeal to the rich and famous from around the world, there's no way Fox Harb'r would have been built. One has to wonder if, in some ways, the resort is Joyce's way of demonstrating how far he's come since dropping out of high school and leaving the area at the age of sixteen, his pockets jangling with loose change and little else as he hit the train for Hamilton, Ontario. It has been a remarkable ride since then.

If there's one thing I've learned about Joyce, it is that the man needs a project to focus his energy and interest. For years, that was Tim Hortons. But once he sold it to Wendy's in 1995, he needed something new. Fox Harb'r filled that void for him for a few years, as did *Destination Fox Harb'r*, his massive sailboat with its 177-foot mast, which he launched from New Zealand in 2002. His autobiography ate up another couple of years before Joyce once again set his sights on changes to his resort. These days, he's focused on promoting real estate sales at the resort, and on new philanthropic endeavours, like building a music facility for performers from Canada's east coast.

He drives the car through the gates near the maintenance facility. The new performance centre will reside across the road, he explains. I ask whether it is his interest in the arts that has led him to create it. Joyce shakes his head.

"It is just going to be a place for people with a lot of talent," he says softly. "I wanted to create something different. Something really different and unique for young people. Nothing like it exists in eastern Canada now. It'll be remarkable, just remarkable."

Truthfully, Joyce can do practically whatever he wants. With his sailboat touring the world (another is on the way), Joyce uses his jets (the most recently acquired includes a bedroom) in the same manner most people use their cars. The question, "So, where have you been?" is never simple with Ron. It may involve a trip to Europe, Calgary (where he has a home), a quick stop in Burlington, and then off to Barbados with friends to spend time on his boat. But even with his crazed schedule, he typically spends Canada's warm-weather months at his home in Fox Harb'r.

After our tour of the resort, including a short stop at the shooting lodge, where his guests have retreated to shoot skeet, he drives back through the course and parks the car in front of the clubhouse.

Joyce admits he didn't know much about golf when he decided in the late 1990s to create a course and resort on his dramatic landscape next to the ocean. He had played some of the best courses in the world—like Augusta National in Georgia, home to the annual Masters tournament—and knew that he wanted a course as finely conditioned as any in the world, with wall-to-wall fairways that looked and felt like velvet, and greens that rolled as if one was putting on glass. But the nuances, the design and its specific features, weren't really on his radar. At the suggestion of former Canadian LPGA star Sandra Post, Joyce gave the job of designing his course to architect Graham Cooke.

Over the next few years, Cooke crafted a track that starts on a high point of land several hundred feet from the coastline, then veers into the wooded area that makes up a bulk of Fox Harb'r's 1,100 acres. It is a solid test of golf, with holes like the tough par-4 second running through tunnels of pines, while others utilize Cooke's large bunkers, the vastness of which match the scale of the facility. But it isn't particularly distinct from dozens of other courses designed by Cooke, at least until the ocean comes into view on the back nine.

That's when the course subtly transforms, yet remains true to its parkland roots. Given his vision for the entire resort, there was no way Joyce was going to create a rustic true links, like the courses of Scotland or Ireland, though he had land that certainly suited it. His taste—in art, homes, and vehicles—runs more upscale, and therefore Fox Harb'r's impeccable aesthetic appearance had to remain consistent with the image Joyce had of the overall facility. That means Fox Harb'r never became the great seaside course it could have been, but that's likely a subtle distinction lost on most of its guests. Regardless, there are some holes on the back nine, especially the stretch that starts near Joyce's home with the short par-3 fifteenth and continuing through the next two par-4 holes along the ocean, that are a delight to play.

The course, buoyed by a warm, dry summer, is in remarkable condition, and Joyce is clearly enamoured of it. He'd do a lot of things differently at the resort if he could do it again, he admits, like passing on the short nine-hole course that gets little play, but he says it is simply too late for that now. Tens of millions have been spent, and he's busy trying to finalize a financial model for the resort that keeps his dream from hemorrhaging cash.

As we prepare to head out on the course, the club's head pro, Elliott Isenor, turns up with Joyce's clubs and shoes and equipment for me as well. Joyce suggests I ride with Isenor—"You two can actually play," he explains—but I simply ignore him and jump in his cart for the ride to the first tee.

Joyce didn't take up golf until he was sixty, largely because he was simply too busy building Tim Hortons to take up a pastime that takes hours to play. Unfortunately, his maturity wasn't kind to his golf swing, which is unorthodox to say the least. Joyce was always a heavy-set man, and even before his back injury, he had very little shoulder turn as he began his swing. Instead, he dips his entire body, taking the club back awkwardly and then rerouting it in a lunging swing at the ball. The result is as arbitrary as the swing itself. There's simply no guarantee the club will meet the ball squarely, which means Joyce rarely broke 95, even when he was playing regularly.

"I don't play much anymore—hardly at all—and I was never really any damned good anyway," he says as we step foot on the first tee, a straightforward par-4 with a decidedly difficult green. "You know that, Robert. I have no co-ordination when it comes to golf."

Legend has it that Joyce has offered all sorts of riches to golf instructors in the hope they could show him the light. But it never happened. Then, two years ago, he fell on the deck of his boat while it was out for a sail near Barbados. He landed with tremendous force, cracking vertebrae. His doctors ruled out surgery, and though his health improved, golf became difficult.* It doesn't hurt to play—at least not immediately—Joyce explains, but the fallout after a game is horrible. The injury has forced him to cancel numerous games,

---

* Joyce would have surgery on his back in the fall of 2007 following a jet crash at Fox Harb'r that made headlines across Canada.

including one with former U.S. president Bill Clinton, who visited Fox Harb'r in 2006. But the former president fell in love with the resort and its course on his first visit in 2004, Joyce says, even taking a cut to his reported $125,000 speaking fee to return.

"I mean, the privacy—for a guy like him, that's important. We couldn't keep him off the course. It was hot, really hot, when he was here, and he just kept playing."

Joyce steps up, and, using a swing that looks like an octopus trying to play piano, strikes the ball cleanly, sending it no higher than fifteen feet in the air, but finding the fairway 205 yards out with a slight cut. Playing from the white tees and downwind, Isenor smacks one nearly to the green. I follow, using a fairway wood from my Nike rental set, hitting a high draw that runs into the rough.

Regardless of whether he's a good golfer, Joyce has made millions from playing the game. It was over a round at Adios Golf Club—the notoriously private course in Florida—with the late Wendy's founder Dave Thomas that Joyce broached the idea of selling Tim Hortons in exchange for millions of shares in the burger chain. The alliance was aimed at giving Tim Hortons a foothold in the U.S., while also allowing Joyce to diversify his wealth, most of which was tied up in the donut chain at the time. The deal, worth more than $600 million, went through on January 1, 1996, making Joyce a major Wendy's shareholder, but essentially costing him control over his beloved restaurant chain.

Joyce remained on the board of Wendy's for several years. By 2002, fed up with battling for changes at Wendy's and having handed daily control of the Tims over to Paul House, his hand-picked successor, Joyce sold out his Wendy's stock and walked away.

Though it has been more than four decades since Joyce joined the once-downtrodden Tim Hortons chain—created by its namesake hockey star in partnership with a would-be entrepreneur named Jim Charade—and more than five years since he had any business involvement with the chain, people still see Joyce as the face of the business. That's not surprising. After all, the former navy shipman turned cop turned restaurateur was the face and backbone of the business after Horton died in a fiery car crash in 1974. Joyce survived high interest rates and a lawsuit by Horton's widow, Lori, for control of the company. Under his guidance, the chain grew exponentially, and many of its famous products—from the Timbit to the omnipresent oval-shaped logo to its coffee--were developed under his direction.

He still gets letters from customers telling him stories about their experiences in the stores, and his picture remains in many of the so-called combo stores that house both Tim Hortons and Wendy's.

But animosity has grown between Joyce and House, especially after the company's public offering in 2006. The problems stem from their philosophical differences. House wants to put his stamp on the business and faces the pressures of growing Tims as a public company. Joyce, on the other hand, sees House destroying the "system" he created, Joyce's often-used term for the interactive way in which Tim Hortons's head office worked with its franchises.

"I don't even exist to Tim Hortons now," he says on the par-5 second hole. "But I'm the company's co-founder, and there's nothing they can do or say to take that away from me. They are like u bunch of kids in a candy store, just taking whatever they can get their hands on. They didn't have to build fuck all. It was given to them."

They may not be able to take it away from him, but they surely have cut him out of the picture. At the company's March public offering, Joyce was notable by his absence. In his place, the company paraded out Jeri-Lyn Horton, Tim's daughter and Joyce's daughter-in-law.

Joyce's concern for the chain isn't rooted in self-interest—he has no investment in the business. He said that he's worried that as a public company, Tim Hortons will focus more on the bottom line than on its stores and customers. To Joyce, the store owners were always his customers, and if he kept them happy and making money, there would be enough success and riches for everyone. He certainly had something there—the waiting list to own a Tim Hortons franchise is years long now. But in his mind, just because there's demand doesn't mean the system couldn't be irreparably damaged.

"It bothers me because management is breaking down the system. I have an attachment to it because it is something I built, something I established and created."

As he talks about Tim Hortons, Joyce's game becomes increasingly erratic, partially attributable to our discussion and partly due to the fact he hasn't played in months. His approach to the second hole flies into the hazard on the right side of the fairway, leaving him to brusquely ask Isenor for a second ball. He hits that one to the left and jumps in his cart, leaving me standing in the middle of the fairway. He putts out, concluding that sooner or later the Tim Hortons franchisees will recognize what's happening within the company: "They gave them dandelions and told them it was roses," he says. "They're going to notice."

On our third hole, a lengthy par-4 that plays significantly uphill, Joyce decides he's going to take a breather. Isenor hits a cut that lands on the left side of the fairway, while I, knowing a score isn't on the line, swing with abandon and hit a high draw past him on the left side of the fairway. We finish up the hole and suddenly, without explanation, Joyce announces he's done, that his participation in the round is over. I suspect his back injury has flared up, but before I can ask him, he's turned the cart around and headed back to the clubhouse, stating he'll catch up with me later.

Does it bother Joyce to have such an elaborate golf course and not be able to take advantage of it? Isenor nods.

"I wish there was something I could do, something I could teach him that would allow him to play. But his back hurts and there doesn't seem to be anything I can do to help it."

I finish the front nine with Isenor, playing a casual game, before heading into the clubhouse to try to find my elusive host. He's gone back to his house, I'm told, but he's asked that I meet him there. I jump in my rental car and drive along the back nine of the course, past the multimillion-dollar homes located along the fairways and the marina next to Ron's home. I knock and push open the massive wooden front door. Joyce is sitting at his dining room table. Though he's known as a drinker, his favourite being a vodka and soda with ice in a Tim Hortons coffee cup, Joyce isn't consuming any alcohol on my visit, and announces that he's quit smoking as well. There's no explanation for the decision other than a quick, "I thought it was a good thing to do." Maybe after years of living a fast lifestyle, he's starting a health kick.

We hang around the house making small talk, with Joyce ducking into his office to take the occasional phone call, before driving back up to the clubhouse for dinner. When we return several hours later, his guests are on the patio, which overlooks the ocean, eating dinner and putting away numerous bottles of wine. Ron sits down for a while, introduces me as the writer of "my book," and before long, as the night cools, the party heads indoors. A dice game suddenly breaks out on Joyce's billiards table, with hundreds of dollars changing hands between Shaw execs and TD's investment bankers. Joyce just watches from a distance, not appearing all that interested in participating, and chats amiably with his guests, before announcing he's heading to bed.

I catch him on the way up the stairs to thank him for his hospitality, especially since I'll be heading for Moncton early the next morning. The party continues downstairs, and Joyce walks into his living room, with its wide, glass window that overlooks the remarkable star-filled vista of the Northumberland Strait. Apparently, he's still thinking about our conversation from that afternoon.

"The chain was improving all those years I was there," he says, sipping on his water. "There's nothing new there now that wasn't in place when I left. The system was always intended to be bigger than the individual stores. It was built to be that way, and that's how it should stay."

Now it appears Joyce is not part of the system at all, cut out of the picture by a company that doesn't want the inconvenience of having one of its founders comment on its present performance.

Does his current relationship and involvement with the company known as "Tims" sadden Joyce? Undoubtedly. Would he do things differently—including keeping control of the company—if he could do it all over again? Most likely.

But would he trade his current lifestyle, with its endless series of jet excursions to exotic locations, boat trips in the Caribbean with friends, and his world-class resort, for a chance to return to his former glories at Tim Hortons?

He says he would, but from my perspective, it looks like he's living the life he always wanted.